W9-BRI-983

Alexandra Harney has been working in Asia as a journalist for most of the past decade. She has covered China and Japan for the *Financial Times*, and was an editor at the newspaper in London. From 2003 until early 2006, she was the *Financial Times*'s South China correspondent. Now a freelance writer, she has contributed to National Public Radio, the BBC World Service, the *Wall Street Journal*, the *Washington Post*, *Slate*, and *The Times*, among many other publications and broadcast media. A graduate of Princeton University with a degree from the Woodrow Wilson School of Public and International Affairs, Alexandra lives in Hong Kong with her husband, the photographer Colin Beere. She speaks Japanese and Mandarin Chinese.

Praise for Alexandra Harney's *The China Price*

"Anyone running a company that outsources manufacturing to China, or is thinking of doing so, needs to read this book. . . . Harney provides a valuable insight into the worst problems of outsourcing and how they occur. Change is needed, and change will come; we must begin to prepare for it."
—Morgan Witzel, *Financial Times*

"*Financial Times* journalist Alexandra Harney has taken what, to date, is the closest and most apposite and readable look at this phenomenon. . . . *The China Price* is a must-read for anyone sourcing or operating in China as well as those engaged in corporate social responsibility initiatives in the country. It's also a book anyone who considers themselves an ethical or concerned consumer should read."
—Paul French, *Ethical Corporation*

"In this book, subtitled *The True Cost of Chinese Competitive Advantage*, reporter and editor Harney, who has spent a decade covering Japan and China for the *Financial Times*, brings to light hidden aspects of China's rise. . . . In unadorned prose, Harney demonstrates what happens when an entire society goes into a feeding frenzy, willing to sacrifice individual and environmental health for the sake of rapid growth."
—*Barron's*

"Harney, a former *Financial Times* reporter who covered South China from 2003 to 2006, draws on her experience reporting on the sources of China's manufacturing miracle to describe how such low prices are possible and why they can't (and shouldn't) continue to fall. . . . Harney is at her best when focusing a sharp eye on the people behind the China price."
—*The Wall Street Journal*

"Harney's book, meticulously researched, is journalism at its highest level, and is remorseless in chronicling human-rights abuses and market caprice."
—David M. Shribman, *The Boston Globe*

"A contrarian offering from the dewy-eyed literature on the China phenomenon. It focuses on the human costs of the China price—both to the people who make it possible and the consumers who thrive on it. . . . An absorbing read . . . thought-provoking." —*India Business Standard*

"If you want to understand China's economic fault lines, pick up *The China Price* by Alexandra Harney. For every business book goggling at the rate and scale of China's growth, *The China Price* is a powerfully needed antidote." —Anne-Marie Slaughter, Dean of the Woodrow Wilson School at Princeton, NPR's *All Things Considered*'s Three Books series

"Behind every two-dollar T-shirt lies the overworked, underpaid human face of a Chinese migrant worker. In her new book, *The China Price: The True Cost of Chinese Competitive Advantage*, Alexandra Harney gives a voice to some of these workers. She tells of the pressures and aspirations that prompted them to join the hundreds of millions of workers migrating from rural China to the coastal manufacturing centers, the many tribulations and occasional triumphs they encounter there, and above all the abysmal labor conditions due to the 'race to zero' in sourcing expenses." —Lisa Movius, *Women's Wear Daily*

"Alexandra Harney's *The China Price* has done for Chinese supply chains what Karl Taro Greenfeld's *Speed Tribes* did for Japanese youth. She has exposed a largely hitherto unknown world via a forensic examination written in a crisp style usually reserved for good novels." —Stephen Frost, www.csr-asia.com

"[An] eloquent and vibrant study . . . the price, the real China price, lies at the core of this meticulously researched and wonderfully readable book. . . . Lots of others, like Harney, with long experience in and around China, knowledge of the language and the grit to scramble beneath the curtains that disguise so much in Chinese life, have written on conditions in Chinese factories. . . . But Harney, who represented the *Financial Times* in Hong Kong and China, draws everything together. . . . She writes, as they used to say, like an angel, and, uniquely, has spent hours with the men and very young women working in China's William Blake–like world. . . . The ghastly point is that Chinese workers work, live, and die in conditions that Charles Dickens could not have described better than Alexandra Harney has." —Jonathan Mirsky, *The Spectator* (London)

"*Financial Times* reporter Harney paints a vivid portrait of factory life in the country that sells consumer goods for the lowest price possible." —*Kirkus Reviews* (starred review)

"A familiar but engrossing tale of Dickensian industrialization. . . . Packed with facts, figures, and sympathetic portraits of Chinese workers and managers, Harney's is a perceptive take on the world's workshop." —*Publishers Weekly*

THE CHINA PRICE

The True Cost of Chinese
Competitve Advantage

ALEXANDRA HARNEY

PENGUIN BOOKS

For my parents

PENGUIN BOOKS
Published by the Penguin Group
Penguin Group (USA) Inc., 375 Hudson Street, New York, New York 10014, U.S.A.
Penguin Group (Canada), 90 Eglinton Avenue East, Suite 700, Toronto, Ontario,
Canada M4P 2Y3 (a division of Pearson Penguin Canada Inc.)
Penguin Books Ltd, 80 Strand, London WC2R 0RL, England
Penguin Ireland, 25 St Stephen's Green, Dublin 2, Ireland
(a division of Penguin Books Ltd)
Penguin Group (Australia), 250 Camberwell Road, Camberwell, Victoria 3124, Australia
(a division of Pearson Australia Group Pty Ltd)
Penguin Books India Pvt Ltd, 11 Community Centre, Panchsheel Park, New Delhi – 110 017, India
Penguin Group (NZ), 67 Apollo Drive, Rosedale, North Shore 0632, New Zealand
(a division of Pearson New Zealand Ltd)
Penguin Books (South Africa) (Pty) Ltd, 24 Sturdee Avenue,
Rosebank, Johannesburg 2196, South Africa

Penguin Books Ltd, Registered Offices:
80 Strand, London WC2R 0RL, England

First published in the United States of America by The Penguin Press,
a member of Penguin Group (USA) Inc. 2008
This edition with a new afterword published in Penguin Books 2009

10 9 8 7 6 5 4 3 2 1

Copyright © Alexandra Harney, 2008, 2009
All rights reserved

ISBN 978-1-59420-157-8 (hc.)
ISBN 978-0-14-311486-4 (pbk.)
CIP data available

Printed in the United States of America
Designed by Amanda Dewey
Frontmatter map by Jeffrey L. Ward

Contents

At the request of some individuals mentioned in this work, the author has changed their names and, in some instances, omitted identifying characteristics.

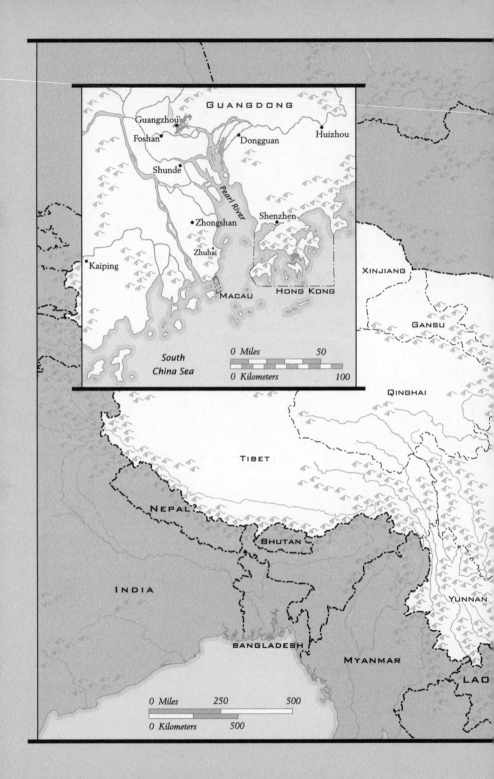

RUSSIA

MONGOLIA

HEILONGJIANG

JILIN

INNER MONGOLIA

LIAONING

NORTH KOREA

Beijing ★

TIANJIN

Dalian

HEBEI

SOUTH KOREA

Taiyuan

NINGXIA

SHANXI

SHANDONG

Linfen

Yellow
Sea

Xi'an

HENAN

JIANGSU

JAPAN

SHAANXI

ANHUI

CHINA

Shanghai

SICHUAN

HUBEI

Ningbo

Guang'an

ZHEJIANG

East
China Sea

Chongqing

uzhou

Changsha

Wenzhou

HUNAN

JIANGXI

GUIZHOU

FUJIAN

Xiamen

TAIWAN

GUANGDONG

Guangzhou

Shenzhen

Shantou

HONG KONG
MACAU

GUANGXI

Area of detail

ETNAM

HAINAN

South
China Sea

PHILIPPINES

© 2008 Jeffrey L. Ward

THE BETTER MOUSETRAP

For two weeks twice a year, trains and planes to the Chinese city of Guangzhou swell to capacity with crowds of foreign men and women. Hundreds of thousands of these people, representatives of the world's importers, fill the city's hotels, bars and restaurants with a babel of Japanese and Arabic and English and French. Every morning, they pile onto shuttle buses and head straight for one of the city's two colossal convention centers.

They've come to pay homage to one thing: the China price.

Inside the many massive halls of the convention centers are thousands of companies peddling countless products made in China. Sweaters, showers, power drills, plates, jacuzzis, cell phones, SUVs, plastic neon palm trees—everything, including the kitchen sink, all for half or even a fifth of what it would cost to make in America.

Over the last several years, the China price has redrawn the global manufacturing map and laid the foundation for the next economic superpower. It has put legions of people out of work around the world and become an open wound in international trade relations. And it has brought unprecedented change to the lives of hundreds of millions of Chinese.

Cheap Chinese goods have made shopping more affordable. By

one estimate, products made in China have saved the average American family $500 a year.[1] But such a savings is of limited consolation to those who have lost their jobs. "The China price," screamed a *BusinessWeek* headline in 2004, has become "the three scariest words in US industry."[2]

The China price touches everyone, everywhere. Since the start of the new millennium, China has come to dominate global manufacturing in a way almost inconceivable before its rise. The prices it offers have been so low that starting around 2003, they have become known simply as the China price.

In August 2007, Mattel recalled millions of toys made in China because of concerns about their safety. Its announcements that some of its toys contained paint with excessive levels of lead and others included dangerously small magnets touched off a global wave of concern about the quality of Chinese-made goods.

The United States has banned the import of certain types of farm-raised seafood from China because of fears that it may have been contaminated with drugs and other chemicals. Chinese-made tires, toothpaste, and pharmaceuticals have come under scrutiny. And traces of pollution from Asia, undoubtedly much of it from China, have been detected on the west coast of America.

Yet beyond the headlines about job losses and product safety scares, what is it we really know about China's manufacturing juggernaut?

The aim of this book is to uncover the true cost of China's competitive advantage. Who are the people behind the China price? How do they make goods so cheaply? At what cost to them, and to us? And how long can they keep it up?

OVER THE LAST DECADE OR SO, China has become legendary for its ability to undercut prices for everything from consumer goods to industrial machinery. The only way for manufacturers elsewhere to compete was to move to China themselves. As a writer for *Fortune* magazine put it in March 2002, "any CEO worth his salt these days is deciding not whether to move manufacturing capacity to China but how much and how quickly."[3]

"China makes you sharp or it kills you," the *Wall Street Journal* quoted Eslie Sykes, manager of a Flextronics plant in Guadalajara, Mexico, as saying.[4] *BusinessWeek* devoted a special report to the China price. "If you still make anything labor intensive," it quoted Oded Shenkar, author and Ohio State University business professor, as saying, "get out now rather than bleed to death. Shaving five percent here and there won't work."[5]

The China price has, in effect, become a brand. To most people, its brand image is a collage: cheap clothing and electronics filling the shelves at Wal-Mart, factory workers at home losing their jobs, the woman on the jacket of this book.

To executives, the China price stirs fears of a new competitor in the East but also conjures soothing visions of hefty savings. To politicians, the term has become shorthand for unfair trading practices including an undervalued currency, intellectual property violations and dumping of cheap goods. To scholars, the China price has become part of a debate on the merits of unfettered trade. And to journalists like me, the China price has looked like a giant, creaking tectonic plate, shifting the way the world thinks about the delicate balance of global trade and national good.

The debate over imports and their effect on the domestic economy isn't new, of course. American companies have been moving manufacturing offshore for decades, and American workers have understandably been upset about it for almost as long. But never has one country yielded such visible price declines on such a wide range of goods in such a short period of time. It is as though the world has been watching a second industrial revolution unfold.

Over the past two decades, China's share of global manufacturing, measured in terms of value added, has risen faster than that of any other country. Its share of the world's manufacturing output by value added was 2.4 percent in 1990; by 2006, that share had grown to 12.1 percent, making China the world's third-largest producer after America and Japan.[6]

China's exports have been posting double-digit annual growth, on average, since the 1990s. China went from exporting $26 billion worth of goods to the world in 1984 to exporting $1,218 billion in 2007. Global Insight, a U.S. economics consultancy, expects China to overtake the United States as the world's largest manufacturer in 2020.[7] In 2004, China replaced Japan as the world's third-largest exporter after Germany and America.[8] China has overtaken America as the world's second biggest exporter after Germany and is expected to take the top spot.

China has challenged the conventional theory of comparative advantage by making everything from basic consumer goods—the shoes, clothing and toys that other Asian countries produced during their export boom years after World War II—to higher-tech products like computer screens, iPods and cell phones. Much of this success is due to the marriage of Chinese labor with foreign capital. China's courtship of international business has drawn the world's manufacturers to its doorstep. Southern cities like Guangzhou, Dongguan and Shenzhen are filled with Indians, Brazilians, Japanese, Israelis, Brits, Irish, Italians, French and Americans who have moved to China to open their own factories or sell Chinese-made goods overseas. Wal-Mart's global sourcing center is based in the southern city of Shenzhen, just across the border from Hong Kong. IBM's chief procurement officer sits in Shenzhen as well.

In 1990, China attracted $3.5 billion of foreign direct investment. By 2006, that figure had soared to $69 billion, according to the United Nations Conference on Trade and Development. Cumulative foreign direct investment in China between 2002 and 2005 alone totaled $239.28 billion. That investment has helped produce the facilities that comprise the workshop of the world.

Wal-Mart buys at least $18 billion worth of goods from China every year. Samsung bought $15 billion worth of supplies there in 2005.[9] Carmakers General Motors and Volkswagen, among others, purchase components from China. Even Boeing now sources parts for its airplanes from China. Between 1989 and 2005, China raised its share of exports to the United States in 41 sectors.[10]

In 2007, China's biggest exports by volume to America were electrical machinery and equipment, including consumer electronics. But it also shipped a lot of toys and sporting goods, clothing, furniture and shoes. That year, America imported $321.5 billion worth of products from China. America's exports to China totaled only $65.2 billion.

Overall, in its trade with the rest of the world in 2007, China exported $262 billion more than it imported. This imbalance has not helped the China price's brand image. It has fueled a continual political backlash that has threatened to undermine the country's competitive advantage.

The China price has stoked fears of a hollowing-out of manufacturing around the world. In a petition to the Office of the United States Trade Representative in 2004, the AFL-CIO, the country's largest labor organization, alleged that China's labor abuses created a reserve of cheap labor that displaced up to 1.2 million American jobs. The Economic Policy Institute, a Washington, D.C., think tank, has estimated that the U.S. trade deficit with China led to the loss of 2.3 million job opportunities between 2001 and 2007.[11]

Senators Charles Schumer, a Democrat from New York, and Lindsey Graham, a Republican from South Carolina, have argued that undervaluation of the renminbi, the Chinese currency, contributed to the loss of three million American manufacturing jobs over five years. "China's emergence as a manufacturing powerhouse at the expense of the United States raises significant economic security concerns and the question of whether a country that loses its ability to produce tangible products will long remain an economic power," reads a foreboding press release by Senator Schumer's office.[12]

Many American manufacturers concur. They have filed a stream of complaints about Chinese competitors dumping their products at below-market prices in the United States, prompting the government to impose duties on Chinese-made televisions, furniture and textiles. "I must tell you that I have seen many companies around me driven out of business and some of them were my customers," Richard L. Wilkey, president of Fisher-Barton, a small components manufacturer in Watertown, Wisconsin, told the House Ways and Means Committee.[13]

"Not all of these companies were dinosaurs—a number of them had made significant investments in technology and modern business methods to remain competitive. They had done all the right things, but were still faced with an environment in which the deck was stacked against them with regard to China."

I first became aware of the China price when I was living in Tokyo, working as a correspondent for the *Financial Times*. In 1999, I joined a group of Japanese journalists on a trip to Honda Motor's operations in China. The carmaker had taken over a plant in Guangzhou and was running it according to the company's exacting standards. Flooring the accelerator in a locally made Accord at a nearby track, I physically experienced China's potential as a manufacturing powerhouse. The car, at least to my untrained eye, looked and drove precisely like an Accord made in Japan—except it was assembled in China.

Not long afterward, for a story on the electronics sector, I interviewed two Japanese semiconductor executives. As an aside, they mentioned that they were studying Mandarin Chinese. I wondered why. The better to understand the people who would one day steal their jobs, they said.

I was used to hearing about *Japanese* people stealing jobs. Having grown up near Washington, D.C., during the height of the fears about Japan, Inc., I remembered the national panic after Japanese investors bought Rockefeller Center and Pebble Beach. Japanese cars were selling like hotcakes in America, but our cars weren't selling well over there. "The Japanese have created an uneven playing field," I remember being told. In high school, I studied Japanese, the better to understand our economic rival.

Now, Japan was running scared. Newspapers were printing accusations that China was "exporting deflation" to the rest of the world. China, it seemed to me, was the real challenge to both Japan and America. I resolved to study Chinese and move to China. In 2003, the *Financial Times* transferred me to Hong Kong to cover southern China.

Other people were having similar revelations. A few years later, hundreds of people in the capital of Spain's shoemaking industry, Elche, staged violent protests against Chinese competitors who they claimed were hurting their business.[14] In Italy, the furniture and shoe industries were distraught about business lost to China. So were Scotland's seafood workers. Poorer countries were also suffering. Mexico's *maquiladoras* watched with dismay as orders drained away to China.[15] Poland's manufacturers, once considered low-cost, were losing ground to cheaper Chinese competitors.[16] The China price had even undercut Nigerian textile factories.[17]

Around 2003, a series of trade disputes over shoes, textiles, apparel and other products began. To mollify critics of the China price, Beijing eliminated the renminbi's peg to the dollar in July 2005 and allowed it to appreciate by 2.1 percent. It loosened the trading band around the renminbi, also known as the yuan, allowing it to rise or fall first by 0.3 percent in daily trading and then, starting in May 2007, by 0.5 percent. This was the start of a rapid appreciation of China's currency. In the first quarter of 2008 alone, the renminbi appreciated by 4 percent.

That wasn't enough to placate people who argued then, as now, that the renminbi is undervalued by as much as 40 percent. The anger—and the wonder—at China's growing domination of global manufacturing continues to spread. In a matter of several years, the China price has become a mighty force in global politics and trade. It has had an equally dramatic effect on China itself.

CHINA'S EXPORT SECTOR has been a powerful engine of growth in the world's fastest-growing economy. China has the world's largest manufacturing workforce: some 104 million people, about twice the number of manufacturing workers in the United States, Canada, Japan, France, Germany, Italy and the UK combined.[18]

Some of these millions of workers are internal migrants from the Chinese countryside. Over the past two decades, China has witnessed one of history's greatest migrations. Estimates vary, but there are between 120 million and 200 million migrants in Chinese cities today. In Guangdong province alone, there are between 17 million and 40 million migrant workers.

Although not all of these migrants work in manufacturing, many do. They log eight-to-16-hour days, sometimes seven days a week, for years at a time, before returning to their villages. Their wages have been a lever lifting families out of poverty, building houses, paying medical bills and sending children to school. By one estimate, between 1994 and 2004, manufacturing accounted for 60 percent of China's economic growth.[19]

China's huge labor pool has, for some time, helped it defy the conventional logic of economics. As investment in manufacturing has soared since the 1990s, wages for the bottom tier of migrant workers have remained relatively low, making China an attractive place to manufacture labor-intensive goods.

Wages in China are extremely low compared to those in developed countries. On average, Chinese manufacturing workers are estimated to have earned $0.57 an hour in 2002, which translates to about 3 percent of the average hourly compensation of manufac-

turing employees in the United States and other developed countries.[20] Chinese labor costs are a fraction of those in Mexico, Brazil
and developed Asian countries.[21] By one estimate, they are even
lower than wages handloom operators earned in the early Industrial
Revolution in the UK or workers in a Chicago lumber yard took
home in the mid-nineteenth century.[22]

And yet Chinese wages are higher than those in countries in
Africa and Southeast Asia. So labor is not the only factor drawing
manufacturing to China. The country's other advantages—lower
costs for land, generous government incentives, a stable political
system, good roads, telecommunications and frequent departures
by container ships—have also helped attract the foreign investment
that has been the catalyst for growth in the export sector.

That investment has helped knit China into the global supply
chain in many industries. Chinese customs records show that more
than half of exports are from foreign-invested firms. Foreign companies bring in components from elsewhere, often in Asia, and set
Chinese labor to assembling them into the final product. Today,
about 55 percent of China's exports are made with imported
parts.[23] Often, these goods are made by contract manufacturers,
companies you have never heard of that produce goods carrying
their customers' brand names.

China doesn't always add much value to a product for export, although its name goes on the label. By one estimate, the value
added in China—including labor, parts and components bought in
China and the profits earned by foreign-owned firms—is only a third
of the value of the output in the whole export processing sector.[24]
Still, what Chinese factories do, they do with great efficiency.

Just as in Industrial Revolution England, certain Chinese cities
and even districts and townships within cities have emerged as
leading manufacturers of specific products. In and around these cities, companies that supply material and components, repair machinery and handle logistics have sprung up to serve factories.

Having materials and services nearby improves efficiency and saves on components and transportation costs. It also speeds up the supply chain because components can be sourced quickly and easily.

China's coastal export regions are littered with more than 1,000 of these clusters.[25] The city of Wenzhou leads the world in the production of cigarette lighters with metal cases. Shunde in southern Guangdong province bills itself as "The Capital of Household Electrical Appliances." One Shunde factory employs 40,000 workers and produces nearly half of the world's microwaves. In Zhili township in Zhejiang province, some 5,000 companies make children's clothing. Datang township in the same province churns out six billion pairs of socks a year.[26] More than 1,000 factories in Shengzhou in Zhejiang province make 40 percent of the world's neckties.

The city of Dongguan in Guangdong province is a leading assembly base for computers and computer parts. "If there is a traffic jam between Dongguan and Hong Kong, 70 percent of the world's computer market will be affected," one IBM executive has said.[27] Clusters like these help make the China price unbeatable, because, as Michael Enright, Edith Scott and Chang Ka-mun have noted, "competitors or potential competitors . . . have to compete not just with a set of end-product manufacturers, but with entire production chains, and in some cases subcultures, found in the region."[28]

Some of China's other advantages are more controversial. Chinese companies' widespread violations of other companies' intellectual property rights, despite promises to protect them, help keep costs down. About two-thirds of the counterfeit goods seized in U.S. ports are made in China. American politicians are right: An undervalued Chinese currency definitely helps hold down the cost of Chinese products overseas.

These factors, well documented elsewhere, all underpin the China price. But this book is about the cost China has paid to sustain these advantages. In order to get to the China price, Beijing has made economic growth its primary aim and let many laws go unenforced.

This policy has created a new kind of uneven playing field, where factories that follow the law are handicapped. Operating without the threat of government censure, factories take shortcuts to save money and lie about their business to placate international buyers.

Widespread ignorance about the impact of rapid industrialization on health and a common desire among government officials, factory managers and workers to make money quickly have caused a widening epidemic of occupational disease. Pollution is contributing to the deaths of hundreds of thousands of Chinese every year. The high costs the country pays to achieve the China price make sustaining it a high-wire act.

THE FIRST PEOPLE to arrive at the Canton Fair, the massive, bi-annual trade show that draws so many importers to Guangzhou each year, are the migrant workers. They are the authors of China's extraordinary growth, the people who build the skyscrapers that dot its city skylines and assemble the shoes that are cheap enough to cause trade wars. The Canton Fair is a showcase of their handiwork.

They turn up just after seven in the morning, two hours before the fair opens, their loose clothing at odds with the crisp glass-and-steel arches of the new convention center. Dragging rusty metal carts, they mill hopefully around the taxi bays. Over the next several hours, the lanes will fill with cars carrying Chinese exhibitors and their foreign customers. The workers, men and women who have come here in search of work from central Henan province, more than 1,000 miles away, wait for exhibitors carrying stacks of corporate pamphlets or product samples. They are hoping for the chance to cart them into the convention center for a fee of $1.31.

Among the workers is a man named Wang. Thirty-nine years old, with thick, dirty nails and tan skin, he wears a brown shirt, black pants and a belt. When he was a child, his parents couldn't afford to send him to school past junior high. Wang is here to make sure his son gets better odds. He wants his son to attend high school, and, he hopes, college, in Henan. Every renminbi he earns carting goods to the convention center counts toward that goal.

The ladies who sell calculators arrive next. They are dressed to move in jeans and sneakers, courier bags slung over one shoulder. When the first taxis roll up, the calculator ladies glide into action, leaning in through the open doors of the cars as the foreigners count their change. At the Canton Fair, where many are speaking a second language and pennies can make or break a deal, calculators are the common language. Handed back and forth between buyer and seller, the calculator speaks the language of money, which everyone understands. "Hello, Casio!" the girls who sell calculators say in English. "Nice nice, good good!" They fish their wares from their bags and thrust fistfuls of calculators toward the foreigners.

Eventually, the sidewalk outside the convention center fills with other freshly hatched capitalists. Young women offer to print stacks of business cards in two hours. Crowds of college kids, some barely able to assemble a sentence in a foreign language, hold hand-lettered signs advertising themselves as interpreters. For every service, there are a dozen or more competitors of similar quality, a miniature replica of the rivalry inside the convention center and across the country every day. Nobody on the pavement seems to mind. This athletic capitalism is the way China works. "There is no development without competition," says Wang, the worker from Henan hauling goods.

The Canton Fair is China's oldest trade fair, held since 1957 in China's historically most important trading hub. For half a century, the world's businesspeople have been traveling to Guangzhou during the fair to make deals. When China was otherwise closed to the outside world in the 1960s and much of the 1970s, the Canton Fair was its window to foreign trade.

After 1978, when the country began economic reforms that opened China to foreign investment and encouraged international trade, the fair took on greater significance. Years later, Guangzhou built a sleek new convention center to accommodate more companies. By 2004, the world's appetite for cheap, Chinese-made goods was so great that foreign buyers crashed through security barriers and shoved aside guards to get into the exhibition halls.[29] The Canton Fair, now known officially as the China Import and Export Fair but still almost entirely devoted to exports, is a capitalist carnival, the world's greatest shopping mall.

Thousands of companies offer products with unfamiliar, tongue-twister brand names. Aki screens. Sope televisions. Zhu Que computers. Cuori vacuum cleaners. PanaVoice speakers. Lamo electrical appliances. Horoad parking meters. JAC automobiles. Huida sanitaryware. Ningbo Golden Fish electrical appliances. There are aisles upon aisles of companies offering identical products: countless manufacturers of streetlights, Christmas tree lights, faucets, toilets and showers with electronic panels that connect to your phone. There are rows of companies making door handles, power tools and MP3 players.

Many of these companies will never make it beyond the low-margin business of contract manufacturing for others. But among them, potentially, are the Sonys and Samsungs of tomorrow.

Some companies try to lure customers to their booths with food: a soft ice cream machine maker plies passersby with free cones, a wine fountain maker touts cups of sour red. Others simply distribute brochures and business cards. One salesman at an electronics manufacturer selling copies of Apple and Nokia products introduces his boss, a 26-year-old man who has chosen to call himself Money. He likes money, he says.

Foreign buyers like money, too. They are here to save it. A Swedish construction executive whose company flew a busload of employees to the Canton Fair says he has cut his procurement costs by 20 percent to 60 percent by switching his purchasing of building materials from Sweden to China. An Australian buyer of windows has lowered his costs by 70 percent. An American restaurant executive says the goods he buys in China cost only a fifth of what he was paying for the same products made in the United States. "Why are all these foreigners coming to the Canton Fair?" asks Li, another migrant worker hauling goods with Wang. "Because Chinese goods are cheap."

UNTIL RECENTLY, the debate about the China price has focused on big, abstract concepts: the undervalued currency, the subsidies to industry, the rampant piracy. This is starting to change.

In early 2007, the Food and Drug Administration determined that the addition of the chemical melamine, typically used to make fire-retardant products, to wheat gluten produced in China caused the deaths of pets in the United States. The contamination led to a massive recall of pet food. More than two million birds and hundreds of hogs also ate tainted pet food, sparking fears of a broader contamination of the food supply.

Then, that summer, the *New York Times* traced the deaths of more than 100 people in Panama to a poisonous chemical used in antifreeze, diethylene glycol, intentionally mislabeled as glycerin in China and then mixed into cough syrup in Panama. Taixing Glycerine Factory, which produced the counterfeit chemical, was not certified to sell pharmaceutical ingredients, the paper reported, an assertion China's foreign ministry later confirmed.[30]

Not long afterward, health authorities around the world warned consumers against using brands of toothpaste made in China that were found to contain diethylene glycol. These warnings were followed in the United States by the recalls of Chinese-made toys coated with lead paint and warnings about car tires from China that were believed to be unsafe. In early 2008, the Food and Drug Administration linked the deaths of dozens of Americans to contaminated batches of the blood thinner heparin made in China.

China's contribution to global warming is of growing concern. Researchers have found traces of carbon monoxide, ozone and mercury from Asia in Oregon and Washington State, and pollution from Asia is believed to be affecting weather up and down the west coast of North America.[31] This series of revelations has driven home the point that what happens in China doesn't stay in China. It comes into all of our homes, every day. The sacrifices China makes to stay competitive in manufacturing affect the rest of the world.

IT WOULD BE IMPOSSIBLE to tell the story of all Chinese factories. China contains an entire universe of manufacturing, from large, highly mechanized, Western-owned factories to tiny local workshops. And every industry has particular characteristics: The dynamics of the semiconductor or automotive industry are distinct from those in the garment or toy trade. In a country as big and complex as China, the conditions in factories in Zhejiang province can differ markedly from those in Fujian, which are again different from those in Guangdong. But certain patterns are common across the country.

To keep things simple, I have chosen to focus on the production of consumer goods—clothes, shoes, toys and simple electronics, the things you use every day—in Guangdong province, the first area China opened to international trade after 1978 and the origin of about a third of the country's exports.

Many of the factories in Guangdong have foreign investors, particularly from Taiwan and Hong Kong. But there are also plants owned by the government, local entrepreneurs and people from around the world. Much of the momentum in Guangdong's economy comes from private and foreign-invested companies.

Guangdong is the most populous province in China, with as many as 110 million people squeezed into an area slightly smaller than the state of Missouri. Its huge population is partly due to the influx of migrant workers from other provinces.[32] Located on China's southern coast, just across the border from Hong Kong, Guangdong is bisected by the Pearl River. The parts of the province not given over to industry look almost tropical: There are palm and banana trees, beaches and farming plots that seem unchanged for centuries. But dotted around the Pearl River, which has been an artery of trade for centuries, are industrial cities containing hundreds of thousands of factories, many of them specializing in light industry.

These factories range in size from single production lines tucked anonymously into office buildings to multistory tiled fortresses with their own cavernous cafeterias, sushi bars, golf courses, bank ATMs, hospitals, massage parlors, swimming pools and hotels. Many sit behind gates manned by security guards. The factories' names or external appearances rarely give away much about the activity inside, since so much of the work is done for other brands behind a curtain of secrecy.

A few times a day, once before eight in the morning, then again at lunch, and once more around six in the evening, the scale of the work happening behind the gates becomes apparent. During these hours, the roads outside the factories fill with a blur of yellow, blue and green uniforms as employees start or finish a shift. They are mostly young Chinese women, often under the age of 25. Between shifts, the girls might eat at a roadside stand or return to the dormitories provided by the factory, where they often sleep 10 or 12 to a room, in bunkbeds, for the duration of their employment. Outside the dormitory windows flutter a thousand pieces of laundry, a tiny hint of the number of people employed in the workshop of the world.

Within Guangdong's borders are some of the largest factories on earth, including an electronics plant with some 270,000 workers; the world's largest television maker, making millions of TV sets every year; the largest sofa manufacturer; the largest artificial Christmas tree factory; China's leading telecommunications equipment makers; and hundreds of thousands of other plants. There are at least 400,000 factories in Guangdong province. In 2007, Guangdong's gross domestic product was $446.7 billion.[33] If Guangdong were a country, its 2007 GDP would have been larger than that of Saudi Arabia, Switzerland or Iran, and about the same as that of Sweden. It would have been on par with that of Norway and slightly smaller than that of Saudi Arabia.[34]

Parts of your computer come from Guangdong. Most likely, so do many of your children's toys. You own shoes, clothes, furniture and electronics that were assembled there—in fact, you're probably wearing or carrying something from Guangdong right now. Guangdong is where China and your life intersect.

Chapter 1
HOOKED

THE STORY OF CHINA'S emergence as the world's workshop starts with the story of one of its most enthusiastic customers: the United States of America. In the aftermath of World War II, American officials decided that the country's foreign policy interests were best served by helping rebuild the global economy. Policymakers were convinced of the economic and security benefits of free trade, and U.S. businesses wanted markets for their products overseas. Washington poured money into reconstruction of industry in Europe and Japan and encouraged imports to rejuvenate foreign economies through "trade, not aid."

Reversing earlier policies that protected American industry by keeping import tariffs high, postwar officials lowered them. President Truman reassured the public that "American labor can now produce so much more than low-priced foreign labor in a given day's work that our workingmen need no longer fear, as they were justified in fearing in the past, the competition of foreign workers."[1]

Over the following years, the American government continued to promote free trade. By the time China emerged from three decades of relative isolation in 1978, American consumers were accustomed to seeing foreign labels on their shoes, clothing and toys. And American manufacturers were in the habit of fighting back.

Long before there was a China price, there was a Japan price, a Hong Kong price, a Taiwan price and a Mexico price, though they weren't known as such.

Japan was an early beneficiary of America's postwar foreign economic policy. Before the war, Japan had built a powerful textile industry, but it was devastated by American bombing during the war. After World War II, American cotton growers lobbied the U.S. government to rebuild Japan's textile industry so that they would have somewhere to sell their product.[2] The U.S. government helped reconstruct the country's textile mills and in the mid-1950s, the Eisenhower administration slashed tariffs on a variety of items imported from Japan. They were working toward political, not economic goals, Ellen Israel Rosen writes in her book *Making Sweatshops: The Globalization of the U.S. Apparel Industry*: "Neither Truman nor Eisenhower had any interest in providing American consumers with low-cost textile products from Japan. Until the late 1950s the reconstruction of the Japanese textile industry was important primarily to the effort to contain communism and promote the political and economic ties that would link Japan to the Western democracies."[3]

Americans pounced on cheap imports of Japanese-made textiles and clothing in the 1950s. Japan's "one dollar blouse" undercut its American-made competition, which was selling for three to four dollars at the time. Under seige from these and other imports, American textile makers pressured the federal government for protection. In 1957, the United States set a five-year cap on Japanese exports of cotton textiles. By the 1960s, checked by these voluntary restraints and shifting into more sophisticated industries, Japan was losing out to other countries in the manufacture of textiles and clothing.

Its economy rebuilt with help from American aid after succes-

sive wars, South Korea was selling long-sleeve dress shirts in the
United States for half the price of the same shirt manufactured in
the United States in 1972.[4] By the middle of that decade, Hong
Kong led the world in the export of clothing.[5] Back at home, American manufacturers continued to take their concerns to Washington,
as imports, particularly cars and electronics from Japan, threatened
domestic producers.

And yet Asian exports to the United States continued to accler-
ate. Asian governments put export industries at the core of their
postwar development strategies. Hong Kong, Singapore, South Korea
and Taiwan, dubbed the "Asian Tigers," achieved double-digit growth
by focusing on exporting to developed countries. Governments in
these areas created special districts just for exporters with tax exemptions on imports used in export manufacturing and other incentives for foreign investors, a strategy that China would later copy.

These countries' lower labor costs made them attractive suppliers to international buyers. In 1975, American apparel workers
earned an average of $3.79 an hour, compared with $0.22 in South
Korea, $0.29 in Taiwan and $0.75 in Hong Kong.[6] These Asian
countries all followed the same pattern: they started at the bottom
rungs of the manufacturing ladder with simple products like toys,
textiles and apparel, and climbed their way up into electronics, cars
and machinery—another model China would quickly replicate.

Liz Claiborne, the women's clothing brand, was an early buyer
from Hong Kong. As Robert Zane, formerly the company's senior
vice president for manufacturing and sourcing, recalls, "Liz and Art
[Arthur Ortenberg, Liz Claiborne's husband] would go to Hong
Kong every two to three months, and they would hold court in
their suite at the Peninsula Hotel, and they wouldn't leave until the
job was done, which meant that the next season's work was designed and production was arranged."[7]

In 1980, domestic manufacturers produced 70 percent of apparel purchased in the United States. A decade later, they were only

making half.[8] In 2006, almost 91 percent of the apparel sold in America was imported. The ratio for shoes was even higher, at 99 percent.[9]

At first, buying overseas was simply a way to lower costs. Eventually, as Japanese and Korean companies began creating their own brands of electronics and cars, manufacturing overseas became a way for multinationals in the United States and Europe to level the playing field by producing in the same countries as their new competitors.

Motorola and Fairchild were among the earliest groups to begin assembling transistors in South Korea in the 1960s. Other semiconductor groups looked to Singapore, Malaysia and Thailand for testing and assembly.

By most accounts, the early days of the offshore manufacturing boom were highly profitable. American retailers were willing to pay premiums to businesspeople, both local and foreign, for introductions to good, cheap Asian factories; and the factories, because of their relative scarcity, had leverage with buyers.

Americans were buying more from other regions as well. As it had done in Asia, the U.S. government was looking to extend its vision for economic foreign policy in Latin America. In 1961, President Kennedy announced an initiative called the Alliance for Progress to fight the communist threat from Cuba and spread democracy in Latin America. As part of the Alliance for Progress, the newly created United States Agency for International Development provided financial support for companies looking to invest in the Caribbean. It advised governments in the region on attracting foreign investment and trained managers. The United States even funded programs to train workers there.

In the 1960s, the government introduced rules that allowed manufacturers to produce components in the United States, send them overseas for assembly into a final product and ship them back to America, paying tax on only the value added abroad. Of course, one of the main reasons U.S. garment makers were shifting production overseas was to take advantage of lower labor costs and overhead, which meant that there was little added value to tax. These rules helped hold down costs for American garment manufacturers by allowing them to source overseas more cheaply.

In the 1980s, the Reagan administration helped make sourcing from the Caribbean even cheaper for American garment producers. It gave unlimited quotas to Caribbean countries shipping clothes to the U.S. market, as long as the textiles used in their production were made—and cut—in the United States. Some considered these measures a way to help American industry compete with lower-cost producers in Asia.[10]

Mexico in particular saw the potential in manufacturing for U.S. consumers. In 1964, Mexico's minister of industry and commerce traveled to Asia and saw the manufacturing by foreign companies already under way there. The following year, Mexico created a scheme to allow investors to bring in materials and equipment for assembly duty free as long as the products would be exported. These factories were dubbed *maquiladoras*, from the Spanish term for the amount a farmer pays a miller to grind his corn.[11] The maquiladoras enabled U.S. companies to take advantage of Mexico's lower labor costs and less onerous labor laws. They quickly became a hub of garment and electronics production for the U.S. market.

As the maquiladoras and the Asian Tigers were packing containers to America, China was hardly a blip on international buyers' radar screens.

FOR THREE DECADES after 1949, when Mao Zedong's Chinese Communist Party, after a bitter civil war, wrested control of the country from the Nationalists, China was preoccupied by its own domestic struggles.

Mao imagined a strong, self-reliant China, powered by modern industry. Under his guidance, the Communist Party emulated the Soviet Union's Stalinist model for economic growth, mimicking its emphasis on central planning and heavy industry. He began by asserting government control over the economy, including factories. New ministries were created to guide industrial development and defense. Peasants were coerced into collectives with other households and barred from traveling without permission.

The government also borrowed from its ideological big brother, the Soviet Union, to fund its investment in massive heavy industry projects. It brought in thousands of Soviet advisers and shipped thousands of its engineers off for training in the USSR. Mao instituted a strict ranking system for the workplace. An "iron rice bowl" of benefits was introduced, including housing, health care and a pension.

Initially, at least, the Soviet model seemed to work well. Industrial and agricultural output rose rapidly. But in their focus on meeting targets, managers often overlooked quality. Employees were unmotivated. To make matters worse, to pay for the machines it needed to import to develop heavy industry, China had to export agricultural products, at the expense of domestic consumption.[12] Agricultural output, while rising quickly, wasn't expanding fast enough.

Mao's thinking began to shift around the mid-1950s. In order to promote simultaneous growth of industry and agriculture, he concluded, the people needed to mobilize en masse. He envisioned an ideal communist society, where everyone was healthy, communal household facilities allowed women to work more productively in the fields and food and clothing were free.[13] His reforms led to what became known as the Great Leap Forward, an ultimately disastrous set of policies enacted in the late 1950s that caused widespread starvation and the deaths of millions of people. Countryside cooperative farms were merged into communes to lift agricultural output and to aid in the mass mobilization. Bands of peasants worked around the clock to build roads, dikes, lakes and other infrastructure. Under orders to dramatically expand steel production, peasants were pushed to build smelting furnaces in their backyards, stripping their homes of metal in order to feed themselves.

The Great Leap brought chaos, famine and devastation. The backyard furnaces were hopelessly unproductive. Officials routinely inflated grain and industrial output figures to please Mao. Managers abadoned factories, leaving them in the hands of workers. China announced ever higher and more unrealistic grain output targets, and officials continued to lie about achieving them. In hopes of importing more machinery to support heavy industry, China tried to expand its grain exports to the Soviet Union, depriving its own rural residents of even more food.[14] Famine and disease spread through the countryside.

In 1960, relations with the Soviet Union, which had started to get rocky in the mid-1950s, took a nosedive. The USSR withdrew its thousands of technicians from key projects, including oil fields and the country's atomic bomb program.[15]

By the time party officials decided to slow down their targets for the economy in late 1960 and early 1961, 20 million to 30 million people had died. China was in a severe recession, with economic output down by a third.[16]

The Cultural Revolution that began in 1966 set off another tidal wave of upheaval. As part of Mao's campaign, young people, intellectuals, teachers and even party cadres were sent to the countryside to perform manual labor. Newspaper editorials warned that some party members at industrial and mining enterprises were "taking the capitalist road" and called for "struggle" against these people. The chaos was highly disruptive for factories.

Groups of factory employees—often ordinary workers, but also party cadres—seized control of factories, in theory to carry out Mao's command but also to settle personal scores. Often they had support from the notorious Red Guards, the young bands of Mao enthusiasts that terrorized the country during the Cultural Revolution. Technical staff with the wrong attitudes were declared "bourgeois technical authorities," removed from their posts and carted off to the countryside. Workers and party faithful with no management experience or training took the helm at factories.

Because of the confusion in the economy, supplies came unpredictably and managers hoarded whatever goods they could procure. And because output volumes, profits and taxes were set by the plan, factory managers had little incentive or freedom to do better. Industrial production and exports slumped, particularly after relations with the Soviet Union soured. Politics trumped all else. One slogan summed up the tenor of the times: "Management is absolutely not a question of production and business operation. It is a question of the political line."[17]

And yet, even during the dark, isolated days of the Cultural Revolution, China's economy was not completely cut off from the outside world. China had traded mostly with other socialist countries between 1949 and 1960, gradually importing more from market economies starting in the late 1950s as the rift with the Soviet Union deepened. In the 1960s, despite its disdain for Western capitalism, China began to step up its trade with Hong Kong, Japan, Europe and southeast Asia.[18] All trade was conducted through government entities.

Exports were wildly unprofitable. During this period, like other socialist governments, China kept its currency overvalued. Because the government paid producers the same price in renminbi for a product whether it was sold overseas or at home, the overvalued currency often ensured that exports sold at below the cost of production. In 1962, China lost $1.50 for every dollar's worth of products it exported.[19]

The Canton Fair, which had started in 1957, was China's window to the world—with a political tint. At the autumn fair of 1967, there were "struggle sessions" against British traders, recalls

John Kamm, then a businessman and now an advocate for Chinese political detainees. "Foreigners were totally segregated from the local population and were accompanied everywhere by stiff and formal escorts. On Sundays, the one day of the week the trade fair closed, they signed up for staged visits to kindergartens, factories, communes, and, most dreaded of all, hospitals, where performances of stomach surgery under acupuncture anesthesia were laid on," he has written.[20]

In the early 1970s, to rebuild its economy from the ravages of the previous decade and shore up its defenses against a feared invasion by the Soviet Union, China began to import more machines and acquire more petrochemical, steel and other plants from overseas. Mao forged links with the outside world again, hosting President Richard Nixon and establishing diplomatic relations with Japan in 1972. Although Mao continued to control China in name, stewardship of the country was passing fitfully by the mid-1970s to more outward-looking officials. Exports began to tick upward, moving away from the agricultural products common during the Mao years and toward manufactured products, including textiles. Bicycles, watches and sewing machines began to trickle out of China, the first signs of the deluge to come.[21]

IT WAS NOT UNTIL Deng Xiaoping came to power, however, that China turned a corner in its trade with the rest of the world. The son of a landlord from rural Guang'an county in southwestern Sichuan province, Deng spent part of his teenage years in France. When he returned home, he rose through the ranks of the Communist Party. Purged during the Cultural Revolution, Deng was rehabilitated in 1973 as a vice premier. Deng's early approach to the economy was to continue the emphasis on heavy industry, this time through the purchase of equipment from overseas. Officials planned to pay for the shopping spree with oil they hoped to discover, but no oil was to be found.

In 1978, after a political struggle that saw him purged and then rehabilitated once more, Deng pushed aside Mao's successor Hua Guofeng to take control of China. The same year, peasants in the countryside began taking matters into their own hands. Starting in Anhui province, farmers began to abandon the collectives and focus on household production in hopes of staving off further famine and hardship. Government policy condoning decollectivization followed later.

Under Deng's guidance, China devalued the renminbi, and lifted taxes on the parts used to assemble exports. Hoping to replicate the success of market-oriented reforms in the countryside, the government gave managers more power to control production and where they bought materials. Enterprises were allowed to keep some of their profits and given more freedom in hiring, firing and promoting workers.

Change was under way around the country, but Guangdong province changed more quickly than anywhere else. For centuries before the Communist Party came to power, trade had been a way of life along the Pearl River, which curls through the center of the province. Canton, the old name for Guangdong, had been a trading hub as far back as the Song dynasty, which lasted from 960 to 1279.[22] It had continued in this role, and by the eighteenth century, British and American traders strolled the streets in white linen suits.

In the nineteenth century, the river teemed with trading ships piled high with goods, sampans and traveling opera troupes. In 1889, Guangzhou opened the first modern mint in China, stocked with machinery from Birmingham, England.[23] Guangdong continued to flourish as an industrial base under the Nationalists.

Guangdong provincial party leaders decided to do everything

they could to promote economic development without alarming their bosses in Beijing. Central leaders saw value in using the province as a way to attract foreign currency, needed to buy technology and equipment from abroad. Most overseas Chinese were from Guangdong and continued to remit funds back to families there; the province was far enough away from Beijing that any unintended consequences of the experiment in capitalism could be contained; and the party leaders in Guangdong seemed game.[24]

Beijing gave Guangdong more freedom to manage its economy. Instead of having to rely on central planning, the province was allowed set its own prices for locally manufactured exports. Instead of having to send all of its foreign currency earnings from trade with foreign countries to the central government, Guangdong could keep most of these profits for itself. The province was also given more freedom to set wages and prices than other areas.[25] Between 1978 and 1980, Guangdong received more than $200 million in foreign investment, some of it flowing directly into factories.[26]

Guangdong also became the staging ground for the Communist Party's first experiment with capitalism. In 1978, Deng named four "special export zones." Three were in Guangdong—Zhuhai, Shantou and Shenzhen—and one in Xiamen, in Fujian province. They were subsequently upgraded to "special economic zones," or SEZs, perhaps to illustrate the government's greater hopes for their potential. Shenzhen was the first SEZ to be officially established, in May 1980.

China's SEZs offered a package of incentives to foreign investors: lower corporate tax rates, exemptions on import duties for parts and material used in export processing and exemptions on export taxes. Hopes for the SEZs ran high. They were intended to serve as a kind of Venus flytrap for technology and investment. They were supposed to encourage reunification with Taiwan, Macau and Hong Kong. And they were to serve as incubators for capitalism.

But at first, the zones were deeply controversial. The SEZs reminded some officials of the humiliations of the "treaty ports" that China had been forced to open to foreigners after the Opium War in the 1840s. Worse, Shenzhen struggled at first to attract investment on the scale that party leaders had hoped.

It was hardly an easy place for foreign investors to work. Local officials sprang additional fees on investors after deals were signed. Labor productivity was low. The transport system was undeveloped and inefficient. Bureaucratic procedures and interference in joint ventures were legion.

Investors had a list of other concerns. How much freedom would they have to repatriate their earnings on the mainland? How easy would it be to find workers and fire them if necessary? How reliable were the Chinese in upholding contracts? What kind of patent protection was there?[27] While some investors, particularly from Hong Kong, did not wait for answers to these questions, many did.

Chinese officials were disappointed, too. By the end of 1984, the SEZs' exports were growing more slowly than the rest of the economy. Foreign investors weren't bringing in all the foreign technology the Chinese had been hoping for. Foreigners were, however, investing in property and tourism, hardly what the planners in Beijing had envisioned.

International buyers also questioned China's potential. A 1986 article in *BusinessWeek* recounted how buyers were upset about poor quality, long lead times and high material costs in China. The piece warned that "many of those most in the know about the China trade—buyers for major U.S. department stores—doubt whether the Chinese will ever be as successful exporters as the Taiwanese and the South Koreans. 'China is walking at a snail's pace, while the rest of the world is galloping,' says one American buyer in Hong Kong. 'They're not catching up.'"[28]

But such fears proved misplaced. Investment from Hong Kong and Taiwan was on the rise. Workers were flooding into Guangdong: By one estimate, there were as many as ten applicants for every job in the late 1980s. In 1987, David Wilson, Hong Kong's governor, noted that there were already at least one million workers in Guangdong province processing goods for Hong Kong companies, more than the British colony's whole manufacturing workforce. Xinhua, the Chinese state-run news agency that served as the mainland's de facto embassy in Hong Kong, called Wilson to say that no, in fact, two million people in Guangdong were doing this type of work.[29]

Quietly, China's factories were taking their place in the global economy. In 1980, Frank Lo, a Hong Kong businessman who had been making underwear and other simple consumer goods since the 1960s, had opened a factory near Foshan in Guangdong province and another in the northern city of Dalian to take advantage of China's lower labor costs. In the first year of operation, Lo's 2,000 employees churned out 14 million bras. He shipped 12 million to America, prompting the United States to create a quota for Chinese-made brassieres. Top Form International, Lo's company, began accumulating market share in the United States and Japan.[30] Top Form is today the world's largest contract bra manufacturer.

One Shenzhen factory stuffed, stitched and assembled dresses for many of Coleco Industries' pudgy-faced Cabbage Patch dolls that flew off the shelves in the United States in the 1980s.[31] Another churned out Sony Trinitron color TVs, most destined for the Chinese domestic market. Sony also relied on a joint venture in Xiamen to make its videotape recorders in the early 1980s.[32] Cheap TV sets made by Hong Kong companies nobody had ever heard of were starting to roll out of Guangdong province into Europe. Philips and Matsushita Electric Industrial, better known as Panasonic, were investing in TV tube factories in China.[33]

"The Chinese market share is shooting up so fast, and they're selling at such low prices, that the situation is becoming intolerable," *BusinessWeek* quoted Jean Caillot, an executive at Thomson, the French TV maker, as saying in 1988.[34] Thomson tolerated the situation for 15 years, until it formed a joint venture with Chinese rival TCL in 2003.

China's manufactured exports began to increase in the late 1980s, rising from 49.5 percent in 1985 to 81.8 percent of total exports by 1993, growing nearly 24 percent per year.[35] Exports of toys, sporting goods, shoes, textiles and apparel accounted for much of this growth, though shipments of electrical equipment like televisions, telephones and home appliances also expanded sharply during this time.[36] In 1988, a Taiwanese businessman named Terry Gou opened a computer components factory in Shenzhen to expand capacity and lower costs. Gou promoted his factory to U.S. and Japanese buyers and acquired a large piece of land. Today, Gou's company, Hon Hai Precision Industry, employs 450,000 people across China and counts Apple, Motorola, Dell and Hewlett-Packard among its customers.[37]

Also in 1988, Yue Yuen, a shoe manufacturer owned by the Tsai family of Taiwan, set up a plant in Zhuhai, in coastal Guangdong. Yue Yuen expanded into nearby Dongguan and Zhongshan and is today the world's largest manufacturer of shoes.

By 1992, when Deng Xiaoping traveled to Guangdong to reinforce his economic reforms on what became known as his Southern Tour, the United States accounted for nearly a third of China's exports, up from only a few percent in 1978.[38] Wal-Mart started buying products from China in 1993.

A mutual dependency was forming. China depended on money from overseas, in the form of either direct investment or orders into its factories. And the rest of the world was developing a taste for cheap Chinese products. In the wake of Deng's visit, local governments in China began vying for foreign investment.

A brazen commercial culture was taking root in southern China, one that was beyond the control, and no doubt the expectations, of the sober mandarins in Beijing who had authorized the creation of the SEZs. Shenzhen, the first and largest of the zones, was by the mid-1980s becoming an oasis of decadence in socialist China, a capitalist playground replete with nightclubs, massage parlors, gambling halls and all manner of illicit financial dealings.

In 1986, the city played host to the National Hercules Cup International Bodybuilding Tournament, including—for the first time in China—Chinese women in bikinis.[39] In 1993, at the height of a stock market boom, a restaurant in the former fishing town hosted a banquet including lobster from Japan, salmon from Norway, turtle, shark's fin and extra-large abalone, at a cost, in today's dollars, of more than $130,000. The banquet was so extravagant that it earned a reprimand from the National People's Congress, China's legislature.[40] Shenzhen's reputation as a wild, lawless Chinese boomtown was sealed.

Chapter 2

THE FIVE-STAR FACTORY

For the crowds of international buyers that flock to Guangzhou each year, the Canton Fair is just the beginning of the journey. Having found factory managers who promised to deliver, the buyers fan out across the country, installing themselves in hotels for several days of visits. One of these hotels is the Shangri-La in Shenzhen, just across the border from Hong Kong. Its lobby fills up early most mornings with buyers, Western men and women in suits, polo shirts and khakis. They wheel their black carry-on luggage behind them, their expressions slack and fogged by jet lag.

The buyers stand beneath the crystal chandelier, making calls on their cell phones to pass the time, squinting through the hazy sunshine at the driveway outside. The murmured talk among them is of shipments to California, the Chicago market and joint venture agreements. Within two hours' drive of this lobby are tens of thousands of factories, filled with millions of workers.

As nine o'clock approaches, the Shangri-La's driveway begins to attract minivans and buses, their dashboards displaying cards printed with the household names of global commerce: Wal-Mart Stores, Hasbro, Sears. The crowd in the lobby swells with well-heeled Chinese men and women, translators and business partners. Gradually, the lobby empties into the vans, which turn onto Shennan Boulevard, the main artery in Shenzhen that runs out toward the factories.

On a bright morning in 2006, a Wal-Mart executive sat quietly in a sedan crawling along Shennan Boulevard. She was on her way to visit a factory that made goods sold in Wal-Mart. Her job was to determine whether the factory was producing according to Wal-Mart's ethical standards—which include a strict ban on child or slave labor and rules on occupational hazards, working hours and payment of the minimum wage. The Wal-Mart executive's visit represented two contrary forces pulling on global supply chains in labor-intensive products today: the demand from consumers and companies for goods at a cheap price, and the fear of news leaking out about the unsavory way they may have been made. Wal-Mart was inspecting the factory to make sure it wasn't a sweatshop.

About an hour later, the car pulled up next to a nondescript industrial building, indistinguishable from countless others in China: Covered in chipped, dirty tiles, with a sad family of plants by the entrance, the factory wasted little on appearances. A manager showed the Wal-Mart inspector to a conference room lined with a glass display case filled with the factory's products.

The inspector asked the manager to retrieve payroll and other records and to choose 15 assembly-line workers she could interview later that morning. "Do it as fast as you can," she said. "I have to finish by one P.M. at the latest." Clipboard in hand, the auditor briskly toured the factory, peering over employees' shoulders and asking them about their work, scrutinizing fire extinguishers and a first aid box. She inspected the factory warehouse. She squinted at quality control records on display at the line supervisor's office.

The factory managers watched her warily, afraid of what she

might find. At the end of her tour, she pronounced the factory
"pretty good." Relieved, the managers treated her to a Cantonese
lunch—steamed fish, rice, soup and vegetables crowded onto a lazy
Susan—at a nearby restaurant. The auditor left early to inspect another factory.

A ten-minute drive away from the restaurant, another factory
owned by the same manager was humming with activity. This factory was making the same products for Wal-Mart as the factory the
auditor saw, but under wholly different conditions and a cloak of
secrecy. Tucked away in a gated business park, the factory is not
registered with the Chinese government. Its 500 employees work
on a single floor, without safety equipment or insurance and in excess of the legal working hours. They are paid a daily rather than a
monthly wage. No one from Wal-Mart has ever seen this factory,
though Wal-Mart buys much of the factory's output, according to
its owner. Officially, this factory does not even exist.

IN THE PIE OF PROFITS made by selling things to people, the
manufacturer often gets the smallest slice. Depending on the product, manufacturers can make as little as a few percent or even less.
Retailers or brands often take the largest piece, marking up the
goods anywhere between two and ten times—or more—between
the time they leave the factory and when they hit the shelves. "We
have a theory," says Bruce Rockowitz, president of the trading arm
of Li & Fung, which manages logistics and manufacturing in China
and around the world for big international companies. "It's called
the soft three dollars. And basically if something is manufactured in
China at a dollar, it then retails at four dollars, in that range.

"What I think Americans don't really appreciate is that a big
portion of the value that is developed by manufacturing in China is
not left with China. It's left with the people that manufacture the

brands, the retailer and the consumer. And the actual factories, they don't make that much money," he says. "The profit that a factory will make in China is very low."

Part of the reason for this is that China's arrival as a mass producer of consumer goods coincided with a dramatic shift in manufacturing processes. Although Western companies have been outsourcing manufacturing overseas for decades, only relatively recently has technology allowed the production of a wide variety of goods to be divided into tiny, standardized steps that could be performed by multiple companies in disparate countries, thereby dividing by three, four or even more the profits to be made from manufacturing.

To make a shirt, a factory in South Korea might supply the yarn, a plant in Taiwan might do the weaving and dyeing and a factory in Thailand might do the actual cutting and sewing.[1] A laptop sold in the United States might contain a graphics chip designed in Canada and made in Taiwan, a hard drive from Japan and a liquid crystal display screen produced in South Korea.[2] Or these factories could all be located within one Chinese province. This so-called modularization of production has made it possible for Chinese factories to specialize and become incredibly competitive in the production of one component of a global supply chain.[3] It has helped turn products that once appeared to be sophisticated luxuries— mobile phones, DVD players, flat-screen TVs—into more affordable commodities.

This shift has also made it easier for companies that control the supply chains—often the Western brands and retailers—to speed up the production process. In industries such as toys, manufacturers are introducing new models faster to take advantage of rapidly changing technology or to stimulate consumer demand. Stephen Dixon, regional director for greater China at consultancy Kurt Salmon Associates, says the apparel industry is moving away from

fixed seasons like spring and autumn and toward the model pio-
neered by Inditex, owner of the apparel retailer Zara. At Zara,
Dixon says, "there is no clear definition of seasonal variation. They
have a continuous flow of merchandise to the stores with an ever-
changing variation to the products in the store." It takes Zara only
three weeks to dream up a garment, produce it and get it into
stores.[4] The treadmill of global capitalism is accelerating, increasing
the pressure on manufacturers to produce goods quickly and, in
some cases, in smaller quantities.

Modularization of manufacturing has also allowed brands and
retailers to switch between suppliers at will. In many light consumer industries, the most salient trend is the lack of loyalty in relationships between buyers and factories. Especially since the advent
of the so-called big box retailers—the discount chains housed in
giant, boxlike buildings—buyers have been looking to save money
wherever they can.

This relentless competition for lower prices has bred what Jim
Straus, an Illinois-based businessman who has been connecting
Western buyers with Chinese factories for more than a decade, calls
"the race to zero." These chains base their business model on providing goods at affordable prices. Shoppers expect continual price
declines, so the retailers, and the middlemen that supply them, demand continual price declines from their suppliers. If one factory
can't provide that, they find another that can. Retailers come to
believe that this process can continue indefinitely. "The mindset of
the big box retailers is the race to zero, because they can't get any
more for their product," Straus says, noting that the trend is particularly striking in electronics. "There's no loyalty. They'll eat you
up for a nickel. They'll eat you up for a penny."

Despite these pressures, there is no shortage of people in China
willing to sign up for a contract to produce for big international
brands. The promise of the annual volume of shipments involved in

supplying to the U.S. or European market provides a powerful incentive to entrepreneurs. And when a product is a hit, contract manufacturers do a booming trade. Some pocket healthy profits.

The world's largest contract manufacturers have found a way to make this competitive pressure work for them. They capitalize on the outsourcing trend by partnering with brands in electronics, apparel and shoes to do more than just assemble products for their customers. They also advise on design and strategy. At the top of the pyramid in the electronics industry are giant contract manufacturers like Foxconn, part of Taiwan's Hon Hai Precision Industry, and Flextronics, which makes Microsoft's Xbox game console.

The garment and shoemaking industries also have their own thoroughbred specialists, many of them descendants of Hong Kong's and Taiwan's booming export trade in the 1970s. Hong Kong–based companies like the Esquel Group, Luen Thai and TAL make clothes for big international brands according to Western management philosophies and with sophisticated technology. But they have diversified beyond traditional manufacturing into research, design and inventory management for customers. Esquel even grows its own cotton in Xinjiang province in northwestern China. Pou Chen, a Taiwanese company, works with the world's leading shoe brands. Its Hong Kong–listed Yue Yuen subsidiary is the world's largest athletic shoe manufacturer and is expanding into retail.

Most Chinese factories are smaller, shakier institutions. The commodification of manufacturing and the Chinese government's emphasis on economic growth have made it easier to gain a foothold in the global supply chain. One European electronics buyer in Shenzhen describes a common archetype for the factory managers he deals with: "Three years before, he was in construction. He was the cheapest factory in his industry, but he didn't know if he was losing money or making money. He stays in business for two to three years," he says. "Anybody can open a factory here."

One Hong Kong businessman brags that with the right connections, he can throw together an assembly line in as little as two weeks. Sometimes, foreign importers or brands supply the tools, the expensive metal molds used in making plastic parts; component or material suppliers provide lines of credit to be repaid (in theory, at least) when the goods are exported. There are consultants in China who will build you a factory, buy your materials, and hire your workforce and management team. All you have to do is wire money.

Foreign investors enjoy greater privileges. In the name of promoting economic growth, local governments will go out of their way—even violating their own laws—to help them. Officials will set aside land, build factories and find workers. They will slash taxes, offer rent-free periods and waive fees. They might even overlook regulations on product quality and health.[5] "Although Chinese law does provide certain preferential treatments to foreign investors, particularly in relation to tax exemptions and reductions," reads an international law firm's newsletter, "it can be the case that incentives offered by local authorities are unlawful."[6]

Partly as a result of these factors, there is fierce competition in the production of many simple consumer products. Log on to Alibaba.com, a leading Web site that connects buyers with factories in China, and type in any item. A search for "lamp" finds more than 2,200 companies making every kind of lamp you could want. Almost 1,000 will make you an MP3 player. More than 17,000 companies produce T-shirts. "Why is it so tough to do business in China?" asks Charle Chen, manager of Zhongshan First Mountain Electrical Appliance, a giant electronic sign factory in the southern city of Zhongshan. "Because you don't have one or two competitors, you have 100 or 200." In the summer of 2005, Andy Rothman, China macro strategist at brokerage CLSA, surveyed 30 owners of small and medium-sized private manufacturing enterprises. Of those he interviewed, 37 percent said they had more than 200 domestic competitors.[7]

In a market like this, buyers often hold all the cards. And they play them well. The largest buyers can demand annual and sometimes even quarterly price cuts from their suppliers. "As things get more competitive, the pressure that comes along with that, yeah, we try to take advantage of it," Gary Meyers, a vice president in global procurement at Wal-Mart, told the *Wall Street Journal* in 2003. The piece dubbed China's export manufacturing sector "survival of the cheapest."[8]

Many export manufacturers in China live order to order, buffeted by vacillating commodity prices and jockeying against aggressive competitors. Rivals copy each others' advances and, once competition erodes profit margins in one product, move herdlike into producing something else. Overcrowding in many product categories is good for buyers, who have more factories to choose from, but hard on manufacturers, who have to endure paper-thin margins.

This kind of pressure can lead factory managers to desperate decisions. Managers, many of whom have little or no management training and sometimes no more than a high school education, often accept orders without considering whether they have the capacity to fulfill them.

One consultant who works with Chinese factories says: "They don't have any strategies. It's seat of the pants, day by day, they survive by some mistake, by some stroke of luck they get by another day and then the next day they get up and do it all again."

China's history of political upheaval and its current business environment, where policies can change overnight, intensify manufacturers' short-term perspective. Some factory managers maintain they operate in the narrow space where the whim of their customers, the favor of local officials and the will of the migrant workforce overlap. A shift in any one of these elements can pitch the business into turmoil.

American toddlers happen not to respond well to a cartoon created to promote a new toy. Hundreds of workers at the factory in Huizhou, Guangdong province, chosen to produce that toy lose their jobs when the order is canceled. An importer in the Middle East falls on hard times and defaults on a payment to a towel factory in central China? The towel factory's young manager takes out another loan, forcing his wife's family deeper into debt.

EUGENE CHAN, the owner of the factory the Wal-Mart auditor visited, grew up in Hong Kong when that city was one of the world's great offshore manufacturing centers. Then a British colony, Hong Kong was so overrun with new arrivals from mainland China in the 1950s and 1960s that many families squatted in hillside shantytowns until the government built public housing estates. Factories farmed out work to local families, and a generation of children grew up assembling plastic flowers, toy motors and jeans on the floors of their apartments after school. Chan, who insisted that his name and that of his business partner be changed to protect his business, was one of those children. Every afternoon at three o'clock, a truck would arrive at his housing estate and deposit in the lobby a pile of products that needed assembling. His mother would snap up the family's share and parcel it out to the children.

That experience gives him a different perspective on factory management from that of the Western companies he started supplying 15 years ago. Then, beating employees was a standard management strategy at factories like Chan's. "This was normal," Chan says. Managers dashed out to eat dinner before dark because all the local restaurants closed at five. The same managers slept at their desks, and when they didn't, they slept in wooden buildings nearby. The factories were their lives.

Several years ago, Chan decided to pitch for a contract to supply Wal-Mart. He knew he was in for a challenge. As we will see in greater detail later, Wal-Mart and other big multinationals began requiring their suppliers to comply with a code of conduct for ethical standards in the 1990s. While codes vary by company, they all contain requirements that suppliers limit working hours, install safety equipment and pay their workers at least the legal minimum wage. And they require suppliers to follow the local labor law. All of these conditions have to be met before a factory will be approved as a supplier. To Chan, the most problematic element of the code of conduct was the working hours. He doubted whether he could meet Wal-Mart's delivery deadlines and still follow China's restrictive rules on hours of work.

Postreform China didn't have a labor law until 1994. Since it came into effect the following year, the law has mandated an average 44-hour workweek, with no more than 36 hours of overtime per month. The standard working day lasts eight hours. Under the labor law, employees are guaranteed one day off a week and at least four national holidays. If a company in China needs its employees to work longer than the standard workweek, it should by law first negotiate with the workers or union. In practice, it can negotiate for a waiver from the local government. Overtime pay on weekdays is one and a half times the regular wage; on rest days it is twice the regular wage; on Sundays and public holidays, it is three times. Employees are to work no longer than three hours of overtime a day.

By comparison, under America's Fair Labor Standards Act, employees who work more than 40 hours in a workweek are entitled to overtime compensation of at least one and a half times the regular wage for any hours beyond that. Although there are some exceptions for certain kinds of workers, there is no cap on the total hours employees over the age of 16 can work. Nor do employers have to pay overtime for work on the weekends, public holidays or rest days, unless the hours worked during those days push the employee over the 40-hour workweek.[9]

China's labor law was created in the midst of an outbreak of worker unrest as the country moved toward a market economy under Deng Xiaoping. After Deng's 1992 Southern Tour, when he asserted his determination to proceed with market reforms, debate began on a labor law that would reflect the new structure of the economy. Part of a broader shift toward improving the rule of law, the labor legislation was intended to reassure foreign investors that China was a stable, well-regulated place to put their money. Chinese officials examined labor laws from other countries, mainly those in Europe.

Auret van Heerden, a former International Labor Organization official who is now president of the Fair Labor Association, a multistakeholder group that monitors working conditions, says Chinese officials had hoped the labor law would address the gap that had emerged between the market economy and the old socialist laws, but even after the legislation came into effect, "nobody knew how to use it. You had a whole load of practitioners—labor bureau officials, trade union officials—whose mind was still stuck in the state-owned economy suddenly expected to manage a market economy and they just couldn't do it."[10]

Chan was fairly sure that if he followed Chinese labor law, he wouldn't stay in business long. "Customers believe they are reasonable but to us the price is not reasonable," Philip Lam, Chan's business partner, said later. "So we have to think of other ways to make our profits reasonable."[11]

Chan's employees are migrants from rural villages who, he told me, consider the legal minimum wage inadequate and prefer to work longer hours to increase their salaries. We were sitting in the factory's conference room, a spartan space dominated by a large table and shelves displaying the factory's products; it was a few months after the Wal-Mart auditor had visited. "The basic trouble is the worker wants to earn more in a short time," Chan told me. "If any factory has overtime in some area, all the workers will go to it. Workers like overtime. They tell me, 'I haven't come here for a holiday. I'm here to earn money.' If you don't have overtime, they will leave."

Chan asked for help from friends who ran their own factories. They explained how they coped with the divergent demands of their workers and customers: They made one set of time cards for Wal-Mart and kept the real ones elsewhere. They coached their workers to give Wal-Mart the answers it wanted to hear. And they set up factories on the side, factories Wal-Mart never saw but that made its products anyway. In essence, they subcontracted.

Chan followed their example. Every night, two of the factory's office employees stayed late to stamp time cards with clock-on and clock-off times that matched Wal-Mart's standards. Real and fake cards were locked away in separate locations to avoid confusion. One manager created forged payroll documents on the office computer to match the fake time cards. Another invited trusted workers to the office for a "party" after work each week and explained how they would be expected to respond to auditors' questions. Underage or uninsured workers were given days off during announced audits. For extra security, new hires were not allowed to work extra overtime, in case they were spies from labor advocacy groups.[12]

The ruse of the falsified records worked beautifully. The workers recited their lines convincingly enough. The time cards exuded authenticity. Wal-Mart never uncovered sufficient evidence to prove that the factory was lying. Chan and Lam suspect that Wal-Mart knew the records were forged and the workers were coached but chose to ignore these facts, although they have no evidence to support this claim. "They need cheap products," Lam said. "If they are not doing it like this—open one eye, close one eye—they can't have cheap products."

"If every factory needs to reach the legal standard, the costs of production will not be that low," he added. "So most factories will have two factories: One is for demonstration, one is for actual production." They are certain the Chinese government is similarly aware of the trade-off behind the China price. Beijing, Chan told me, "only sets a very beautiful number for working hours to show the world. The government already knows everyone cheats, even themselves."

BUT THE FORGERY MADE Chan uneasy. He worried about being caught, which would have consequences for his relationship with Wal-Mart. Even if the workers were well trained, "how can you prove that they will say the right things?" Chan thought. And yet he knew his competitors were working in excess of the legal working hours and still managing to pass the code-of-conduct audits. If eight out of 10 factories followed the rules and two didn't, you might as well not have rules, he thought.

So he switched to a new strategy. Quietly, even as he was masterminding the document forgery at the old factory, Chan cut a deal with a powerful local entrepreneur to rent a floor in an industrial building in a nearby business park. He ordered simple equipment and recruited workers willing to work for longer than the maximum legal working hours, without insurance or labor contracts. Because the factory wasn't registered with any authority, it wasn't bound by any cumbersome rules on health and safety and it didn't have to pay taxes. Very few records were kept. Chan made sure the factory, which isn't listed on his business card, stayed a secret from Wal-Mart and the vendors he contracted with to sell to the U.S. retailer.

Chan decided to keep the first factory operating as it was, but to run it strictly according to Wal-Mart rules: no more fake time cards, no more coaching workers. Instead, he would farm out more work to his second factory. Everything Wal-Mart saw would be real; it just wouldn't represent the whole picture. In China, they call them "five-star factories"—as good as a five-star hotel. Sometimes they're known as "model" or "demonstration" factories. Their unregistered cousins are "black" or "shadow" factories. But shadow factories are ultimately subcontractors. As America outsources to Chinese factories in pursuit of cheaper prices, Chinese factories outsource to other Chinese factories for the same reason.

Paul Midler, president of China Advantage, an outsourcing and supply chain management company, says subcontracting is a common practice in China, often without the knowledge of the customer. One auditor who has been monitoring factories in China for over a decade estimates 99 percent of factories have a "shadow" to help them meet retailers' demands.

Chan shifted 40 percent of his production to the shadow factory, recruiting 500 migrants to work there. Staff who wanted to work the legal hours remained at the five-star factory. "This factory is for the lazy workers," Chan says. Employees in the shadow factory earn about $165 a month for working 11- or 12-hour days, seven days a week, while the "lazy" workers at the five-star plant take home at least $127 for eight- to 10-hour days, six days a week. "Seven days a week, every day overtime for four hours, they will be happy," is how Chan describes workers at the shadow plant. Employees at the five-star factory are paid by the month; at the black factory, wages are paid daily.

The workers asked to be paid by the day, Chan says, and even accept a lesser wage in exchange for the privilege. Getting the unregistered workers their money that regularly is a hassle. Every morning, a driver who doubles as a bodyguard brings the manager to the bank, where he withdraws enough cash to pay the second factory's workforce. Still, it's worth the trouble: Chan reckons the shadow factory is 20 percent to 30 percent more productive than the five-star plant because of its longer working hours. He has started outsourcing 20 percent of his production to a third factory and plans to invest in a fourth—both are shadow factories.

"I must make our factory stronger," he says. "Without these other factories, we wouldn't have a chance." More than half of Chan's production capacity is now off the books, off the Chinese government's radar screen and out of sight of Wal-Mart.

SUBCONTRACTING LIKE THIS is a common practice in manufacturing around the world, often for good reasons. It frees factories to focus on what they do best, outsourcing the operations where they are least efficient. It can cut costs and accelerate production. But unless buyers of the goods monitor their suppliers' subcontractors, the practice also means that customers have no guarantee where or how their product is made. A subcontractor could be substituting cheaper parts or materials, adding unapproved chemicals or skipping safety features. "You can't control for quality that you can't see," says Midler, the outsourcing executive. "Anything you're trying to monitor, you can't monitor if the product is being made somewhere else."

But for Chan these issues are beside the point. Subcontracting to a shadow factory simply allows him to tap one of China's most important resources over the past few decades: laborers who work long and hard.

Good official data on the hours Chinese manufacturing employees spend on the line is difficult, if not impossible, to get. Judith Banister, a consultant with Javelin Investments in Beijing who also works for the Conference Board, a business research group, has made her own estimates based on publicly available information. Using the results of a government study, she found that during two weeks in 2002 manufacturing workers in cities worked an average of 45.4 hours per week.[13] Manufacturing workers in so-called town and village enterprises, which are companies introduced in the 1970s that are collectively owned by or closely associated with rural communities, worked on average 50 hours a week.[14] As Banister concedes, these numbers may well underestimate the hours worked in Chinese factories, particularly in export plants on the coasts.

Some Chinese factory workers regularly log 360 hours or even 400 hours in one month, according to the ethical trading consultancy Impactt. That's a 12- or 13-hour day, an 80- or 90-hour week. With no days off. Under Chinese law, workers should not be on the job more than 204 hours a month, including overtime.[15] By comparison, the average American manufacturing workweek in the United States was 41.1 hours in the fourth quarter of 2006.[16]

Excessive overtime is not an exclusive vice of Chinese factories, nor of sweatshops producing for big retailers. It stretches across the supply chain. But in China, it is extremely common. Of the 142 Chinese factories Amherst-based nongovernmental organization Verité surveyed for international brands between 2002 and 2003, 133—an overwhelming 93 percent—were working longer than legal limits. Of those 133 plants, the largest percentage were working more than 100 hours of overtime a month.[17] During the busiest months in Pearl River Delta factories, working days can stretch to 18 hours or even longer. More than half of the workers Verité interviewed said they wanted to work overtime to earn more money. Nearly three quarters said they considered this extra work "important," "very important" or "essential."[18]

"It's an incongruous law," says one Western factory owner in China of the labor law's overtime restrictions. "Because you know they are asking people to work eight hours and they all say what do I do with the extra four or five hours? Sit on my bum? That's their logic."[19]

Factory managers believe there is no other way to meet customers' demands. Buyers often introduce essential design changes late in the production process without extending the production deadline, forcing their suppliers into overdrive. Or they drag their feet in approving the final product specifications. Buyers and factories often misunderstand each other. Materials are late in arriving at the factory. In the absence of vigorous enforcement of the labor law by the Chinese government, each of these factors contributes to widespread violation of working hour requirements.

So, too, does a shortage of managers who understand the importance of knowing how to manage people. Says Auret van Heerden of the FLA: "I think even today the major problem is that in the labor field, you've just got so few people who have an understanding of human resource development, human resource management or labor relations. The mentality of those managers that we were meeting in 1996 is the same as the mentality of the manager you're meeting in 2006."[20]

For all the extra hours they are working, Chinese employees are not always adequately compensated. A survey by the Guangdong trade union found that 35 percent of workers were not paid proper overtime wages, and this surely understates the problem.[21] In interviews with workers in the southern city of Dongguan in 2004 and 2005, Hong Kong NGO China Labor Bulletin found that "managers basically regarded the payment of overtime as an internal matter to be decided on by the factory, and not as a statutory right of the workers. Indeed, many of them seemed to award overtime pay as a kind of 'discretionary bonus' entirely untied to the actual number of overtime hours worked."[22]

Nor is overtime always optional. China Labor Bulletin found that many managers set production quotas so high that they were impossible to meet during a regular working day. Employees were not paid for the overtime they worked in order to meet the targets. What overtime they were paid for constituted a significant portion of their earnings: some 30 percent to 50 percent, according to CLB.[23]

As anyone who has ever pulled an all-nighter can attest, all this overtime can't be good for workers' output. The longer the hours, the higher the risk of accidents. Productivity also declines during long overtime work. And even if managers are not paying the full overtime wage, having workers on the line for longer costs money. Half of managers surveyed by Verité for its overtime report admitted that while they worked overtime to meet production deadlines, they were losing money by working overtime. Sixty percent admitted productivity declined during excessive overtime.[24] In *China Blue*, a documentary by filmmaker Micha Peled about a jeans factory in southern China, workers try to hold their eyes open with clothespins during long shifts.

Yet for many factory managers, the case for illegally long overtime is much more persuasive than that for working within legal limits. With so many competitors and so much pressure from buyers on price, factories cannot afford to miss a shipment deadline. Their livelihood depends on it.

CHAN'S FIVE-STAR FACTORY is not somewhere you would want to stay overnight. There are footprints on the walls. It's poorly lit, with low ceilings and slippery floors. Like most factories in southern China, only the offices are air conditioned. If that was five-star, I wanted to see what one-star looked like.

Though they often sit just down the road from their five-star brethren, China's shadow factories are generally off limits to most foreign visitors. Most buyers, auditors, government officials and journalists see only the model factories. It took time, then, to convince Chan to take me to one of his shadow factories. He insisted on one condition: Allowing a foreign woman onto the production line was too risky; I had to be content with a drive-by. So one sticky summer afternoon, we left the model factory and drove for about ten minutes, passing tired-looking, tiled factories with thirsty palm trees out front, a few restaurants and new apartment buildings.

The car slowed and we turned into a narrow road blocked by a metal gate manned by a guard. The first tall commercial building had reflective windows and looked, like many in the area, entirely empty. Chinese cities are filled with mystery buildings like these, thrown up in a froth of real estate development, their intended or actual uses unclear. We drove past that building and pulled into a narrow paved area behind it in a valley between two industrial buildings tall enough to block the sunlight. Workers streamed past us, headed back on shift. Chan, visibly nervous, got out of the car and pointed out the lack of fire extinguishers—except for one fire hydrant outside the building—and the stairs, which had been broken but were recently fixed.

Chan had told me that if I asked his employees at this factory where they worked, they would tell me they were unemployed to protect the factory's anonymity. If government inspectors arrived, employees would shut the door to the factory to keep them out. Chan didn't like to come here, he said, because it made him uncomfortable. He preferred to have his local managers deal with this factory. "You like to eat chicken, but you don't want to see how the chicken was killed," he said, hurrying me back into the car.

WAL-MART EXECUTIVES acknowledge that they are aware of the practice of subcontracting. Rajan Kamalanathan, vice president for ethical standards, says the retailer asks all suppliers to declare any other factories they will be using to complete the order so that those factories can be audited to the same standards.

When presented with Chan's argument that he can't stay in business and make a decent profit and follow Wal-Mart's code of conduct, Beth Keck, director of international corporate affairs, objects. "There's no bones about it, we're tough negotiators," she says. "It's very clear that we see ourselves as the advocate for the consumer in bringing the consumer the best value possible. But a business, a supplier, a factory that's doing business with us, it's by their choice. If they see terms that they can't meet, then they have a responsibility to not take the order. They've got a choice there."

In spite of his chicanery, Chan's business is not getting any more profitable. Skyrocketing oil prices and rising demand from other manufacturers in China's booming economy have driven up material costs, which account for 60 percent to 70 percent of the total production bill. Power shortages two to three days a week have forced Chan to buy his own generator, which can double his electricity costs. At the same time, the government is raising the minimum wage quickly.

Worker turnover continues to increase, as employees at Chan's model factory leave for better pay elsewhere. He is losing 20 percent to 30 percent of his workforce every month. "If your factory has too many holidays, they will go to another factory without holiday," he says. Not all of his former employees stay in industry, however. Since almost all of his employees are women, some leave for entertainment, others for the ever-booming business of prostitution. That's why "you don't find a beautiful girl on the production line."

To encourage workers to stay longer, Chan has been holding barbecues for his staff at the five-star factory and taking them to the beach—tactics he calls "updated management." But he admits he can't compete with the benefits larger factories are offering, their movie nights showing pirated DVDs and their karaoke rooms. He has resorted to paying his staff $39 for every new worker they bring in. And he is spending hundreds of thousands of dollars on machinery to replace his workers and relieve the headache of high turnover. Employees have to pass Wal-Mart's audits for working hours and pay, but machines don't, he says. Plus, machines make visiting customers think he's "very high-tech."

For now, Chan's company has hundreds of competitors. He believes some of them routinely lower their prices below the cost of production to win business. He also suspects mainland Chinese businessmen are moving into his sector with government help: One new competitor who is undercutting him on price drives a car with license plates from the People's Liberation Army, China's military. His concerns are difficult to verify. Chan says his gross profit margins, a healthy 20 percent five years ago, are 10 percent to 15 percent and falling.

Recently, local officials appear to have decided to turn the area where his factory is located into a luxury property district; a high-rise apartment building is already under construction nearby. "The local government wants the factories to leave and all of them build beautiful apartments or business centers, just like Hong Kong a few years ago," he says.

Having watched his rent rise 10 percent to 20 percent annually for the past three years, Chan has been looking to move his first factory. For months, he traveled to cities in the Chinese interior. Officials in these areas courted him, he says, "like a man dates a girl," promising a ready supply of workers, good power supply, the flexibility to work around the clock. Just as he was about to settle on one city in northern Guangdong province, a rainstorm flooded local factories. The officials had failed to mention, over the mao-tai liquor and stuffed pig, that they were living in a flood plain. Chan put the search on hold.

And through this, Chan is spending more than $19,000 a year to be audited by Wal-Mart and his other customers. Many multinationals have started charging their supplier factories for audits, particularly if previous inspections have uncovered code violations. For factories like Chan's that must pass dozens of audits a year, these inspections are a substantial, resented business expense.

Like other Chinese factory owners, Chan fervently believes that the code of conduct and compliance programs are a conspiracy, a ploy by America to make China less competitive. He suspects, incorrectly, that factories in other countries do not have to undergo audits. "In other countries, they don't have this. This is because the government, they don't want China to be the only [country supplying America], so they give you a lot of trouble."

Chan feels he is making the best of a difficult situation: Caught between the demands of his workers and the demands of his customers, he is just trying to survive. Chan says his employees and customers leave him no other choice. "If you need . . . to be competitive with other factories, you must follow the rules of the game. First is the workers, second is the game of overseas orders."

"The biggest problem, I think, is the culture of the Chinese. Everyone wants to earn more and then go back home," he says. Everyone, including Chan. His margins may be falling, but his profits from the factory are still enough to buy luxury cars and trips around the region.

Just as he worked after school as a child to earn money for his family, migrant workers actually want to work beyond the law's limits. "This is a very, very deep culture. All Chinese people want more money because it's the culture . . . the workers like to work and earn money because they don't want to stay here very long. After a few years, they'd like to go home and have a very small business."

This desire is part of China's competitive advantage, he explains. "Why haven't the factories gone to Africa?" he asked me one day. "Because only Chinese work like this. In Thailand, Malaysia, the workers are lazy. And in Africa." His uncle had been to a factory in Africa, he said, and the workers there only worked four hours a day and slept the rest of the time. "Because the history of

China has always been civil war, people think saving money will make them safer."

Chan reckons he is like everyone else in China: just trying to survive. Going behind his customers' backs to subcontract work to sweatshops is just part of doing business. "Everyone knows that everyone cheats," he says. "Everyone knows this is only the rules of the game."

Chapter 3

THE PHYSICAL COST

Every morning for a decade, Deng Wenping awoke at dawn and crept out of bed for a run. When he returned, his wife would have a bowl of watery rice porridge waiting. One rainy morning in the summer of 2000, Deng arrived home from his jog exhausted, having wheezed and puffed his way through his daily ritual. "That's because you've gotten so fat," joked his wife, Tang Manzhen.

Deng's waistline had been expanding along with the couple's fortunes over the last few years. As the pair's savings from the Guangdong jewelry factory where they both worked rose, Deng, always a good eater, had ballooned to a plump 190 pounds. Here near China's southern coast, more than 1,400 miles from their hometown in western Sichuan province, Tang and Deng were living the Chinese migrant worker's dream: buying a home in their rural hometown, sending their children to school in new clothes, saving for the future. Life had never been better. They grabbed their factory badges and reported for work.

Today, Tang traces her despair back to that morning, when the first crack appeared in their handmade portrait of prosperity.

Within six months, Deng was diagnosed with silicosis, an incurable lung disease he contracted grinding semiprecious stones, and was out of a job.

As Deng's health deteriorated, the pair drained their life savings and fell deeply into debt fighting their former boss for fair compensation. They spent days in government agencies and lawyers' offices and courtrooms before their case won a hearing. Then, months after a judge ordered his former employer to pay him almost $30,000, Deng died. He was 36.

Dotted across the Chinese landscape are "cancer villages," towns full of widows whose late husbands worked in the same toxic industries, enclaves where women give birth to babies with deformed limbs and other disabilities. Eastern Jiangxi province's Shangshan village was once renowned for its gold mines. Today the village is heavily in debt caring for hundreds of farmers who contracted silicosis working in the mines.[1] Some of these "widow towns" owe their fate to environmental pollution; others to a common workplace.

More than 200 million Chinese workers in 16 million companies are exposed to dangerous working conditions.[2] As of the end of 2005, China had recorded 665,043 total cases of occupational illness; of these, 606,891, or about 90 percent, were pneumoconiosis, an umbrella term for a group of debilitating lung diseases. The most common of these are "black lung," common among coal miners, and silicosis, the illness that claimed Deng Wenping's life.[3] The actual incidence is probably much higher: Yi Jintai, head of the public health school at Shanghai Medical University, has put the number of pneumoconiosis victims at more than one million.[4]

In a sign of the seriousness of the problem, Beijing has become increasingly frank about the long-term effects of the country's rapid industrial growth on public health. "In the past few years, people ignored work safety amid fast economic growth," Su Zhi, deputy director of the Ministry of Health's law enforcement and supervision department, said in 2004. "But vocational disease cases will increase in the coming years. . . . The troubles planted in the past will be exposed in the coming few years."[5] The *Workers' Daily*, a Chinese newspaper, has warned that pneumoconiosis will be the most serious social problem in rural China by 2010.[6] One official claims that the spread of pneumoconiosis is sparking popular protests.[7]

One effect of this emerging epidemic is a wave of litigation from workers who fell ill as a result of their jobs. A growing number of Chinese workers are responding to government calls to make use of the legal system by taking their employers to court. Surprisingly enough, the workers are winning.

ON A BRIGHT JANUARY morning, Deng's widow, Tang Manzhen, and a friend buy paper and firecrackers at a corner store in Xujia, a poor, remote town set in the terraced hills of Sichuan province. They set off into a muddy field, their sneakered feet deftly navigating around sticky holes and puddles. For forty minutes, they weave their way deeper into the countryside, around glassy rice paddies and lazy water buffalo, past golden rapeseed fields and one-story brick houses. There are no roads here. A local official hit residents up for money to build one, but the money vanished and the road never materialized.

At a small, grassy slope overlooking a clump of trees and rice fields, the women stop. Deng's tomb sits here, a large red and white structure painted with traditional Chinese funeral wishes: "Your story will be everlasting," reads one. "This man's children and grandchildren will be prosperous," reads another.

Tang and her friend set fire to the paper they bought and ignite the firecrackers, snapping echoes through the valley to honor Deng.

It's almost a year since he passed away. "You should be pleased," Tang says aloud to her late husband's tomb. "A lot of people have come to see you today."

Tang and Deng were born and raised in these hills. Tang's family ran out of money to pay for her schooling before she learned to read well. Still teenagers when their marriage was arranged, they moved into Tang's gray brick family home and continued to farm, as generations had done before them in fertile Sichuan. There was no running water, no electricity. The toilet was a hole in the ground in the corner of the pig shed. So it was with great hope that Deng set out at 21 to find work in the booming coastal province of Guangdong: hope for money and a better future.

Millions of other hungry farmers had the same idea, though, and as they poured out of the countryside into the coastal cities in the early 1990s, factory work was hard to get without a personal introduction. Deng worked his way up from planting trees to a factory job. By the mid-1990s, he was earning $25, sometimes $40 a month and was father to two children he rarely saw. Tang decided to leave the kids with relatives and join her husband. Deng had found her a job at Perfect Gem & Pearl, a small jewelry factory where he had been working since 1997 in the dusty city of Huizhou, near the border with Hong Kong. They would be processing artificial and semiprecious stones including quartz, onyx, aventurine and carnelian used in costume jewelry and ornaments for export.

The products may have been pretty, but there was nothing glamorous about the work. Tang remembers nearly 12-hour days, seven-day weeks and sealed windows that held in the dusty air. In jewelry factories in the area, it was common for workers to be fined for forgetting their factory badge, or taking a day off, or washing their hands minutes before their shift finished. Factories regularly required deposits worth half a month's or a month's wages from new workers. In the gem drilling section at Perfect Gem, Tang says she earned at most $2.50 to $4.00 a day, or about $100 a month. Deng, a more experienced worker, took home closer to $200.

Tang recalls how government labor inspectors would warn her boss before they came. "They would clean everything up until it sparkled," she said. The government officials "would never know there was anything wrong." Not all jewelry factories in China are like this, but some are.

Perfect Gem & Pearl has since ceased doing business under that name. Company executives say the company changed its name to Perfect Silver Jewelry in 2005 and stopped processing gems. The company now focuses on the manufacture of silver jewelry. Where the products that Deng and Tang made were sold is still unclear.

Company executives at a Hong Kong jewelry fair were reluctant to discuss their customers. "You mean exactly where we sell the goods? Exactly the place?" Aaron Long, a salesman for Perfect Silver, responded when I asked where his goods were sold. "I don't remember exactly." He turned to his colleague, and in Chinese repeated my question and said that he wasn't supposed to tell me.

Tony Lee, his colleague, offered that the company's products were sold in the United States and South America. He suggested I speak to the company's wholesaler, Decal Jewelry. A man named Alpha Chi from Decal told me that when the company was still processing gems he sold their unfinished goods to bead stores, catalogs and other wholesalers. Most of what the factory made was unfinished goods; it also made some finished products, which Chi initially told me were sold at chain stores including JCPenney and Wal-Mart. Later, in an e-mail, Chi insisted that he only sold to other wholesalers in New York, and that he never dealt with retailers.

When I contacted JCPenney, the retailer denied that it had

ever done business with the company. Wal-Mart said it had "no record of our suppliers having used the factory in question. As you know, whenever these situations come to light, we quickly investigate."

Such inconsistency is not surprising. Unlike the gold and diamond industries, where large companies are the norm, smaller businesses are common in the gem sector. Gemstones also come from disparate countries. "The colored gem supply chain is probably the most complex and difficult to monitor," says Peggy Jo Donahue, director of public affairs at Jewelers of America, the national jewelry retailers' association.

What is clear is that China is a major jewelry and gemstone manufacturer, and its products are increasingly attractive to international buyers. China exported $6.87 billion worth of jewelry to other countries in 2006, a 25 percent increase from the year before. In terms of volume, jewelry accounts for only a small portion of American imports from China, but shipments are growing quickly. In 2007, the United States imported $1.76 billion worth of jewelry, including watches and rings, from China, a 36 percent increase since 2003, according to U.S. Census data. Imports of gemstones were up 51 percent over the same period to $1.16 billion. But the fastest-growing category of imports was gem diamonds, which have risen 91 percent since 2002, to $77.16 million in 2006. "As China has done in other industries, it has a transforming effect on jewelry and how and where it's produced," Donahue says. Guangdong province, where Tang and Deng worked, is the country's largest jewelry production base.

After months of trying to contact the company to discuss Deng's case, I received a letter from a lawyer at a Chinese law firm known as Guangdong Province Lichen Law Firm that said it had represented Perfect Gem. The letter stated that Perfect Gem provided health checks for its employees before they started working at the plant and conducted annual health checks. It said the factory had

provided "relatively complete" dust-removing equipment and facilities, trained its workers in safety procedures and bought injury
insurance and contributed to pensions on behalf of all of its employees. The Chinese Center for Disease Control and Prevention
had "failed to identify the employees' potential health problems in
a timely manner due to a lack of professional staff and equipment."
The lawyer's letter also noted that Deng had worked for seven years
at other jewelry plants before he started work at Perfect Gem and
had kept his case history a secret. Tang says that while her late husband did work at other jewelry factories before Perfect Gem, earlier medical examinations did not uncover any evidence of the
disease. Given the poor quality of medical check-ups at many Chinese factories, it's hard to say for sure whether Deng contracted
silicosis before he started working at Perfect Gem.

Tang recounts that weeks and months at Perfect Gem sped by
so quickly that she and Deng forgot their own birthdays. All their
savings went back to Sichuan, into a house and new clothes at Chinese New Year for their children.

But then Deng came home breathless from his run that rainy
summer morning. In the following weeks, the man who never
caught colds came down with a deep and persistent cough. A local
doctor diagnosed him with tuberculosis. Incredulous, Deng sneaked
away from the factory one day and traveled to the provincial
capital, Guangzhou. It was there, at the province's occupational
disease hospital, that he learned what his work had done to
his lungs.

That night, Deng was too overwhelmed at first to tell his wife
what he had heard at the hospital. One of the world's oldest occupational illnesses, silicosis is caused by the inhalation of crystal-
line silica dust produced by the grinding, crushing, drilling or
breaking of rocks, sand, concrete and certain ores. Inhaled in great
quantities, silica dust causes inflammation and scarring in the lungs,

which continues even after exposure has stopped. The severity of the disease depends on the intensity and length of a person's exposure. In later stages, silicosis can lead to lung cancer, tuberculosis and heart disease. It has no cure.

Deng's silicosis was already at an advanced stage. He was told he had five, maybe 10 years to live. The next day, Tang says, he returned to work. Factory policy was to deduct three days' wages for every day missed without management's approval, a pay cut he could hardly afford.

The idea that working in dusty areas could be harmful to your lungs was a health problem among miners and workers in other dust-producing trades in the UK and South Africa in the nineteenth century. It became a national issue in the United States during the Depression, when workers began to sue their employers for silicosis-related liability.[8] The deaths of hundreds of laborers as a result of exposure to silica dust while building a tunnel in Gauley Bridge, West Virginia, for Union Carbide in the mid-1930s caused a public outcry.[9]

Silicosis is preventable. Good ventilation, safety equipment and the isolation of operations that generate silica dust can all help reduce the risk of exposure. Developed countries have put programs in place to prevent silicosis in the workplace.

And yet the disease persists as a public health issue around the world. Personal injury lawyers in the United States have targeted silicosis as a potential source of workers' compensation claims. A rise in silica-related litigation has fueled discussion of the illness as "the next asbestos," a reference to the huge number of lawsuits filed by people who suffered from exposure to the fibrous mineral asbestos, used in insulation and fireproofing since the 1960s. While the number of Americans dying from silicosis is falling, there were still 187 deaths from the disease reported as recently as 1999.[10] Germany was reporting 3,500 cases a year as recently as the 1990s.

Japan records 1,000 cases annually. There are some 600,000 former miners in South Africa with the disease.[11]

China has recognized silicosis as an occupational disease since the 1950s. As far back as 1956, the government issued regulations to limit dust exposure in industry. It apparently achieved some success in controlling the disease, although figures from this tumultuous period of Chinese history are particularly suspicious because of frequent misreporting for political purposes. The average age of patients being diagnosed with silicosis reportedly rose from 35 in the 1950s to 51 in the 1980s, which suggested that patients were being exposed to less intense amounts of silica dust.[12] In the late 1980s, the number of new cases reported each year had apparently started to decline.[13]

But any improvements were temporary, if not illusory. From the illegal coal mines in the north to the jewelry factories in the south, the China price has multiplied the threats to workers' health. Today, according to official statistics, China records about 10,000 new cases of pneumoconiosis, the umbrella term that includes silicosis, every year. About 5,000 people die from silicosis annually, although the actual figure is no doubt much higher.[14] And the victims are getting younger. The average age of diagnosis has slipped to 40, and patients as young as 20.[15] China Labor Bulletin, a Hong Kong NGO that published a report on silicosis among jewelry workers, calls the disease an epidemic.[16]

Deng had never heard of silicosis, much less how to prevent it. His education came directly from the doctors who diagnosed him.

After several of Deng's colleagues, suffering similar symptoms, visited the same Guangzhou hospital, authorities there sent a team to Perfect Gem to examine the staff, Tang recalls. Six male employees, including Deng, were immediately hospitalized. When they were released almost a month later, the factory offered Deng employment doing light work, Perfect Gem's law firm said in its letter. Tang remembers it differently: She says the newly discharged workers were not welcome back at the factory and were told they would be compensated and dismissed. Deng would get almost $13,000.

While it is difficult to know for sure what was or wasn't offered to Deng and the other workers in terms of "light work" after they were released from the hospital, one thing is clear: It wasn't enough to satisfy Deng. His life, sacrificed over dusty machines, was worth more than that. He wasn't going down without a fight.

CHINA'S MILLIONS of migrant workers are very vulnerable to occupational disease. Some 90 percent of victims of occupational disease in China are believed to be migrants.[17] Migrant workers tend to take the most dangerous, dirty, exhausting jobs—those least likely to adhere to national laws for health and safety. Many lack labor contracts to formalize their relationship with a factory. They often live in cramped, unsanitary conditions—prime breeding grounds for infectious disease.

Even in relatively good factories' dormitories, many workers in southern China's industrial cities sleep 12 to a room and share one bathroom. Sometimes there is only one bathroom per floor, a damp open room with squat toilets and showers and sinks. The stench is so bad workers limit their visits. Housing outside the factory gates can be even worse: piles of trash in the stairwells, filthy shared kitchens, communal toilets that are rarely cleaned. Dirty, crowded living conditions like these are thought to be the reason tuberculosis, cholera, smallpox and other diseases spread so quickly through the cities during England's Industrial Revolution.

Migrants' working conditions also make them susceptible to injury and illness. Most export factories pay by the piece. An employee's speed determines her salary, and in turn the amount she sends home to needy relatives. Safety equipment is a hindrance, a drag on productivity, to people working under that kind of pressure.

To compound the problem, many migrants are unaware of the risks they face on the job, often because their bosses fail to warn them. Under Chinese law, companies in industries with a high risk of occupational illness are required to provide medical exams for their workers and keep records of their health before, during and after employment. But factories often skip all of this. Former workers from Deng's factory claim that employees in the stone-cutting and polishing division had no such examinations, though the company, through its lawyer, denies this.[18] Those factories that do provide exams don't always allow staff to see their results, though there is no evidence that this was the case at Perfect Gem.

To illustrate the problem, Auret van Heerden, president of the Fair Labor Association, describes a hypothetical case of a woman working in a factory where the production process exposes her to carcinogens that might not lead to cancer for 20 years. Former workers who subsequently fell ill have long ago left the factory. "So we come in and say, you know, you've got to wear the mask. Nobody explains to her why she must wear the mask. If they do, probably they don't explain it in terms she can understand, and within a week or two, she's forgotten all that. Because in her day-to-day experience, nothing seems to merit, nothing seems to warrant those precautions."[19]

China has a law on the prevention and treatment of occupational disease that came into effect in 2002. Responsibility for inspecting Chinese workplaces is dispersed across various government bodies. Very roughly speaking, the Ministry of Labor and Social Security is responsible for enforcing labor law, and so it is concerned primarily with labor contracts, hours of work, wages and social insurance. The State Administration of Work Safety, also known as SAWS, is in charge of making sure Chinese workplaces

are safe. Among the Ministry of Health's tasks is identifying potential workplace health risks. Enforcement, however, is left to local
governments. There are simply not enough people to monitor the
factories where migrants work. The country had only 22,000 full-
time labor inspectors as of the end of 2006, overseeing the workplaces of some 764 million employees—one inspector for every
34,727 workers. Government regulations mandate one inspector
for every 8,000 workers. Shenzhen, home to thousands of factories
and 5.8 million employees by official count, had only 136 inspectors as of the end of 2005. The numbers of labor inspectors are increasing, but not nearly fast enough to keep pace with the growth
of China's industrial sector.

One former Chinese government labor inspector recalls that he
and three colleagues were expected to supervise about 500 companies. They were so busy investigating complaints that the inspectors
had little time to proactively inspect factories; to reduce their workload, they hired external contractors. Some of these contractors
were ethically challenged. "These guys, because they're not very
formal government officials, cause lots of corruption cases," says the
former inspector. "People pay money, then they close their eyes."[20]
Given the scale of corruption reported among officials in China, it
is safe to assume that the government's internal inspectors were
accepting bribes as well.

Bureaucratic procedures can also lengthen the amount of time
it takes for inspectors to reach a factory. Drew Thompson, director
of China studies and the Starr Senior Fellow at Washington, D.C.,
think tank the Nixon Center, says that the devolution of responsibility for enforcement to local officials adds layers of bureaucracy
in a government where most employees still insist on faxes rather
than e-mails. If a Ministry of Health official were to observe a health
violation at a factory near the ministry's offices in Beijing, he says,
"they wouldn't normally send their inspector into that factory. They
have to send a letter to the Beijing municipal government" request-

ing an inspection. The Beijing government then sends a letter to the municipal health bureau and the municipal health bureau sends a letter to the district health bureau.

China also has a shortage of people who have the technical qualifications to examine workplaces for occupational hazards. Compounding the problem is the state social insurance system, which fails to cover many migrant workers. Private insurance is still relatively new to China and does not cover a substantial portion of the population. While the figures vary, every statistic paints the same picture: Only a minority of migrant workers has any formal protection from the consequences of health hazards on the job.

One in five migrant workers has medical and injury insurance, according to one Hong Kong NGO that works on occupational health and safety issues. According to another study, 21.6 percent of migrants had medical coverage, 31.8 percent had employment injury insurance and 10.3 percent had unemployment insurance.[21] A study by the International Institute for Labor Studies, part of the International Labor Organization, concluded that only 10 percent of migrants have medical insurance.[22] An even smaller number have pensions.[23]

Under China's labor law, workers are entitled to social insurance benefits to cover maternity care, unemployment, occupational illness or work-related injury, general illness or retirement. Typically, a factory manager buys a package of social welfare benefits on behalf of the employee, who also makes contributions to the scheme. The package of benefits includes unemployment, medical insurance, pension, work injury and maternity care.[24] These benefits cost money. Under reforms introduced in 1997, employers must contribute about 20 percent of their wage bill to the pension and employees must part with 8 percent of their wages. Unsurprisingly, to save money, some managers skip insurance entirely for some or all of their workers. Government officials in heavily industrialized areas often allow factories to purchase insurance for some but not all workers, according to factory auditors. Recently, under pressure from foreign buyers, some factories have started to buy private insurance for their employees. Some will only buy accident insurance, however, which does not cover occupational illness.

Some migrants volunteer not to be covered by insurance. Workers may recoup their social security contributions, but not their employers', which local governments keep. China's social insurance benefits are not reliably portable across provincial boundaries. Some workers, fearing they will not be able to recoup their social insurance contributions in other provinces, don't bother paying into the scheme. Local governments around the country are trying to improve migrant workers' access to pensions, but the rules are still complex. Under the current system, workers are required to contribute to their pension for at least 15 years before they become eligible for benefits. For some workers, that prospect is too distant, and their family's financial needs too urgent, to pay into a pension.

Another reason migrants are denied social services is the *hukou* system, China's 1950s-era household registration scheme. Every Chinese person is required to register with the police for a *hukou*, which logs him or her as part of a household unit in a certain place. One's *hukou* is either rural or urban, and for decades, that distinction has determined that level of benefits received: Urban *hukou* holders got more.[25] Although reforms have relaxed the *hukou* system in some cities, migrant workers commonly hold rural *hukou*, which officially bars them from accessing many state-subsidized public services in the cities where they work. As a result, many migrants pay out of pocket for health care and their children's education.

Left out of the formal health care system, living as temporary or undocumented immigrants in their own country, unaware of the risks they may face and unprotected by insurance, China's migrant workers are on their own when illness strikes.

AFTER HIS DISAGREEMENT with the factory, Deng began looking for a lawyer. He had heard from fellow patients in the hospital that he might have a case.

Before China's labor law came into force in 1995, there were no formal procedures for resolving labor disputes. The law established a set of procedures for workers to redress grievances with their employers, and suddenly it became clear that Chinese workers were no longer as docile as they had once seemed. Labor disputes have risen an average of 24 percent every year since 1996, according to official data.

At the vanguard of this wave of litigation was Zhou Litai, a tall, gregarious man with a military flattop and round belly. In the late 1990s, Zhou, a self-taught lawyer from Sichuan who once worked in a brick factory, represented the family of a couple killed by a delivery truck at the factory where they worked, winning them more than $40,000 in damages. The case set a new standard for awards for victims of accidents of this kind. Zhou became one of the first lawyers to specialize in workers' rights in postreform China.

Zhou set up shop in Longgang, a booming industrial district in Shenzhen. Zhou would take workers' cases for a contingency fee. He was part of a new phenomenon in China: the American-style personal injury lawyer. But Zhou added a local twist. He rented a building where his clients could live as their cases traveled through the legal system. Word about his work spread by rumor and through the media. Since 1997, he claims that his offices in Shenzhen and Chongqing have represented workers in more than 7,000 cases.

The day we met at his Shenzhen office, Zhou greeted me at the front desk and showed me to a room in the back. As we spoke,

Zhou interrupted every few minutes to shout orders through an open window at a colleague next door or to greet another visitor. Men filtered in and out of the office, delivering business cards, tea and documents. The phone rang constantly.

Zhou's practice helped make litigation an option for migrant laborers. "The biggest effect of the cases we have handled is that we have raised awareness of the issue in the Chinese government and among workers," he told me. "Shenzhen's worker rights issues are now national issues."

He also helped raise the value of lost lives and limbs in southern China's industrial cities. Standard compensation in Shenzhen for a hand lost on the job used to be about $3,900, he said. Now, it's between $25,000 and $38,000. Zhou's success also paved the way for a new breed of Chinese lawyer, the ambulance chaser.

His services were not universally appreciated. In 2002, officials in Shenzhen effectively ran Zhou out of town by accusing him of practicing in the city without a license. Zhou believes government officials felt he was hurting the local investment environment by defending workers' rights. "They hated me," he says. Zhou also sparked a national debate when he sued a former client who didn't pay his bill. Zhou claims that more than 500 clients have disappeared without paying, and that he has lost almost $800,000 in potential income as a result. Some of these deadbeats, he believes, were encouraged by the local government. Others, he says, "were not so honest."

Originally, it was the Chinese government that drove workers into the courts. In the mid-1980s, Beijing began a campaign to familiarize citizens with the law. Strengthening the rule of law enhances the government's legitimacy, in the eyes of both its public and the world, and provides the formal channel for complaints necessary in a market economy. In official documents, the government encouraged the public to "use law as a weapon." China's state-controlled media picked up on the slogan, covering cases filed by ordinary people, usually in a positive light. Zhou's cases often made the news, according him celebrity status.

Press coverage also raised people's awareness—and hope—for justice through the legal system. Mary Gallagher, an assistant professor of political science at the University of Michigan who specializes in Chinese law and politics, surveyed four Chinese cities and found that people's willingness to go to court was directly linked to their level of media exposure.

IN JANUARY 2001, Tang says, she and Deng were fired without compensation. To pay the rent on a new apartment, the couple borrowed from friends and family. Tang picked through trash heaps. As he petitioned local authorities for assistance, Deng fasted during the day to save money on food. The pair was getting desperate. One labor official from whom Deng sought help threatened to beat him up. Deng consulted a lawyer and concluded he had no choice but to accept the factory's offer. It was a fateful decision: A Chinese judge would later argue that Deng's acceptance of these funds freed the factory from further responsibility.

Perfect Gem's lawyer says that in April 2001, Deng and the company reached a mediation agreement through the local county labor bureau whereby Perfect Gem would pay Deng $9,200–$10,500 to cover his medical fees, disability compensation and pension. In addition, the company volunteered to pay another $4,600 for "other fees . . . not requested by law." Only then, the lawyer says, was the labor contract between them formally terminated.

Tang remembers that weeks passed after Deng agreed to accept the money, but Deng still hadn't received anything. He was furious. Deng tried calling the factory's general manager, but Tang says he refused to take his calls. He even considered bombing the factory. One day, Tang recalls, Deng dialed the general manager's number and identified himself as Liu, the name, he knew, of a Perfect Gem customer. He was asked to hold.

When Deng identified himself, the general manager told Deng he'd look into it. Nothing came of this promise, though, until Deng agreed to give another manager at the factory a cut if he would help, Tang recalls. This bribe whittled the payout to about $11,000, a sum too modest to cover both the medical bills and his family's needs. Deng would have to keep fighting.

Shortly after Tang and Deng moved into their new apartment, it was burglarized. Fortunately, they had stashed their evidence—Deng's factory identity card and health and attendance documentation—at a friend's home. For the next four years, as they made the rounds of the legal system, Tang and Deng guarded their documents closely. At first, Tang followed Deng to court, carrying his evidence in a 16-pound bag. As his health worsened, Deng became too weak to walk, bathe or even dress himself. Tang began to carry him to court on her back, his oxygen supply by her side. The evidence traveled in a backpack fastened across her chest.

Fighting a labor case in China takes time, energy and financial resources. At the time Deng decided to contest the labor bureau's decision, labor disputes in China were resolved in three stages: mediation with the company; arbitration by a local committee composed of representatives from the local union, labor bureau and employers' organization; and litigation. Workers could skip the first stage. But arbitration has traditionally been mandatory. Since then, the government has tried to streamline the process to make it easier for workers to file suit. In August 2006, China's Supreme Court issued a judicial interpretation that allowed employees to go straight to court without submitting to arbitration or mediation if they had pay slips from their employer. It has also lowered the court fees for filing a labor lawsuit to just over one dollar.

In part because of the historical weakness of the All-China Federation of Trade Unions in representing workers' interests, there is ample opportunity for collusion between companies and the arbitration committee to push away labor disputes. The fact that the committees are administered by the government makes them more vulnerable to official interference.[26] The process is expensive, and arbitration committees, which are often understaffed, have not been allowed to rule on personal injury compensation. Nor have their judgments been legally binding. A growing number of Chinese workers appeal arbitration decisions in court.

The government is also trying to improve the mediation and arbitration process to make it easier for workers to get the compensation they deserve. In May 2008, a new law on labor disputes came into effect. It gave employees up to one year to file a labor dispute, and even longer under certain conditions. The law also waived all fees for filing labor arbitration cases, allowed arbitration committees more power to compel employers to produce evidence in a labor case within a certain period of time, and made arbitration committee awards final.

Back in 2002, there was no such law in China. After a year of selling phone services, Deng applied for arbitration. The committee rejected his application on the grounds that he had waited too long. At that time, the labor law required that requests for arbitration be made within 60 days of a labor dispute, a detail many workers had never heard of. Over the next three years, Deng filed suit against the company twice. Both times, the lawsuit was dismissed. His appeals were also rejected.

For Deng, as for many others, the weapon of the law had jammed. By 2005, Deng had sold the home he and Tang had worked so many months and years to build. He was sicker than ever, in and out of the hospital. Friends and family would visit his bedside to ask him for the money he had borrowed, anxious that he would die before they were repaid. When he could no longer afford treatment, the hospital declared him recovered and kicked him out.

DENG'S CASE WAS IN some ways unusual. Most cases involving migrant workers' claims against their employers never make it to court in China. Most migrants are too poor to afford legal representation, too poorly educated to navigate the labyrinthine regulations of the legal system, too scared to challenge authority. They are no match for their wealthier, better-connected bosses and local officials hoping to attract foreign investment by limiting labor disputes. Factory bosses often persuade officials that there was "no working relationship" between their company and an aggrieved worker. Or they move the factory to another town or city and set up shop under a different name, complicating workers' attempts to file suit against them. Cases drag on for years, beyond migrant workers' ability to afford legal advice.

Many judges avoid labor cases, says Fu Hualing, director of the University of Hong Kong's Centre for Comparative and Public Law. A labor-related case is "political, it's quite sensitive, especially if large groups file suit together," Dr. Fu says. "Normally migrant workers are not represented, they don't have lawyers. The judges have to help them a lot."[27]

One of the reasons judges in small cities dislike labor cases is because the litigation fees are so low. Litigation fees in China are set by the Supreme Court and vary by the type of case. Courts depend on litigation fees as a source of income, which in turn determines a portion of judges' salaries. Because the fees for labor cases are set intentionally low—just over one dollar in most provinces—judges shy away from them in favor of more lucrative cases.[28]

As a result, the cases involving migrant workers that make it to court are generally based on the most incontrovertible evidence. While weak enforcement of the law contributes to the high rate of workplace injury and illness, Chinese laws on occupational health and safety are actually clear and strict. The country has a fairly comprehensive set of occupational health and safety standards introduced since economic reforms began. It has a law on preventing occupational diseases and regulations on preventing and treating pneumoconiosis, on diagnosing occupational disease and workplace injury and on work-related injury insurance. "If you have evidence that the factory has not complied with the laws and regulations, and you have a law on the books saying that this is illegal, then it's very hard for a judge to ignore," says Robin Munro, research director at China Labor Bulletin, the Hong Kong NGO that published the report on silicosis.[29]

Between 1986 and 1990, workers won less than 40 percent of labor disputes. By 1997, they were winning more than half, according to Professor Gallagher. Between 1995 and 2001, in the city of Ningbo in eastern Zhejiang province, a rapidly industrializing area, and Zhongshan in Guangdong, workers won over 90 percent of their cases.[30] Fittingly for a nominally communist country, Chinese guidelines dictate that judges should favor the worker in labor disputes, because workers are considered the weaker party.

IN THE SUMMER OF 2005, Deng got a lucky break. China Labor Bulletin and other Hong Kong NGOs learned of his case and organized protests outside the offices of Perfect Gem and other jewelry companies where workers had contracted silicosis. Tang and the daughter Deng had left behind in Sichuan when he went out to work so many years ago were there.

Shortly afterward, a member of the Guangdong Provincial People's Congress, the local legislature, ordered the court to review its decisions on Deng's case. The court found it had erred and ordered Perfect Gem to pay Deng about $30,000, now a common award for a silicosis victim in China. Compensation awards for silicosis range between $26,000 and almost $40,000, according to a lawyer who works with these cases.[31]

Perfect Gem's lawyer contends that Deng asked friends to appeal to higher authorities for assistance, initiated demonstrations overseas, distributed leaflets and threatened the company's leaders, and that Deng and the other workers "adopted some unreasonable words and actions that were in conflict with the law." Perfect Gem agreed to pay the money on the condition that Deng stop threatening the company and organizing protests and "to demonstrate its understanding for and its cooperation with the government as well as its consideration for humanitarianism," the lawyer wrote. He maintained that Perfect Gem had followed the government's orders despite the "extreme words and actions adopted by Deng Wenping and other workers"—unlike other jewelry companies that simply disappeared after they encountered similar problems. "As an attorney," he concluded, "I would like to express my admiration for Perfect Gem and its owner!"

Tang and Deng returned to Xujia to repay their creditors. They moved in with Deng's sister, a wiry woman with a big smile, in a four-story house built with money from her husband's career as an itinerant construction worker. Every day, Tang would take Deng to the local hospital, sometimes by hired motorcycle but more often by herself, hoisting her husband onto her back and carrying him down the town's main street. Silicosis had ravished his body. Deng weighed half what he had five years earlier.

"I would put him down, rest for a while, then pick him up again," Tang remembered as she walked down the same street a year after Deng's death. Xujia is a quiet town populated mostly by young children and the elderly. Nearly everyone of working age has decamped to the coastal cities to work in the factories or in construction, leaving evidence of their departure everywhere: Farm

plots are abandoned, a building under construction is an investment of income earned down south. The aged who remain in Xujia
sit outside, hands clasped around their knees, faces like oatmeal
cookies, watching with vacant eyes the few passersby. "People would
look at us and feel uncomfortable," Tang said.

The hospital commute was a financial and medical necessity.
Deng's settlement had quickly disappeared into creditors' pockets.
He needed daily treatment for his illness, but he couldn't afford the
$1.30 fee for an overnight hospital stay. Deng stopped eating spicy
food, a Sichuan staple, because it aggravated his illness. He slept
little, because his coughing kept him awake most of the night. And
he cried, knowing he would leave his wife a widow and his children
without a father. In January 2006, he passed away, almost five years
to the day after he was diagnosed.

PROFESSOR GALLAGHER calls the attitude of Chinese workers
who have sparred in the courts "informed disenchantment." Despite the fact that many have disappointing experiences navigating
the Chinese legal system, most workers say they would do it again.[32]
In a survey at a legal aid center for workers in Shanghai, Professor
Gallagher found that 80 percent of plaintiffs said they would sue
again. Their responses were not closely correlated with the results
in their case—88 percent of those who lost said they would sue
again, versus 100 percent of those who won. Many workers Professor Gallagher interviewed saw their first experience in the legal
system as an education, and most went on to give legal advice to
others, planting the seed for future lawsuits. Some even appeared as
witnesses in cases filed by other laborers. Professor Gallagher calls
these workers "little experts."[33]

Feng Xingzhong grew up in the same area of Sichuan as Deng,
though the two had never met before they both fell ill with silicosis

and decided to fight for better compensation. He arrived in the factory towns the year before Deng and eventually found work at another jewelry factory. Conditions there were horrible, Feng recalls:
Employees would emerge at the end of the day covered in dust the
color of the stones they had been grinding, only their eyes visible
through the powder. Former colleagues died young, but nobody
knew why.

Feng, who has a thatch of thick black hair, stayed at the factory
for a decade. He met his wife there, and the couple raised two children with the money they earned at the factory. "My whole life was
in that factory," he told me. We were sitting in a Starbucks in Shenzhen, its soft lighting and gentle-mannered staff at odds with
Feng's memories.

Like Deng, Feng was bundled off with a compensation package
after he and other workers were diagnosed, first with tuberculosis
and later with silicosis. In his fight for a just payout, Feng even enlisted Zhou Litai as his lawyer. But his case, too, lingered unresolved
in the courts until Hong Kong NGOs and provincial officials took
notice. With their help, Feng received almost $40,000 from his for-
mer employer. He believes it is the highest compensation awarded
to a silicosis victim in China.

Inspired by the NGO staff he met in Hong Kong, Feng, whose
disease has not yet progressed to the advanced stage, stayed on in
Shenzhen to help other occupational disease sufferers get justice.
He has become a "little expert" himself. Twenty or 30 times a day,
his cell phone rings, the ring tone a recording of Feng's son singing.
On the other end of the phone is yet another worker in trouble.
Feng, whose formal education stopped after one year of junior high
school, tells them where to get a medical examination, how to file
a lawsuit.

Workers today don't have to struggle the way he did, Feng says.
They are more aware of their rights and Chinese courts are more

willing to defend them. "When I took legal action, it took a long time and I made a lot of mistakes. Many of my coworkers died before they got a ruling," he says. "Now I feel things are much better. A lot of workers know how to file suit. And it doesn't take such a long time."

Judges in developed coastal areas are becoming more generous with their awards. The government is increasing legal aid to migrant workers and trying to attract more lawyers to their cause.[34] In 2006, the All China Lawyers Association, a professional organization, barred lawyers from accepting contingency fees in labor cases, in what one Chinese lawyer characterizes as an effort to prevent lawyers from taking too much of workers' awards. This lawyer expects the new rule to further lower the cost of filing suit, since workers will pay only a flat fee instead of parting with 10 percent or 20 percent of their winnings. Zhou Litai worries the decision will discourage workers who can't afford the flat fee from going to court.

There is still a long way to go in defending workers' rights. In less developed inland provinces, to which China's factories are relocating as costs rise on the coasts, the system still tilts heavily in favor of management. Because of the Chinese government's desire for economic growth, employers everywhere still have the upper hand in disputes with their employees.

"If you sacrifice workers' rights, you get a much higher GDP," says a lawyer who works on labor rights cases. "The central government cares about this issue very seriously sometimes, but the problem is with the local governments. Because the local government needs to improve their economy, and get a higher rate of GDP growth, and attract more investment."[35]

However, some observers caution that as laborers become more aware of their rights, they may become less understanding when things don't go their way. China will need to create other channels through which workers can get help more reliably and efficiently, or face increasingly violent and frequent labor uprisings. Beijing is already gravely concerned about maintaining social stability amid a wave of popular protests over everything from property seizures to pollution. But the government has to balance the need to give workers and other disgruntled citizens more of a voice with its desire to retain a firm grip on power and to keep the economy growing.

There is always the possibility that Beijing will decide that all the demands for justice have gotten out of hand. "I think there will be continued pressure and the government will have to make a choice: do they want to continue to try to have markets without political freedom?" says Professor Gallagher.[36] Labor conflicts continue to multiply. In 2006, arbitration committees accepted 317,000 cases. The number of labor cases handled through arbitration has risen 28.2 percent on average every year since 1991.[37]

Perfect Gem, Deng's former employer, "suffered great loss and could not keep on with its business due to high risks associated with jewel processing and the huge sums of compensation made for occupational disease," its lawyer wrote. Its businesses under that name have been terminated in both Hong Kong and mainland China. Perfect Silver has moved into new premises in Huizhou. Government officials are believed to have pressured the company to improve working conditions there.

However, Monina Wong, executive director of Labor Action China, a Hong Kong NGO that has worked with silicosis victims, says that even if factories have improved ventilation, employees may still be exposed to excessive levels of dust if working hours are too long. Factories may now arrange to have regular medical examinations for employees, but they may not share the results with workers. And some jewelry factories are now subcontracting gem processing to smaller workshops to avoid scrutiny. "The factories where the main production is look good," Wong told me. "But in fact a lot of subcontracting is being done in more and more places in northern Guangdong where the implementation of the law is even worse than Huizhou."

Perfect Silver subcontracts its gem processing to Haifeng, in northern Guangdong, according to Tony Lee, one of its salesmen at the Hong Kong trade fair. Alpha Chi, the wholesaler from Decal Jewelry, said that the situation in Chinese jewelry factories was more nuanced than it might seem. Insisting that he was not speaking on behalf of Perfect Silver, he said that in China, workers moved from one factory to another, making it difficult to determine where they might have become ill. "Nobody wants to hurt their employees," he said. "They are your partners."

He added that foreign-invested factories are at a competitive disadvantage. Uneven law enforcement means that foreign-invested companies are held to a higher standard than their local Chinese rivals. As a result, the local factories have lower costs and are more competitive.

The jewelry industry has created the Council for Responsible Jewelry Practices, a nonprofit group that represents more than 60 companies in the gold and diamond industry. The group aims to promote more ethically, socially and environmentally responsible practices. It has drawn up what it calls a "code of practice" for its members.

Zhou Litai, the activist lawyer, returned to his Shenzhen practice in 2005. He says he now operates freely. "Now, when Zhou Litai helps a worker, it's not a big deal," he said, speaking of himself, as he often does, in the third person.

He says that the number of serious injuries, such as those in which workers lose arms, is falling. "With the increase in compensation, the cost to [factory] bosses will increase, and that will force the bosses to realize the need for better safety." But he concedes that occupational illness, which he calls "invisible" illness, is now more common than visible injuries.

CHINA IS ONLY STARTING to come to terms with the occupational disease epidemic created over the last three decades of rapid industrial growth. For decades under the planned economy, state-owned enterprises oversaw their own occupational health and safety. Now, the economy has moved on, but the government has lagged behind in its responsibilities. Even the Ministry of Health describes the country's occupational disease situation as "grim." In a report to the National People's Congress released in 2007, the ministry gave the country a failing "F" grade for its lax oversight of companies and poor coordination among government departments with regard to occupational disease.[38]

This neglect comes at a price. Beijing estimates occupational illnesses and injuries cost the country more than $13 billion a year. Indirect costs could bring the total cost to twice that figure. Pneumoconiosis alone costs China $1.8 billion in direct economic losses, and an additional $79 million every year, according to the state-owned media.[39]

But acknowledging a problem and solving it are two different things. Prevention and early detection of work-related disease are still insufficient. Despite the increasing amount of auditing by foreign buyers and litigation, many factory managers' awareness of occupational health has not significantly improved.

Government supervision of workplaces is too lax. Even China's state-controlled media admit the country's 2002 occupational diseases prevention law is widely ignored.[40] Su Zhi of the Ministry of Health has noted that only one million of the six million workers exposed to dangerous working environments got checkups in 2001.[41] "China has a long way to go in controlling hazardous dusts in the workplace, and in reaching the WHO's goal of eliminating pneumoconiosis," conclude two doctors at the Harvard School of Public Health.[42]

Part of the problem with illness as well as injuries in Chinese workplaces, say labor advocates, is poor coordination between government ministries. In an interview, Su Zhi told me that the Ministry of Labor and Social Security, the State Administration of Work Safety and the ACFTU needed to strengthen their cooperation. As it tries to make workplaces safer, China will also have to invest in training more people in occupational health.

Caring for sick workers will place an additional burden on China's overtaxed health care system. Government spending on health care has been rising as a fraction of gross domestic product, but falling as a percentage of total public and private spending on health care.[43] When the government doesn't provide, ordinary people pay for their own health care.

Much of the burden of treating Chinese workers who get sick on the job could well fall on hospitals in rural areas in or near migrants' hometowns. There are more than two dozen provincial occupational health institutions in China, but they tend to be in urban areas. The quality of health care is severely compromised in the countryside, where the quality and number of doctors has been falling.[44] Most of China's government spending on health care goes to the cities.[45] "Ever since the inception of the economic reform programs in the early 1980s," writes Liu Yuanli, assistant professor of international health at the Harvard School of Public Health, "the attitude of the Chinese government towards rural health financing can best be described as *laissez-faire*. The dominant thinking of policymakers has been that voluntary community financing schemes would emerge with economic growth."[46]

Patients' access to health care in China is determined by their ability to pay. Nowhere is this more true than in the countryside, where the vast majority of residents lack health insurance. About 80 percent of rural residents were uninsured as of 2003, compared with about 50 percent in the cities.[47] Tian Chengping, minister of labor and social security, has said that China's social insurance system covered just 6 percent of its population.[48]

China is trying to fix the situation with new schemes for health care in the cities and the countryside. But migrants who lack urban *hukou* are left out of the new urban health care program.[49] And critics say the new rural cooperative medical scheme does not do enough for the country's poorest residents.[50]

Concerned about the threat to social stability angry workers pose, Beijing is trying to expand insurance coverage for migrant workers. In 2004, the State Council, China's cabinet, introduced a regulation that made it mandatory to have occupational injury insurance in every type of enterprise. Two years later, the Ministry of Labor and Social Security introduced a three-year program called "Safety Action" to provide injury insurance for migrants in dangerous jobs.[51] The government also established a pilot program in ten provinces to monitor and report occupational diseases among migrant workers.[52] These programs are already raising labor costs for Chinese factories in some areas. In Shanghai, which has been trying hard to improve coverage for workers, welfare costs are rising rapidly.[53]

But this is only the beginning of the rise in welfare costs. Even though the government has been trying to insure more migrants, by its own calculations, only a fraction of migrants were covered by work injury or medical insurance as of March 2007.[54] In characteristically ambitious fashion, Beijing has said it hopes to have 140 million migrants insured by 2010.[55] It seems highly unlikely to come close to meeting that target. But as it strives for greater protection for its workers, China will be turning to factories to pick up more of the tab.

Su Zhi of the health ministry says that China needs to raise the level of worker protection, to find a level appropriate to China's economic situation. "We have to pay the price for economic development," he told me. As it does this, China will need the help and understanding of the rest of the world. "Especially the multinationals," he said. "They brought dangerous work and pollution and left with the profits."

BACK IN SICHUAN, Tang has begun socializing with other wives of silicosis victims. At a dinner of soup filled with eels, tofu and lotus root one cold winter night in a nearby town, Tang and Feng Xingzhong's wife, who met as a result of their husbands' legal battles, discuss how Chinese factories became dangerous enough to kill strong, healthy men. "Isn't it because you Americans have brought all your bad factories to China?" Feng's wife asks me. "I heard it's because China has so much corruption, and it needs the money so it wants foreign investment," Tang offers.

A year after Deng's death, Tang is still consumed by the loss—not only of her husband, but of the comfortable life they worked so hard to build. A benefactor in Hong Kong pays her children's school fees, but Tang is still in debt. Sometimes, she thinks she'd like to go back and ask her former employer for more money, tell him it wasn't enough.

"When we went out to the factory, we had no idea that this disease existed," Tang says. "If I had known that we would suffer from this kind of disease, I wouldn't have come out to work there. I would have stayed home and continued to work on the farm." Tang is poor again, living in her sister-in-law's home and scraping by selling vegetables. She worries for her children. "I don't mind tasting bitterness," she says, using the Chinese expression for hardship. "I just don't want my kids to have to."

"What I really want is for my kids to get good grades so that in the future, they don't have to go out to the factories to work," she says that night over dinner. "The hours are long, the salary is low, and when you get sick, you get fired."

The following summer, Tang's daughter, who is 16, passes the entrance exam to high school. Tang, who fears the money from her Hong Kong patron will not be enough, will pull together the money to pay her tuition. She will do whatever it takes to ensure her daughter never has to go south, to the factories.

Chapter 4

THE GOLD RUSH

H<small>IGH IN THE HILLS</small> of northern Shanxi province, beyond the reach of roads, above the frenzy of civilization, the air is still. Shrubs and trees cling to the steep, dusty cliffs. A forested valley spreads below and then rises to another row of hills in the distance. There is little evidence of human life here, no signs or houses or power lines. Just a lone, insistent sound, so soft it is barely audible at first. *Tok. Tok . . . tok. Tok. Tok . . . tok.* The noise is coming from a large, dark hole in the mountain, tucked anonymously into a ridge. Next to the hole is a black, greasy pile the size of a dinner table, glinting in the late afternoon sun.

Coal.

Ma Jianguo, a short, thin man in a soot-covered brown uniform and black rubber boots, winds his way expertly around the cliffside until he arrives at the hole, a tiny coal mine. He calls into the opening toward the noise, which by now is clearly someone scraping the soft coal from the mountain.

A moment later, the scraping stops and a man's face appears, floating in the black and smudged with coal. The man is wearing a tan shirt, brown pants and a hard hat with a head lamp. He is startled to have visitors. Ma greets him and turns his attention to the heap of coal, turning over a few pieces in his hand. "I can get $24 for a ton of this," he says proudly.

Coal has been Ma's life for more than two decades. He came to this mountain outside Taiyuan, the capital of Shanxi province, as a teenager to work in the mines. He has been here ever since, cutting into the seam deep underground in a state-owned mine where he is a supervisor. At 41, he is married with three children, two boys and a girl. He lives in a modest one-story house near the mine.

In the summer of 2006, Ma decided that the $263 he earned every month at the state-owned mine wasn't going to be enough to support his dreams for his family. Ma took time off work and started hiking the hills up behind his employer, combing the quiet mountain for evidence of coal deposits. By August, he had six men working on three deposits near the surface. Ma had become the small-town version of a national scourge: an unlicensed private coal mine owner.

COAL, more than any other product, lies at the heart of the China price. More than two-thirds of China's energy supply comes from coal, a higher ratio than either Japan or the United States.[1] The country is the largest producer and consumer of coal in the world. Coal keeps China's economic engine—including the export factories, pumping like pistons near the coasts—turning over.

It is also China's dominant source of air pollution and a growing environmental threat to the rest of the world. Burning coal, the world's cheapest and dirtiest source of energy, produces a nasty cocktail of emissions: nitrogen oxide, mercury, carbon dioxide and sulfur dioxide. China is the world's largest emitter of carbon dioxide and sulfur dioxide. The country's coal-related pollution is blowing around the globe, turning up as far away as the west coast of the

United States. But China feels the effects of its coal habit most acutely: It produces 70 percent of the smoke and dust in the air in China, and 90 percent of the sulfur dioxide is from coal.[2]

Carbon dioxide emissions lead to global warming. Sulfur dioxide, when combined with water, causes acid rain, which affects waterways and crops. Nitrogen oxide contributes to smog, and mercury can cause neurological damage in infants and children.

Coal is a threat to China's people in other ways as well. China has about 16,000 coal mines, of which some 90 percent are small.[3] These small mines produce about a third of China's coal supply. But they are also dangerous: As larger, state-owned mines gradually modernize, installing machines to replace human labor and improving safety procedures, many small, private coal mines continue to rely on riskier, more traditional methods. As a result, they generate more than 70 percent of China's coal mine deaths.[4]

Which is also to say that small Chinese mines produce most of the world's coal mining deaths. China produces 35 percent of the world's coal and 80 percent of its reported coal mine deaths. In 2006, 4,746 people died in the country's mines. By comparison, U.S. coal mining deaths the same year totaled 47—and that was the highest level in a decade.

Once useful to Beijing because they helped meet the country's burgeoning demand for coal, small, private mines had become a nuisance by the late 1980s. Underground mines were sneaking their product onto the already-clogged railway system illegally, taking capacity away from the large, state-owned mining companies.[5] They were inefficient and produced lower-quality coal. By the 1990s, they were adding to an unwanted coal surplus.[6] And they were unsafe. China has been trying to shut them down ever since.

Small mines without licenses, like Ma's, survive by a combination of corrupt means, including bribing local officials. Often, the same local officials who are supposed to be supervising the sector have stakes in mines themselves.[7]

But China's small mines also prosper because they meet a crucial need. China is so hungry for power that it is building at least one coal-fired power plant every week to keep pace with demand. Rising coal prices have made mines a lucrative investment.

People in Shanxi province live and breathe coal's twin effects. Shanxi is China's largest coal-producing region, generating about a quarter of the country's production each year. The resource is a mainstay of the local economy, along with iron and steel, chemicals, cement and electricity. Shanxi ships nearly 80 percent of its coal to other provinces, sometimes on railway cars and sometimes over power lines after it has been turned into electricity.[8] The area's power stations supply Beijing, some 250 miles to the northeast of Taiyuan.[9] Coal mining and refining provide the main source of income for 80 percent of the counties in Shanxi province.[10]

Beyond the trucks full of black lumps, the most visible legacy of the area's coal deposits is a thick, noxious blanket of smog. In 1998, the United Nations Environment Program (UNEP) declared that Taiyuan had the most polluted air in the world. Measured concentrations of particulates, tiny particles of liquid or solid suspended in gas, were six to seven times World Health Organization (WHO) standards.[11] Exposure to particulates is believed to increase susceptibility to respiratory illness or aggravate existing lung or heart disease.

Taiyuan became a focus of the international aid community and one of Beijing's first test cases for experiments with proenvironment policies. In 1998, China's National Development and Reform Commission and what is now known as the State Environmental Protection Administration (SEPA) declared Taiyuan the first pilot city in an effort to encourage "clean" production. The UNEP helped the city develop a "clean" production program, an effort to encourage polluters to reduce emissions and conserve resources. The Asian Development Bank loaned Taiyuan money to fight air pollution. Resources for the Future, a nonprofit Washington, D.C., think tank, even advised the city on creating a sulfur dioxide emissions-trading program.

Local companies responded, at least initially. Taiyuan Steel Group, a major local employer, banned the use of sulfur-heavy coal. State media reported that the city forced thousands of polluting companies to shut down. Coking plants, which release unhealthy emissions when they burn off impurities from coal, were closed south of the city.[12] Coal is baked to make coke, which in turn is used to smelt iron ore into iron.

Eager, no doubt, to show results, the state media cheerfully reported that people had started to exercise outdoors again.[13] Liang Liming, director and Communist Party chief of Taiyuan's environmental protection agency, was celebrated for her contributions to improving China's environment.[14]

But the smog never really disappeared. Companies continued to build new, polluting projects without government approval. Others purchased equipment to reduce environmental damage, but rarely used it.[15] People still used coal to cook and heat their homes.[16] And in the hills outside the city, private coal mines continued to pop up, producing ever more coal under treacherous circumstances.

Today, on a summer day, when pollution is supposed to be lighter, Taiyuan's gray air is sour, acrid and bitter. The stench gathers in your nostrils and at the back of your throat. Instinctively, you try to avoid yawning or gulping down too much of it. After a day out near the mines, the smell reappears as a black stain in your tissue when you blow your nose. It collects in your ears, in the corners of your eyes and on your skin. Taiyuan's air pollution is clearly a serious threat to public health. A 2001 report by the WHO and the United Nations Development Program found that particles with a diameter of less than 10 microns—which are more dangerous than larger particles—composed between 74 percent and 87 percent of the total suspended particles in Taiyuan's air.[17]

Unsurprisingly, pollution affects people's health in Taiyuan. In the winter, respiratory illness and colds are common. One survey published in 2002 found that 64 percent of children tested in the city had excessively high levels of lead in their blood.[18] Exposure to lead can lead to neurological damage, particularly in children.

Four of the world's 20 most polluted cities are in Shanxi. Today, nearby Linfen, another coal-producing Shanxi city, has claimed the title of the most polluted city in the world. Taiyuan, however, has traded one notorious title for another: once the most polluted city in the world, Taiyuan is now the city with the highest incidence of death from lung cancer in Shanxi province.[19]

TAIYUAN IS A MICROCOSM of China's environmental disaster. The prioritization of economic growth above all else led officials and companies to neglect the environment, with horrendous consequences. Even in places like Taiyuan, which face obvious threats to public health and the safety of the workforce and where the government has tried to address the problem, the desire for development still wins out. The hunger for wealth trumps concern for health and safety, with catastrophic results.

A third of the people in Chinese cities are breathing polluted air.[20] More than half of 696 cities and counties covered by a national monitoring program in 2005 were affected by acid rain from sulfur dioxide pollution. All of the rain that fell in certain coastal areas in Zhejiang and Fujian provinces was considered acid rain.[21] Only six of 27 of China's largest cities provide drinking water that complies with government standards.[22] The World Bank has put the annual bill for China's air and water pollution damages at $54 billion.[23] By China's own account, environmental damage already costs the country the equivalent of 10 percent of GDP a year.

In rural areas, the destruction of the environment is so bad that it is creating what SEPA vice minister Pan Yue calls "environmental refugees"—people evicted from their land by pollution. In the 1990s, an estimated 20 million to 30 million farmers left their plots as a result of environmental deterioration. Another 30 million to 40 million more may be on the move by 2025, according to one estimate.[24] Pan Yue has warned that China may ultimately have to deal with 150 million environmental refugees. Many flock to the cities for work, joining the crush of migrant workers.

Those unable to migrate are increasingly willing to challenge polluters with public action, adding to China's mounting protest statistics. Demonstrations often lead to violent clashes with police, arrests and the deaths of protesters. "In some places, environmental problems have affected people's health and social stability, and damaged our international image," Zhou Shengxian, SEPA's head, has acknowledged.[25] Pollution played a role in some 50,000 protests in 2005, according to SEPA, that's nearly 1,000 protests a week.[26] Sometimes not-in-my-backyard protests force the government to move factories into less populated areas, where there will be fewer people to complain. Often, the government is less responsive, compelling some people to take their grievances to court.

In 2006, some 1,700 residents of Xiping village in southeastern Fujian province filed what is believed to be China's largest environmental class action suit to date against a chemical factory. They argued that the factory had polluted the river and wrecked their crops. The Center for Legal Assistance to Pollution Victims, a pioneering nongovernmental organization in Beijing, has advised on other cases and, its founder Wang Canfa has said, is now winning more lawsuits than it loses.[27]

The effects of environmental pollution on China's health are only starting to be understood. Some of the "cancer villages" and towns with abnormally high rates of birth defects, described in chapter three, are the products of local pollution. At the same time, doctors and researchers report a rising incidence of asthma and lead poisoning among children in polluted cities. The pollution is equivalent to letting children smoke two packs of cigarettes a day.[28] More than half of children in 28 cities surveyed in China have levels of lead in their blood that exceed the World Health Organization guidelines, leading to widespread blood poisoning.[29] Air pollution now contributes to at least 400,000 deaths every year in China, perhaps many more.[30] It costs Shanghai more than one billion dollars a year in health care expenses, according to Fudan University's School of Public Health.[31] "There's an environmental health crisis in China," says Jennifer Turner, director of the China Environment Forum at the Woodrow Wilson Center, a Washington, D.C., think tank.

The central government, increasingly aware of the costs of prioritizing economic growth over the environment, is trying to do something about the problem. It has set targets (which it has missed) to reduce the country's energy consumption and cut pollution. Among its other initiatives are encouraging coal-burning power plants to install scrubbers to limit sulfur dioxide emissions and promoting the development of alternative sources of energy. It has also drafted a comprehensive set of environmental protection laws. But, as with laws on labor and other issues in China, the problem is enforcement. One reason for the lack of enforcement is the heavy emphasis on economic growth. Local government officials are still evaluated primarily on the amount of growth they record in gross domestic product.

This is starting to change. Environmental protection is quickly moving up the agenda of policymakers in Beijing. In 2004, as the country's environmental problems deepened, Wen Jiabao, the Chinese premier, introduced the concept of "Green GDP," which would deduct the costs of environmental damage from traditional GDP. Green GDP data would be used to show the environmental costs of growth, so that officials' promotion would better reflect the quality, rather than simply the quantity, of growth.[32] But Green GDP remains controversial. Some provinces are unwilling to participate, and even the National Bureau of Statistics has opposed the public disclosure of Green GDP figures.

The communities where the complexity of China's environmental crisis is most clear are those where the local economy depends so heavily on polluting industries that change is harder to effect.[33] These communities lie at the crossroads where China's environmental disaster and its widespread labor abuse meet.

Covered in soot, sucking down smog, the people in these communities live with pollution in part because their livelihood depends on the very industries that are making them sick. The hills outside Taiyuan, in northern Shanxi province, are among these places.

IN THE MOUNTAINOUS AREA outside the city where Ma lives, mines continue to churn out coal to feed a nation hungry for power. Enormous orange and blue trucks wobbling under the weight of huge heaps of coal trundle down the potholed road out of the district every day, passing a sign that reads STRENGTHEN MANAGEMENT TO PROTECT THE ENVIRONMENT. The air outside is thick with dust and smoke.

At the state-owned mine where Ma works as a supervisor, soot-faced miners in brown and black jumpsuits emerge into the daylight and find relief in cigarettes. They mill around the tracks where the miniature trains they ride down into the pit are parked. Inside the mine office next door, coal dust shed by off-duty miners covers the floor and cigarette butts litter the hallways. Women do the ceaseless work of scrubbing soot from the toilets.

In the hills above, beyond rows of one-story red brick homes with firewood stacked outside and dirty-faced children sucking on Popsicles, Ma leaves his pile of coal and strides across the hill. He, too, has just finished a shift at the state-owned mine, and he is covered in soot. Everything—his fingernails, his furry eyebrows, even his identity card—is coated in a thin layer of black powder. In the car on the way up the hill, he covered the seat with a towel to protect it from his blackened pants in what seemed like an old habit. Ma agreed to show me his mines on the condition that I take no pictures. To protect his identity, I have changed his name.

Ma operates three mines and employs a staff of six migrant workers to work in them. The mines are in varying stages of development—two are still shallow holes, not reinforced by wood or metal, and one is more developed. Ma arrives at the most developed mine. He is proud of it, proud enough to memorize its dimensions: two meters wide at the bottom and 1.8 meters wide at the top, it is 1.3 meters tall, a black horizontal chute into the side of the mountain. It's hard to tell how far back it runs, but it is deep enough to swallow three men.

The tunnel has no ventilation system besides the wind. Wooden beams reinforce the mine's opening and the dark horizontal tunnel that burrows into the hillside. On the wooden beams over the entrance are the Chinese characters for safety and life, written in pink chalk. In the center is a hand-drawn pink Christian cross. Ma is Catholic, a relatively unusual set of beliefs to hold in China. He claims to speak Latin, which he demonstrates in a fluid, staccato stream.

Ma calls into the mouth of the mine, but no one answers. The seconds tick by. He calls again. More silence. If anyone is in there, they don't want to be found. Beijing's campaign against illegal mines has driven these miners deeper into their tunnel. A hard hat lies by the entrance, and Ma picks it up, gets on his hands and knees and crawls inside.

A few moments later, he crawls out and walks toward another opening so snugly tucked into the hillside you would have to know it was there to find it. A miner, his face smeared with soot, emerges from the hole. He is wearing black pants and a brown shirt and flimsy slip-on shoes. He has no visible safety equipment.

The miner, who declines to give his name, left his family in Hubei province nearly a decade ago to work in Tangshan, another industrial city in Shanxi. He arrived in this area only two months ago, hoping to find work in more shallow mines.

Migrant workers do some of the most dangerous jobs in the Chinese mining industry. Workers in private mines generally have no insurance, no safety equipment and no job security. In the state-owned mine I visited, migrants often worked the closest to the seam and the farthest underground. Permanently employed, better-educated staff worked closer to the surface. As one miner described it to me, you can tell the rank of a Chinese miner by the amount of soot on his face.

Officials have been trying to shut down private mines in this area. They have even asked people living along the main road not to rent rooms to migrant workers. But the migrants have simply moved higher up the mountainside, closer to the mines. They need the money and the mines need them. The hills are still dotted with illegal private pits, where explosions and other accidents are still common, according to an employee at a state-owned mine. "It's all about enormous profit," he said.

Ma's employee says he has no choice but to work in the illegal pits. At 50, he's too old to be hired by a state-owned mine. But he needs the 1,000 renminbi a month he can earn up here in the hills: He has three children to support, although one of them has already started working in a factory in Shenzhen. He is desperate to keep his job. "My workers can eat a lot of bitterness," Ma told me.

IN THE BLEAKNESS of Taiyuan's rust-belt economy, private mine owners live well. They are the speculators in the country's gold rush for coal. One local journalist says everyone knows who the mine owners are because they drive the nicest cars: Humvees, 7-series BMWs, Rolls Royces.

Private mine owners are new money. They own apartments and entire buildings in Beijing, wear expensive watches, buy cars for their friends and relatives. They spend lavishly on entertaining, particularly of the government officials who regulate the sector. Their children attend private school, in China or overseas. Their car and home purchases are often made in cash. According to one Chinese media report, a third of all millionaires in China are coal mine owners.[34] With all their cash, coal mine owners make attractive targets for kidnappers. Some hire bodyguards for protection.

Ma is just a baby mine owner, only a few months into his venture, so he has little to show for it so far. He lives in an immaculate, modest, one-story brick house along a dirt path streaked with trash and reeking of urine. He hasn't sold any coal yet, because, he says, he is still examining the quality of the deposits. For now, he is stockpiling the coal his workers produce. He won't say where the coal is stored. But Ma knows what he will do once he starts selling it: put the profits aside to send his younger son to university in the United States. Wide-eyed, with a military-short haircut and impeccable manners, Ma's son attends a nearby school with other miners' children. He is only ten, but his father's mine is an investment in his future.

It was Ma's desire for upward mobility that brought him to the hillside above his mine, and his employees' hope for the same that compelled them to work for him. The same ambition helps Ma keep his illegal mine open, despite frequent sweeps by government inspectors. Bribes to the right officials go a long way. "If you have money, you can keep working and use money to get rid of trouble," Ma says.

Corruption is endemic in the government agencies in charge of coal mines in China. Despite an obvious conflict of interest, many local officials invest in mines. When the Communist Party's Central Commission for Discipline Inspection issued a mandate in August 2005 that all government officials and executives in state-owned enterprises relinquish their stakes in coal mines, over 5,370 officials came forward to confess 755 million renminbi worth of investments.[35] It's safe to assume this was hardly full disclosure—a point that even the central government's mouthpiece, the *China Daily*, concedes.[36] Not to mention that many officials have invested in coal mines in their relatives' names.

In the rush for coal, some entrepreneurs in Shanxi have even set up illegal coal inspection stations that take a cut before the coal leaves the area.[37] Corrupt village officials are also involved in the transportation and sale of illegal coal.[38] Officials who aren't paid off have been known to turn up at a mine and demand bribes on the spot. The underground dealings of coal mines are replicated elsewhere in the country's energy supply chain: A fifth of China's power plants are illegal.[39]

The hunger for wealth around China's coal mines has even perverted the watchdog role of the media. The beating death of a Chinese journalist at the orders of a mine owner in a major mining area outside Taiyuan in January 2007 shed new light on the phenomenon of "fake" reporters. These are people who arrive at the scene of a mining accident and extort money from the owner in exchange for not reporting it—a different breed of ambulance chaser altogether.

Keeping this wealth machine of illegal coal mines running requires a heavy cloak of secrecy. "When there is an incident, I pay more than 100,000 renminbi, or several hundred thousand renminbi, or even as much as one million renminbi" to muzzle the media, one mine owner interviewed by the *Beijing News* said.[40] Reporters from larger media organizations are reportedly better paid than those from smaller, local groups. Authentic reporters are regularly beaten, harassed and detained for investigating mining accidents.

Mine owners resort to ghoulish means to cover up accidents, burying bodies far away, bribing family members with hush money, claiming that the workers died of disease, keeping other employees in the same mine in the dark about the incident. The larger the accident, the greater the need to collude with government officials to keep it quiet.[41]

While the executives at the state-owned mine I visited were surprisingly friendly, one cautioned his colleagues that Chinese mines were full of secrets best kept from Americans. Even Ma hung up the phone the first time his colleagues suggested an interview with me. (He later capitulated.) "If we say that Chinese coal is tainted with blood and the news reaches the United States, what will they think of China?" the executive asked the other people in the room with us, presumably assuming I couldn't understand.

Ma's employees are terrified of media exposure, more terrified, it seems, than of the possibility of contracting respiratory disease, being injured or dying in the mine. "Please don't publish this in the newspaper or I will lose my job," one of Ma's miners, who said he felt safe working in the mine, begged me. "We are working for the boss and I'm afraid if you publish something, that will harm the boss's well-being. We need money and our boss needs to survive, too."

Ma is less concerned. In exchange for his bribes, he is notified when inspection teams are coming to his area for a crackdown. On those days, he tells his employees their services won't be required. The holes his staff is digging in the mountain remain quiet and anonymous, the only sign of activity a wheelbarrow parked outside. "When supervision is tight, we stop mining, and when the situation improves we start again," Ma explains. In the few months he has been operating, Ma hasn't had to suspend production once.

COAL IS THE LIFEBLOOD of Ma's community. The resource provides employment for at least 10,000 people and their families in
one community alone. But it is also creeping into residents' bodies
in unhealthy ways.

"It feels terrible when I sit still," says Xu, a miner's son who
works as a driver. Xu is at home on a Saturday morning, lying on a
bed covered with a red and pink striped blanket. His arm is hooked
to an intravenous drip hanging from a wire strung across the ceiling.
The television drones from the opposite side of the room. Xu has
rhinitis—a stuffy, itchy nose, coughing, sneezing, postnasal drip. The
intravenous drip helps alleviate the symptoms. It's a minor ailment,
but his father and friends have it, too. One friend joined the army
and moved to the southern province of Yunnan. His rhinitis disappeared. Ma's wife has rhinitis, too. Rhinitis can be caused by aller-
gens, including pollens and mold. In these cases, it is commonly
called hay fever.

In the hills outside Taiyuan, it's not clear what is causing the
rhinitis. The air is certainly full of soot. But it is also common in
rural areas in China for people to use coal-burning stoves, which
cause indoor pollution. "A lot of people in Shanxi have rhinitis because of the coal," Ma explains. "When we were young, we got it
because of the smoke of burning coal."

It's highly unlikely that rhinitis is the only health problem in
Ma's community. Coal mining can lead to pneumoconiosis; indoor
pollution from coal-burning stoves is known to increase the incidence of respiratory diseases and infections; mines discharge toxic
wastewater without treatment, which affects local crops.

And yet the area seemed poorly equipped to handle health
problems. A teacher at Ma's son's school says many of his students
have rhinitis as well as trachoma, an infectious eye disease caused
by bacteria that can lead to blindness. The most gravely ill students

are sent into town for treatment. The teacher would prefer if these problems could be treated locally. He asks whether I know of any good treatment for rhinitis.

Most everyone else I meet, though, seems willing to sacrifice some of their health in exchange for a piece of the profits from the country's coal rush. Who has time for rhinitis and respiratory disease when there is so much money to be made? And yet Taiyuan is a sober place, hardly the kind of town that seems to be in the middle of anything exuberant. Perhaps the human sacrifices involved in powering China's economy does weigh on people's hearts.

When I first met Ma in an office at the local coal mine and asked him about his decision to open his own mines, he wrote down a poem in my notebook. I never figured out whether it was something he wrote himself or he had borrowed it from elsewhere.

No one cares about other people's concerns, so don't complain about your fate

People lend you money when you have it, and they turn you down when you need it

When it rains, an umbrella is welcome, but it seldom comes

When you're doing well and expect more, someone vicious will always do his work.

IN 2006, Shanxi province shut down 3,550 illegal coal mines.[42] In November of that year, the Ministry of Supervision and the State Administration of Work Safety published new regulations spelling out penalties for government officials or employees of state-owned enterprises whose corruption leads to workplace accidents that cause injuries or fatalities.[43]

In May 2006, five department chiefs in Taiyuan's safety audit department were forced out of their jobs. A year later, seven safety audit department heads were in prison, most for corruption.[44] Shanxi plans to lower the number of coal mines from 3,500 to 2,500 by 2010.[45] The central government wants to shut small mines—not only coal, but also other minerals including iron ore, gold and copper—as part of an industry consolidation.

The campaign to improve mine safety and clean up the environment continues, but the country's appetite for coal only intensifies.[46] Its demand for the energy source is expected to more than double by 2025.[47]

The rise in demand is helping propel prices for coal ever higher, making it harder to close small mines. Coal prices doubled between 2003 and 2007. With these kinds of prices, "there's not a lot of incentive for small coal mines to stay shut," says Trevor Houser, director of the energy practice at China Strategic Advisory, a New York consultancy. China is investing in other sources of energy, including hydropower, natural gas, nuclear plants, wind power and clean-coal technology. With help from foreign investors, Shanxi is building a power plant that will harness methane produced in coal mining. China is also moving toward coal liquefaction, in which coal is converted into liquid fuels such as gas or diesel.

But even as China develops alternatives to coal, the amount of energy needed to power its economy is so great that most new sources can only provide a fraction of total demand. Even the gigantic Three Gorges Dam, the hydroelectric dam built across the Yangtze River that is five times the size of Hoover Dam, doesn't provide enough power to unseat coal. "It's hard to scale up any alternative technologies," says Houser. "In the medium term, it's still coal."

That means more pollution, and higher clean-up costs down the line. Investment in scrubbers for coal-fired power plants will cost the industry money. That could make power more expensive, which would in turn raise costs for manufacturers. These additional costs could well affect the competitiveness of Chinese factories. Or the increase in costs might be so universal that Chinese factories are able to pass it on to foreign buyers—and ultimately, perhaps, to foreign consumers of Chinese-made goods.

The effect of air pollution on health will lead to countless lost work days and contribute to the early retirement of employees. Caring for people made ill by pollution will add to China's health care costs and tax the already struggling health care system. Without substantial health care or legal reform, families will end up picking up the tab for the health costs that result from China's worsening environmental pollution. That might be enough to make people in and around Taiyuan take to the streets in protest.

Chapter 5
THE STIRRING MASSES

L I GANG FELT HEAVY with apprehension as he boarded the bus. It was an old clunker, an overnighter with narrow bunk beds beside the windows. Other people from his village lumbered aboard, filling the beds until the bus was so swollen with passengers and their sacks of local delicacies that they could hardly move. As the bus groaned into motion, Li considered his situation.

Seventeen years old, he had just quit one of the best high schools in the province only months shy of graduation. Li was a star student, at the top of his math, chemistry and physics classes. Graduates from his high school had a shot at admittance to Tsinghua and Peking Universities in Beijing, the best in the country, and a world apart from his family's rice, corn and sweet potato plot.

But Li's mother had fallen ill, and the family savings would have to go toward her medical bills instead of tuition. College, which Li's grades, if not his parents' finances, would have made possible, was no longer an option. In this poor, rural county in Sichuan province, the birthplace of Deng Xiaoping, father of capitalist China, there was only one thing for a teenager in Li's position to do: head south and look for work in the boomtowns Deng's vision created.

Everyone on the bus was making the same pilgrimage. At the start of every year, after the festivities of Chinese New Year have wound down in February or March, an exodus of millions of farmers pours out of the Chinese countryside onto buses and trains. The peasants, most of them young, clutch bags of freshly preserved pork, oranges from the family farm, grandma's special marinated tofu—tastes of home, reminders of the people they are leaving behind. A day or more later, the exodus arrives as a weary, dirty, blinking mass on the other side of the country, deposited at a bus depot or train station filled with pickpockets and policemen.

It took Li's bus a week to reach coastal Guangdong. Ordinarily, the journey would have taken only 24 hours. But because the bus was illegally overloaded, no doubt to take advantage of the surge in passengers at that time of year, it could only travel at night, when the police were less vigilant. By day, Li and his two friends from home wandered around, bleary-eyed and penniless, in the towns where the bus stopped. By night, they caught snatches of sleep as they trundled toward their new lives in the city.

Some peasants feel awed and excited, jealous even, when they arrive in the new, modern cities of the south for the first time. Stepping off the bus in the sprawling industrial city of Dongguan that morning in March 2000, Li was unmoved. He yearned for his place back at Peng'an High School with his schoolmates. Two years, he promised himself, two years down here in the factories and I'll have earned enough money to go back to school. I'll work hard, get promoted, get a raise, save money. And then I'll be back to studying. With what remained of his $50 deposit from his school and only the clothes on his back, he set off to find a friend from home who was working in one of the factories that lined the streets of Dongguan.

Three days later, Li had a job at the same factory. He was lucky: With so many workers descending from the countryside at the same time, jobs were hard to come by. Li's friend had put in a good word for him. The factory was small by Chinese standards, about 100 people, run by a businessman from coastal Fujian province who had emigrated to Hong Kong. It produced cheap plastic bags—shopping, garbage—for export. Their manufacture produced a strong smell that permeated the factory, only to be held in by doors the management kept locked.

Li accepted the stench, and the $39 monthly salary, and his position as a *zagong* or dogsbody, the lowest-ranking job in the factory, as part of the deal. He vowed to give this factory two years of his life, and in return, it would give him the money he needed to go back to school. Even if someone had mentioned that everything about the factory, from the pitifully low wages to the locked doors, was illegal, Li wouldn't have complained. He was grateful just to have a job.

Li worked mindlessly at his new position, putting in 18 hours a day, seven days a week. For overtime work, he earned all of 10 cents an hour. When he clocked off, he collapsed, exhausted, in an apartment he shared with seven or eight other migrant workers. The days and nights began to blur with fatigue.

Li was assigned to a machine that melted recycled plastic into tiny pellets, which would then be reheated to make plastic bags. Late one night, sometime after 11 o'clock, he grabbed some plastic and thrust it into the machine with his right hand. It was a routine procedure, one he had probably done 1,000 times that day.

But when Li tried to remove his hand, it wouldn't budge. He could feel himself slipping into shock. Li's colleagues rushed to help. They pulled him from the machine and drove him to the hospital in a minivan. When Li woke up, just two weeks after arriving in China's industrial heartland, his right hand, half of his forearm and his dreams of returning home to study were gone. Half a country away from his family with not even a month's income to speak of, Li had limited options. Like most undocumented migrant workers, he had no insurance. No factory would give him a job now. His welfare depended entirely on the generosity of his boss. Even a country boy like Li knew factory managers were not known for their compassion.

The next day, Li's boss arrived at his bedside. He assured him he would cover Li's treatment and pay him two years' salary in compensation. Seven thousand renminbi, or about $900: the value of a hand at that time in the Pearl River Delta.

For three weeks, Li lay in his hospital bed, thinking, watching. In the beds around him were factory workers whose fingers, hands and legs had been consumed by China's industrial machine. All of their fates hung on their bosses' whims. Li resolved to improve his odds. When friends from home came to visit him in the hospital, he asked them to bring him magazines and books related to Chinese law. He asked his fellow patients about their injuries and how much compensation they expected their bosses to pay. He had always been interested in the law. Here was a clear reason to study it. "I had to find a way to survive," he said later. As his arm healed, Li studied. He learned about his rights and how the law entitled him to compensation. By his own calculations, his boss owed him almost $13,000—after he had paid his hospital bills. Li realized he needed a lawyer.

FOR TWO DECADES AFTER China opened the door to reform, most of its workers personified the global manufacturing ideal: docile, diligent and willing to work under almost any conditions at great length for little pay. But by the turn of the century, the Chinese worker had begun to change.

The second wave of postreform migrant workers, many of them from smaller families born under the one-child policy, arrived on factory floors with some awareness of the risks and rewards of life in the workshop of the world. These were the children, the nieces and nephews and the neighbors of migrant workers. They had grown up listening to stories of dirty, dangerous factories, trickster bosses, fingers ground up in machines. They knew better what they were getting into.

That knowledge is making the Chinese manufacturing workforce more closely resemble that of other countries. Today, Chinese workers are more likely to shun factories with poor conditions, more prone to protest or strike, and more willing to sue their employers than in the past. China's government may not be able to enforce the law, but its workers are starting to take on that job themselves.

This all has an inevitable effect on China's competitiveness. The low wages, uneven law enforcement and suppression of workers' rights that helped create China's competitive advantage in the first two decades after economic opening are, by providing the impetus for labor unrest, creating conditions that are beginning to erode that advantage. "There are not too many factories in some supply chains that haven't experienced some form of protest or worker action," says Stephen Frost of CSR Asia, a Hong Kong–based research and consulting firm. "Every worker that takes a company to court is another issue that a brand or a retailer has to deal with."[1]

By the standards of labor rights movements in the rest of the world, the shift under way in China is subtle. There is no national labor movement, no nationally coordinated strikes or sit-ins, no collective consciousness of the daily struggle of a Chinese factory worker. There is not even a charismatic leader. China keeps a tight grip on labor activists, harassing, arresting and imprisoning those who overstep the blurry line. In part because of these efforts, many Chinese workers still remain unaware of their entitlements under the law or too scared to do anything about violations of their rights.

And yet the stirrings of activism among Chinese workers are already creating challenges for the country's manufacturing sector.

Protests are on the rise. Factories around Guangdong province where workers once lined up to work now regularly hang red HELP WANTED banners.

Worker activism has helped spur the government to introduce the most sweeping changes in labor legislation in more than a decade and to encourage the creation of branches of the national labor union, the All-China Federation of Trade Unions, at foreign companies, starting with Wal-Mart's stores.

Demographic shifts that will tighten the supply of workers will only strengthen labor's leverage. China's one-child policy is already starting to winnow the supply of young workers. In the country that is expected to be the world's largest manufacturer within about a decade, the country that is already the dominant supplier of countless consumer goods, these are changes of international significance. China's labor issues are the world's labor issues.

THE FORCES THAT BROUGHT Li Gang to Dongguan began with a series of policies China instituted in the early 1980s. By returning land to the peasants in the countryside and creating investment incentives in the cities, Beijing set the stage for what is believed to be one of the largest internal migrations in human history.

In 1983, the State Council, China's cabinet, issued the blandly named Regulations Concerning Cooperative Endeavors of City and Town Laborers, giving rural peasants official approval to move into "market towns"—as long as they ate food they brought themselves and didn't consume rations reserved for city residents.[2] What had been a trickle of people moving from rural areas to the cities swelled to a flood. Regulations and documents the central government created to control this population shift barely kept up with the flow.[3]

Inland provinces encouraged the flood of people. Market prices for grain began to fall in the mid-1980s, after the government adjusted the prices following a particularly good harvest. Ironically, as has happened in other countries, with the spread of efforts to improve efficiency, Chinese farms became less profitable. Farming required fewer people and made less money. But there weren't many other job opportunities in the countryside, as industry at the time was concentrated in the east.[4] Corrupt and underpaid rural officials further narrowed peasants' income by skimming off state resources for themselves. Incomes in the city began to grow rapidly compared with those in the countryside, a trend that continues today.[5]

Senior rural officials saw exporting labor to other provinces as a painless way to generate much-needed income. "We consider migrant labor to be a kind of cooperation between eastern and western parts of the country," Xie Shijie, Communist Party secretary in Sichuan province, reportedly said at the time. "They leave empty-handed and return rich—it's like making money from nothing."[6] Migrant workers have since become known as "factories without smoke."

Migrants were—and are—a powerful lever in pulling rural China out of poverty. Labor migration contributed to 16 percent of GDP growth between 1987 and 2005, according to one estimate.[7] Annual remittances sent through the post office of one poor county in rural Sichuan were equivalent to five times the revenues of the county government—and remittances sent through the post office generally represent only about half the money migrants send home.[8] Remittances help build homes, pay for children's education and put food on the table for rural residents.[9]

And so rural provinces played an active role in shuttling their people to the cities. Migration became a profitable business for poor inland governments. Labor departments in the countryside organized peasants and arranged jobs for them as construction workers, factory hands or nannies in eastern provinces, and collected fees for their services. Some provinces even put offices in Guangzhou, capital of Guangdong province, to manage the export of their populace.[10] These arrangements "operated to shunt what could be termed the troops of China's rural labor reserve army from places where local bureaucrats considered them a useless burden to spots where their cheap toil was a valued good," writes Dorothy Solinger, a leading scholar on Chinese migrants.[11]

Most migrants, however, arrived through introductions from friends or relatives. They tended to be "middle class" peasants—not the poorest, nor the most wealthy—from areas with good transport links to the destination province.[12] They were often better educated than their peers back in the villages.[13] Manufacturing, including handicrafts, and construction absorbed the largest numbers of migrants.[14] As immigrants often do around the world, China's migrant workers typically took jobs locals didn't want: dangerous, exhausting, low-paying work.

But not everyone was happy to see them. Official policy in the cities was, and still is, to maximize employment opportunities for legal locals. Many urban officials saw migrants as burdens—impossible to control, prone to criminal activity and disruptive to social stability. City officials expressed dismay at what they called *mangliu* or "blind wanderers" from the countryside. The *hukou*, or household registration, system provided a way to keep these blind wanderers in check. It also greatly benefited the Chinese export manufacturing sector.

Under the rules of the system, anyone leaving his or her *hukou* zone for more than three days must register with the police. In order to legally leave the Chinese countryside and move to a city, migrants need to submit to the police proof of employment from a city labor bureau, an official document of acceptance by a school in the city or a relocation permit issued by the city where they are moving.[15] Once in the city, migrants must apply for a temporary residence permit.

The system has provided ample opportunity for corruption. In

Shenzhen in 1992, black-market prices for temporary residence permits reached 30,000 renminbi—about $4,000 at current exchange rates.[16] Even the police inflate the prices. The official fee is between $26 and $66, depending on the city. But as recently as 2004, police in Shenzhen and Dongguan were reportedly charging additional, one-off fees of $20 to $28 for temporary residence permits, rather than the 65 cents they were supposed to charge by law.[17] These fees have fallen sharply in more developed cities like Shenzhen.[18]

Even armed with such permits, migrants are still denied subsidized housing, unemployment and other welfare benefits. They still pay exorbitant fees to send their children to school.[19] Unsurprisingly, many migrants don't bother registering at all. Today, less than half the migrant population in Beijing is registered, according to one academic.[20] Only a fraction of migrants across the country have temporary residence permits, contends another.[21] The Ministry of Labor and Social Security has been trying to simplify the procedures for migrating.

Failure to register can have serious consequences, however. Migrants are required to carry three pieces of documentation at all times: an identity card, a temporary residence permit and a work permit. Those without these certificates are known as "three withouts." For two decades after economic reforms began, police regularly harassed migrants, detaining them and shipping them back to the countryside if they lacked proper documentation. Migrant workers represented "the vast majority" of people detained under this system, according to a report by Human Rights in China.[22] Before the Asian Games in 1990, Beijing rounded up some 200,000 migrants and deposited them in the countryside to make the city look more attractive to foreign visitors.[23]

The most famous case, however, involved a young, university-educated designer from Hubei province named Sun Zhigang. On March 17, 2003, police arrested Sun, who was legally employed, in

Guangzhou for failing to produce a temporary residence permit. They took him to a police station and then a detention center for migrant workers, where he died days later. An autopsy showed Sun had been severely beaten. When his death was reported by a gutsy local newspaper, it provoked a national outcry. The uproar prompted the State Council, China's cabinet, to eliminate the Measures of Detaining and Repatriating Floating and Begging People in the Cities, which had governed the detention and deportation of undocumented migrants since 1982. The risk to migrants of dying in police custody has diminished, although they are still subject to harassment by police.

The *hukou* system was designed to help Beijing shape the country's development, to handpick who would get to live in the socially and economically important cities. One internal *hukou* police handbook from 2000 describes the system this way: "[We should] make it easier for high-quality people to relocate, harder for low-quality people; easier for professionals to relocate, harder for general labor; . . . [We should] work especially to prevent national blind floating of low-quality people."[24]

Wang Fei-Ling, associate professor at the Sam Nunn School of International Affairs at the Georgia Institute of Technology, argues that the system has been a key factor in promoting China's economic growth since the 1980s. "It is the constant and continued sacrifice of the excluded majority in the Chinese villages that makes the Chinese economic miracle possible," he wrote in his overview of the *hukou* system, *Organizing Through Division and Exclusion: China's Hukou System*. "The *liudong* (migrant) rural laborers are highly mobile and responsive to market demands for cheap labor. They create only temporary, minimal burdens for the cities and usually have no means of raising their own demands for benefits, promotion, job security, or asserting their right to get the promised pay."[25]

Critics of the *hukou* system have drawn unflattering comparisons with South Africa's apartheid and American Jim Crow laws. One Chinese professor of labor relations likens the situation of the country's migrant workers to India's untouchables.[26] America's largest union, the AFL-CIO, has cited the *hukou* system as one way China represses workers' rights in its repeated petitions to the Office of the United States Trade Representative.

Professor Wang contends that the *hukou* system has been integral in widening China's income gap, by denying some people privileges and rewarding others.[27] Today, that income gap has become a source of popular unrest that worries central government leaders.

China has been trying to reform the *hukou* system for at least a decade. Some provinces are experimenting with eliminating the distinction between urban and rural residents. Other reforms appear to have been targeted at allowing more wealthy people into the cities, rather than making it easier for ordinary workers to migrate. In most areas, household registration tied to a place still determines the level of state benefits to which a resident is entitled.[28]

Professor Wang argues that the *hukou* system provides too many benefits to the Chinese government—in terms of social control, economic development and governance—ever to be allowed to disappear completely. Some cities that have experimented with allowing rural *hukou* holders to upgrade to urban *hukou*, like Fenghua in eastern Zhejiang province, could not handle the increased cost of providing social services to all their new residents. When Fenghua gave 13,000 select rural *hukou* holders urban *hukou* over a period of eight months in 2001 and 2002, $2.6 million in extra school fees these migrants were paying dried up overnight. The city also had to find ways to pay for all of the social benefits these new citizens required.[29] Other provinces have also suspended their *hukou* reforms because the cities were unable to cope with the resulting increase in population.[30]

"To lift the *hukou*-based institutional exclusion for so many people and in so many realms, there must be either a massive spending of public funds or a massive resource reallocation and redistribution—neither, however, is easy, since the interest of the minority but powerful and organized urbanites will be directly impaired," Professor Wang argues.[31] Nor do all migrant workers want to surrender their rural *hukou*, because the rural registration gives them land-use rights in their hometowns. Land is the ultimate source of security for migrant workers, who can always return home to work the fields if they can't find work in the cities.[32] The household registration system, or some variant of it, seems unlikely to be abolished. As long as it remains in place, a legal framework for discrimination against migrants will, too. And discrimination, history shows, plants the seeds of unrest.

AS LI'S ARM HEALED, he flipped through the reading his friends had brought him in the hospital and came across an article in a magazine about Zhou Litai, the self-taught lawyer who became a celebrity by winning record payouts for workers injured on the job. It was about four years since Zhou had won his first case in Shenzhen by arguing that the family of a couple killed by a delivery truck at the factory where they worked deserved both accident and occupational injury compensation. Zhou was already on television, where Li had seen him before his accident.

From the hospital, Li dialed the mobile phone number listed for Zhou at the bottom of the article. When the lawyer answered, Li explained his case. Come see me in my office, Zhou said. So Li, still checked into the hospital, found a bus to Zhou's office in Longgang. It took him three hours to get there.

He found Zhou surrounded by maimed migrants. Legal battles leave many victims of occupational injury poor and unemployed in

China—hence Zhou's decision to rent a building where his clients could live while their cases moved through the legal system. The day Li visited, there were more than 40 other injured workers crowded into Zhou's building. Zhou spent only a few minutes with him that day, Li recalls. But it was long enough for the lawyer to agree to take on Li's case. And that was enough for Li, who was thrilled to have his case in the hands of the country's best-known workers' rights defender.

Li returned to the hospital. When he was released two months later, his first concern was money. Legal battles in China are notoriously drawn out, and Li was broke. With only one hand, factory work was out of the question.

Instead, Li became a peddler, selling apples and oranges out of a stand in a residential area in Dongguan. For a while he set aside the fruit business and, in the spirit of "if you can't beat them, join them," tried to become a trading agent for factories around the Pearl River Delta. It was an ironic choice for a man who was now fighting a factory to win fair compensation for the hand he lost on the job. His father, a government official in the family's village in Sichuan, moved to Dongguan to help his son get back on his feet.

After ten months of living on fruit money, a friend of Li's, a worker from Fujian province, suggested he try again at his childhood passion: studying. "You can make money when you're older," she told him. Li took her advice. Returning to the sciences, which had so captivated him as a student in Sichuan, was out of the question. Science, he realized, required two hands. The law was both relevant to his life and more accessible.

In March 2001, Li moved in with Zhou. Being at his lawyer's side would be useful for his own legal defense and for his studies of the law. A year after his accident, Li's case still lingered unresolved in the courts. Both Zhou and the Chinese courts were too busy with other legal battles.

At Zhou's, Li shared a small room with seven other injured factory veterans. There were more people than beds. In these crowded rooms, the onetime science whiz began an unconventional apprenticeship. Li invested in law books and threw himself into his studies. When he came across something he didn't understand, he would ask one of the team of lawyers working with Zhou for clarification.

None of it came easily. Not only was Li learning the law, he was also learning to adjust to life with one hand. He had come to Guangdong to earn money for his family. Before he even had a chance to send anything home, a machine stole his best chance at steady work. Now, he was relinquishing what little income he made selling fruit and trading goods to study the law.

Li was not given to self-pity. But he took long walks in the neighborhood, turning over in his head the direction his life had taken. "The hardest part was putting aside these thoughts and focusing on my studies," he remembers.

His time with Zhou was an education in other ways, too. The lawyer's fame brought him in contact with the world of international nongovernmental organizations. NGOs were still a new concept in China, and Li had never heard of them before he met Zhou. But his time in Zhou's building introduced him to these groups, and eventually, he began to think about creating one himself. He could start, he thought, by visiting injured workers in the hospital to tell them what he had learned about their legal rights.

One day, while Li was studying at Zhou's, visitors from Hong Kong arrived. They were from the Hong Kong office of Oxfam, the international charity that focuses on poverty alleviation. Oxfam was funding Zhou's office at the time, helping him house the workers during their legal battles. Li heard the visitors arrive and went to listen in on their conversation. When the Oxfam executives asked him for his thoughts on the situation with workers, he told them his idea about visiting injured workers. Nearly a dozen meet-ings, phone calls and e-mails later, Li had talked himself into a sti-pend from Oxfam to provide legal advice to workers in the hospital. In less than two years, he had gone from star student to factory grunt to amputee to aid worker. Li was 19 years old.

LI'S TRANSFORMATION was unusual. But it was also a sign of the times. By the day he arrived in Dongguan in the spring of 2000, a generation of migrant workers had already rotated through the fac-tories on the coasts.

The path is well worn between poor inland provinces like Si-chuan and industrial Guangdong. The countryside around Li's hometown is sprinkled with signs advertising long-distance phone service, a luxury necessitated by the exodus of local peasants to the coasts. It is dotted with bus stations selling rides to precise locations in Guangdong province, districts and towns and cities like Zhang-mutou, Shunde, Longgang: places only migrant workers, their bosses and sourcing agents have ever heard of.

By the year 2000, the Chinese government's campaign to edu-cate the public about using the law as a weapon was well under way. China's state-controlled media had taken up the cause of mi-grant workers' rights, highlighting the potential for abuse and the recourse available through the court system. The coverage of labor disputes came as reporting on other contentious issues, including land seizures, was also rising.

In the late 1990s, rural peasants, largely left out of the economic boom under way in Chinese cities, became increasingly aware of their rights. They were more willing to challenge the government when they felt they had been violated. Official corruption, illegal taxation and land seizures and environmental pollution were fuel-ing peasant unrest. Peasants were petitioning the government, appealing through the legal system and trying to elect leaders who would serve their interests. As a last resort, they were also protesting. In 1993, there were 8,706 popular protests in China. By 2005, there were 87,000. About 40 percent of these protests occurred in the countryside.[33]

An exposé by Chen Guidi and Wu Chuntao, Chinese journalists, details the abuses in the countryside in nauseating detail: the murder of auditors of a town's accounts; the arrest of an entire family because the grandmother dared to question excessive taxes. The book, published in Chinese as *Zhongguo Nongmin Diaocha* and translated into English as *Will the Boat Sink the Water?: The Life of China's Peasants*, sold 10 million copies on the black market in China.

Li also benefited from being born under the one-child policy, a generation of children more doted on than others in the past. The phenomenon is most noticeable in China's wealthier classes, where solo offspring known as "little emperors" are spoiled rotten, but the trend applies in its way to poor, rural families as well. While labor advocates and academics who study China's migrant population have noted a gradual evolution in attitudes over the previous two decades, the generation of migrant workers born after 1979 seems to represent a sharp change.

"These workers understand the concept of employment better," says Zeng Feiyang, a former lawyer who has been working with laborers in Guangzhou since 1998. "They not only want a job, but they also want work that is relaxing, with less overtime, a higher salary and satisfactory working conditions. They're also looking for further development and personal growth in their life outside their job. . . . They don't want to be an assembly line worker their whole life."[34]

While the first generation of migrant workers just wanted money, many in this generation already want something closer to a career. They are not happy with earning enough to eat and support the family back on the farm. Could this rapid change in mentalities undermine the foundation of one of the pillars of China's economic miracle, the manufacturing sector?

Second-generation migrants tend to go straight from school to the factories, without tending the family farm as the last generation of migrants did before they moved to the cities. As a result, they don't see themselves as farmers and have fewer ties to the village. These migrants are more likely to have relatives or friends from home already living in the cities. As the amount of available land in the countryside declines, some families have moved to the cities entirely, only returning to the countryside once every several years. Some of these migrants have a place to stay and family to borrow money from when they first arrive in the city or are between jobs, a safety net the Chinese government doesn't provide them.

Some second-generation migrants know more about the labor law than their predecessors. Some avoid factories with excessive overtime and dangerous conditions in favor of those with higher wages and shorter hours. Many are interested in cultivating skills: learning how to use a computer and how to speak English.

They keep more of what they earn, instead of sending most of their salary back to relatives in the countryside as workers before them did. They tend to stay longer in the cities, making a life there instead of rushing back to the countryside to get married or help out on the farm after a couple years' work in a factory. They are more aware of and willing to stand up for their rights.

Han Dongfang, a labor activist who was imprisoned for his role in the protests centered on Beijing's Tiananmen Square in 1989, argues that one reason for migrant workers' increasing assertiveness is that they have no choice. The diminishing supply of farmland in the Chinese countryside means that today's migrant workers have little or nothing to return to. "They have nowhere to go," he said in an interview. "That is the reality."[35]

Ching Kwan Lee, an assistant professor of sociology at the University of Michigan who specializes in labor politics and protest, agrees. "The countryside has become a huge force compelling workers to leave and stay longer in the cities," she says. "The idea of having an insurance policy in the land is not as universal as it was ten years ago. They are going to be more resilient in fighting for their rights because they don't have any choice."[36]

As a result of family planning policies, Li came to Dongguan after China's population of young people had already peaked. Starting in the late 1990s, China's young rural population began to fall rapidly, according to United Nations data.[37] That trend has continued since then and shows no sign of letting up, even as the need for employees is greater than ever. The rapid growth of the Chinese economy and its attractiveness as an assembly base has spawned a frenzy of investment not only in manufacturing but also in services. And when the first wave of peasants left the countryside in the 1980s, Guangdong was essentially the only place to go to look for work. Jobs were hard to come by.

But peasants migrating in the new millennium have much greater choice: In addition to Guangdong, there were now ample job opportunities in the Yangtze River Delta (centered in Shanghai), in eastern Fujian province and even in many inland areas. There were so many jobs, in fact, that factories in Guangdong province, where pay and working conditions were worse than in the Yangtze River Delta, were desperate for employees.

By 2004 and 2005, the streets of Dongguan were filled with colorful banners advertising factory vacancies. Factory managers began offering perks—basketball courts, Internet cafes, more air conditioners—to attract and retain workers. One toy factory in the city of Huizhou even installed a roller skating rink complete with revolving disco lights and loud dance music on its roof. In April 2005, many factories gave employees a day off to celebrate the Qingming festival, when Chinese pay respects to deceased family members. Qingming is a big holiday in China, but usually not for factory workers. Managers hoped by giving staff the day off, they might inspire them to stay longer.

Increasingly, factories have been tempering their preference for young workers, advertising jobs for workers as old as 35 or 40. In 2004, government officials estimated Guangdong's factories needed another two million workers. Some southern Chinese factories have started to need workers more than their workers need the factories. The balance of power, long tilted in favor of factories, has begun to shift, slightly but inexorably, toward labor.

WITH HIS MODEST STIPEND from Oxfam, Li and a few other industrial accident victims he met through Zhou began making the rounds of local hospitals. He looked for workers like himself, injured in the line of duty.

Li told them how to hire a lawyer, how much it would cost, how long it would take to get their case heard and win compensation. He taught them how to pick the real lawyers from the con artists who preyed on accident victims: by checking their lawyer's registration number against a publicly available list. For this service, he earned nothing. A cook at Zhou's shelter, paid by Oxfam Hong Kong, made his meals.

Li became friendly with some of the workers he met on his hospital rounds. "These workers needed support," he said. He and the other accident victims from Zhou's house discussed the idea of organizing activities for workers that would teach them about the law and provide them other skills they couldn't learn in the factories. They aspired to set up their own NGO, though they had no idea how to run one. Li also felt that while his time in Shenzhen had helped him understand the issues workers were facing there, he was still unfamiliar with the problems in other cities in the region. If he was going to start a workers' organization, he needed to get to know his clientele better. "I knew about workers in Shenzhen, but I wanted to know what workers in Guangzhou, Shunde, Foshan were like," Li recalls. So Li hit the road. He spent the next three months interning at workers' rights organizations around the province.

Guangdong's proximity to Hong Kong has allowed the province unusual access to international groups interested in labor issues. Their support has been instrumental in creating organizations that educate and defend the rights of migrants in southern China.

Most are small, ragtag groups. One is in tucked in a corner across from a guitar store in a strip mall frequented by migrants; another above a Christmas ornament distributor on a main artery for container trucks; a third on the top floor of a factory building. Their founders have diverse backgrounds: factory work, government, journalism.

In an illustration of the globalization of labor issues, American, European and Hong Kong donors are the main source of funding for most if not all of these labor advocacy groups in Guangdong province. Hong Kong labor rights organizations, which work closely with partners in mainland China, also rely heavily on funding from the West. The ideologies of these funders have helped shape the agenda of labor groups in southern China. Not all of their imported Western notions fit with China's unique situation. "In the 1990s, international organizations planted the idea of labor rights in China, and local people developed the idea," says Li.

The U.S. government has been supporting labor rights programs in China for several years. Among the main sources of general assistance are the State Department's Bureau of East Asian and Pacific Affairs and Bureau of Democracy, Human Rights, and Labor (DRL). The funding mostly goes to U.S. NGOs with operations in

China, which then provide funding for Chinese NGOs. Some of the monies for China programs come through DRL's Human Rights and Democracy Fund, which was created by Congress in 1998 and promotes democratic development abroad.

Congressional appropriations for the fund are rising, from $13 million a year on average in fiscal years 2001 and 2002 to $33.7 million on average every year between 2003 and 2005. According to the Congressional Research Service, in 2006, Congress allocated $63 million for the fund. About a quarter of the Human Rights and Democracy Fund's spending goes to China-related programs.[38]

The Department of Labor's Bureau of International Labor Affairs also funds activities in China, including a four-year, $4.1 million grant, awarded in October 2002, to help the Chinese government raise awareness of the law, improve industrial relations, develop laws that protect workers and expand legal assistance to female and migrant workers. The grant was given to the group Worldwide Strategies and included the Asia Foundation and National Committee on United States–China Relations as subcontractors. The department also gave a four-year, $2.3 million grant to the National Safety Council to improve mine safety in China.[39]

Among the other foreign organizations providing support to migrant workers in China are the United Nations Development Program and the Belgian embassy in Beijing, which helped fund a Chinese government program, announced in 2006, to train lawyers to defend migrant workers and establish legal aid centers in 15 provinces. The UK consulate in Guangzhou has organized a series of seminars on corporate social responsibility. The Asia Foundation, a San Francisco–based nonprofit, funds several projects to help the migrant worker community. Oxfam Hong Kong has also been involved with migrant workers in southern China.

Li took turns at many of the nongovernmental labor organizations in Guangdong, learning how to design projects, how to write grant proposals and how to manage the employees and accounts of an NGO. He went as far as Beijing and the city of Wuhan, studying briefly at universities there.

In 2002, two years after his accident, Li's case finally made it to court. The day the Dongguan People's Court of First Instance heard his case, Li testified about what had happened that night in the factory. His former boss calmly argued, perversely enough, that Li set out to maim himself. The hearing was over in two hours. Months later, the ruling was announced. Li won compensation of just over $6,000, an amount he believed was less than half the standard award in Dongguan for injuries like his. Li attributed the small payout to differences among judges in China. Li sent most of the money home to his parents. Some of the remainder went to setting up his NGO with his friends. A Hong Kong labor advocacy group provided the rest of their initial funding.

Everything was a challenge. Later that year, Li went to court for the first time as a legal adviser. His client was the husband of a woman from central Henan province who was severely injured in a hit-and-run accident at the entrance to her factory. The case went on for months. Li was so nervous that he had to read out his statements in the courtroom. Even the verdict didn't bring an end to Li's responsibility. After the judge awarded the husband and wife compensation of about $26,000, it fell to Li to find the driver of the truck that had struck her.

In cases of this kind in China, both the driver and his employer, which owned the truck, were expected to contribute to the payout. Thrust into the role of private investigator, Li successfully tracked down the driver, who had disappeared after the accident, using videotapes at tollbooths in the area.

Meanwhile, Li's NGO was struggling for approval from a government that views independent organizations suspiciously. It wasn't until 2004 that the group was granted an official registration.

ON A HOT, rainy weekend afternoon two and a half years later, a group of migrant workers dug into boxes of rice and vegetables in a common room at Li's office on a busy commercial artery in Shenzhen.

Outside, public buses careened down the road, swerving, honking, curtains flapping out the windows. Container trucks streamed past, their trademark blue boxes painted with names that testified to the road's global relevance: Yang Ming, Hanjin, Cosco, Mediterranean Shipping Company, China Shipping. Inside the office, it was dark and damp, filled with the noise of conversation and scraping chairs.

Li had invited the workers here for a day of instruction in self-expression, supported by a Guangzhou arts group. All morning, the group dutifully sang along with the teacher, a young Chinese woman in a pink T-shirt that read, YOU CAN MAKE A DIFFERENCE. But the moment the teacher announced a break for lunch, the talk turned to labor issues, irresponsible factory managers and uncaring local officials.

"I went to the labor bureau to complain about my factory several times, but the officials said that they had no time to see me," said Chen Wei, a lanky, voluble young man from Chongqing who worked at a nearby toy factory. "I waited there for the whole morning, but no one helped me. The officials were just drinking tea and chatting. The central government claims it is protecting the rights of enterprises, but who protects workers' rights?"

The discussion homed in on the issue of profits. "In the factories here, the profits are low and some of the profits are withheld by the owners, so even the factory managers aren't paid all that they're owed," another worker said.

"I've been working on labor rights and workers' rights for several years, and I've learned more about the situation," Li interjected. He spoke calmly, with authority, his Sichuan accent seasoning every word. "To be honest, there are many factors involved. The labor law is a social issue. And the problems are related to the way these factories are managed."

Another worker agreed that management was part of the problem. "In those factories, if you haven't been working for a long time, the boss can't make any profits from you, so he often withholds your salary," he said. "If they followed the law, they would make no profits, because the order has passed through several people before it reaches them, so the profits are divided among those people."

Li conceded this point. "In the global production chain, the poorest people are the workers," he says.

"It's a cycle," a fourth worker, a woman just out of her teens, volunteered. She was already jaded by her time in the workshop of the world. "Some people take away your profits and you take away other people's profits."

Li struck a more optimistic note. "I think there is a clear change in China's protection of labor rights. There has been significant progress because of several factors—better worker awareness, more support from the public and society and better understanding by government and enterprises. These days, serious occupational injuries don't happen that often and fewer people hide the truth."

The discussion is part of Li's new initiative. While he still provides legal advice to workers injured or unfairly treated in factories—Li handled five cases of unpaid wages and contract disputes this year—he goes to court less often.

The government's enforcement of the labor law has improved, he says. He can help workers pursue justice in the courts by simply advising them on what to do. What this generation of migrants needs is something beyond the salary they get for repeating the same task hundreds of times a day on an assembly line. "The workers need an education," he insists. That education, as Li's organization defines it, is a combination of life skills and legal knowledge. Li still conducts classes in the Chinese labor law, training ranks of workers who, as he did a few years earlier, want to learn more about their rights.

But now, every Wednesday evening, he also opens his office to what he calls a "salon," where workers can have tea, socialize and relax. Other days, he offers training in basic life skills: how to use a condom, how to handle relationships with the opposite sex, how to communicate effectively.

He encourages his students to build connections to give them options beyond factory work. He tries to build their self-confidence. Some of this he does through activities, like the one today, that give workers the opportunity to practice expressing themselves. By giving workers a sense of their potential and individuality, some would argue that Li is weakening a key component of the Chinese export machine, tampering with the China price. Others would contend that he is building a base of creative, independent thinkers—just what China needs as it accelerates away from labor-intensive manufacturing. "They shouldn't look at themselves just as a low-level worker," Li says. "There is a lot more they can do."

For this work, Li says he has received funding from people in the United States. But Li now believes that China's labor issues are unique and require programs designed with local interests in mind. In the seven years since his accident, even as he has promoted the empowerment of workers, Li has come to argue that labor rights are a Western idea that has been imposed on Chinese NGOs by foreign labor groups.

He now advocates less talk of rights and more of channeling disputes through the Chinese government, through either meetings with the labor bureau or lawsuits. He stresses the importance of not upsetting social stability through holding strikes or demonstrations or organizing workers. "In China, stability is the utmost concern. Of course, this is the official line, but the public also believes it," Li says.

It's unclear how or why Li has come around to this way of thinking. He insists it is a reflection of his personal beliefs. But this approach also makes his organization less threatening in the eyes of the Chinese government.

THE SUPPORT LI PROVIDES to Chinese workers with American funding should, in theory, be provided by the All-China Federation of Trade Unions (ACFTU), China's sole union. With 134 million members, the ACFTU claims to be the world's largest union. But it is essentially made toothless and discredited by the contradictions of its role as both a defender of labor and a government institution. The union's failure has been China's gain as an investment destination.

Founded in 1925, the ACFTU has always been closely aligned with the Chinese Communist Party.[40] The year after the Communists came to power in 1949, the government passed a law authorizing the creation of a national union. The party has always directed the union's activities: In the early 1950s, union leaders who tried to assert a role for the institution independent from the party were removed from their posts. The ACFTU became what was known as a "transmission belt" of party propaganda and an enforcer of labor discipline. The *danwei*, China's work units, looked after workers' interests. In the frenzy of the Cultural Revolution of 1966–1976, unions were declared "economist" and "welfarist" and their meetings suspended. The union was marginalized by the time economic reforms began.[41]

Economic reforms transformed the labor market: State-owned enterprises privatized and went bankrupt, laying off millions of workers in the process. Migrant workers filled jobs at foreign-invested and private firms. The ACFTU's constituency and the

economy at large had changed dramatically, but the union remained a bastion of the old establishment. The union was once
described as resembling a person trying to board a moving train
when one foot is being dragged along by the train and the other is
tied to the platform.[42]

Attempts to make the ACFTU, the only union allowed in China,
more independent ended with the bloody crackdown on the student protests centered in Tiananmen Square in 1989. Students had
created their own independent unions, to the horror of Beijing officials. Fearing political opposition, the Chinese government has
adamantly refused to allow independent unions. The ACFTU's senior leadership is dominated by political appointees.

Although Chinese law says trade union officers must be elected
by workers or their representatives, in practice they are often ap-
pointed by the government or the party. Even when workers do
elect their own union leader, the leader often turns out to be the
government's or party's nominee.

Often, a factory manager or party secretary also serves as the
union leader, removing any pretense of independence or partiality
to workers' interests. In a 1993 survey of 250 company unions in
the Shekou district of Shenzhen, one of the first areas to open to
foreign investment, only two had full-time union officials. But 143
had union officials who also served as general or deputy manager of
the company. Some, it should be noted, were also workers.[43]

The logic makes perfect sense to factory managers. "Why do
some factory heads become the head of the trade union as well?
Because if something bad happened, the factory head could communicate with the government," a union representative and manager at a Guangdong shoe manufacturer explained. "In our factory,
the chairman of the trade union is the factory head as well. But he's
a nice man."

This union representative added that her role was to make sure
the factory treats employees in accordance with the law—a narrow

vision of a union by international standards. By Chinese law, the ACFTU has much broader responsibilities, including investigating workplace hazards and possible violations of workers' rights, providing legal aid to workers, advising employees on the signing of labor contracts and representing workers in labor disputes.[44]

Unsurprisingly, many international unions have not historically had much time for the ACFTU. Workers don't rate it very highly, either. Surveys conducted in the 1990s consistently showed that workers were unaware of or dissatisfied with the union.

The ACFTU does intervene in labor disputes, mediating between employees and management or advising workers on their legal defense in cases where their rights have been obviously and verifiably violated. It represents workers in collective bargaining with management for pay and conditions. But it refuses to support worker protests, because that would represent too large a challenge to the government.[45] When workers do demonstrate, union officials are expected to get them to stop.[46]

Part of the problem the union faces in representing workers' interests is a lack of resources, argues Chen Weiguang, chairman of the ACFTU in Guangzhou. Chen sits at the top of a pyramid that includes grassroots unions district-level unions, and industrial unions. Together, these groups claim a membership of 1.2 million workers and pledge to help any worker, union member or not.

But when Chen and I met in 2005, the union's legal department, created to help workers resolve disputes with management, employed only six people and was hiring temporary staff to cope with its workload. The union relies heavily on dues, equivalent to two percent of payroll, that it collects from companies with an ACFTU branch. But those dues often are not forthcoming. "It's hard for us to collect membership fees," he told me. "Many enterprise owners are reluctant to pay the fee. Under the Trade Union Law, we could sue them, but generally speaking, we don't do that." Less than 40 percent of private and foreign companies that have a union branch in Guangzhou pay their dues. To raise much-needed cash, the union opened a travel agency in its lobby.

The ACFTU's weakness has left a vacuum of representation for workers, a substantial, if relatively pliant, constituency since the 1980s. That gap left room for the growth of small independent unions and local organizations like Li's, a particularly worrisome development to Beijing.

The central government's desire to maintain one-party rule means it takes a skeptical view of all NGOs. Those that receive foreign funding are an even greater cause for concern. Beijing worries that overseas organizations might help local NGOs foment a democratic revolution, as happened during the so-called Color Revolutions in former Soviet republics in 2003 and 2004. As a result, the Ministry of State Security, China's version of the Central Intelligence Agency, and the Public Security Bureau, the police, have increased monitoring of labor groups in Hong Kong and the mainland. In 2005, officials formed a task force to increase scrutiny of NGOs.[47]

Officially, NGOs in China must register with the government. To register, they need to comply with several requirements, including having a government agency sign on as their sponsor. "The government is quite clear that the Americans and other countries are using work injury statistics to negotiate about trade," says one Hong Kong employee of an NGO that works in the mainland. "They are very sensitive to these American and European comments that China is abusing labor rights."

Representatives of Hong Kong NGOs that receive funding from overseas say they have been approached by mainland Chinese who present themselves as representatives of a "research institute" and then ask questions about their activities. Financial support from religious organizations or U.S. sources, they say, attracts the highest level of scrutiny.

Labor advocates in Hong Kong believe their phones are tapped and their e-mails monitored. They allow the possibility that their offices are bugged. Under the "one country, two systems" doctrine that has governed relations between China and the former British colony since its return in 1997, mainland officials have no legal authority to independently tap phones in Hong Kong.

Officials in the mainland continue to harass NGOs and their leaders. In November 2006, government officials investigated five labor NGOs in Shenzhen for participating in a petition drive to lower labor arbitration fees. Officials seized computers and closed down two of the NGOs.[48] The prominent founder of a legal aid center said he received regular calls and visits from security officials. These officials asked about the nature of his work and warned him not to meet with other prominent labor advocates or attend certain conferences on labor issues. Because of the government's sensitivity to these issues, Li only agreed to have his story told if he could use a pseudonym.

This harassment extends even to U.S. companies that promote workers' rights in a way that displeases Beijing. After a U.S. company that sourced from China began to promote branches of the ACFTU in its suppliers by proactively organizing elections for union officials, people who said they worked at a research institute began calling the company's offices to interview employees involved in the union drive, according to two former executives. The executives believe the people making the calls were from China's government security apparatus, though their claims are difficult to substantiate.

These people asked for personal information about an American executive involved in the union elections, including this employee's home telephone number and the names of the hotels where the employee stayed on visits to the mainland. They stressed that their questions were confidential, never to be discussed with anyone. After his first meeting with these people, one terrified employee broke the rules and told his wife. "Be prepared," he remembers telling her. "If some bad thing happens, please believe I did nothing wrong."

The harassment creates an invisible electric fence for many labor groups. Instinctively, they know what is within the realm of the acceptable and what will cause trouble. Cooperation between labor groups in the mainland is not acceptable because it would give officials the impression the groups were creating a network independent of the government. "We can't keep direct contact with each other in China," says one labor advocate in Hong Kong who insisted on anonymity. Instead, they communicate through informal channels in Hong Kong.

Occasionally, the Chinese authorities lower the charge on the invisble fence, only to turn it up again unexpectedly. One labor group in Guangzhou was allowed to organize a conference in 2004, only to have it forcibly canceled at the last minute. Another Guangdong labor advocate scheduled a meeting with a foreign journalist around the same time, only to be visited by government officials reminding her that she was not to meet with foreign reporters. She canceled the meeting.

At other times, resistance to labor-related NGOs comes from other sources. Authorities at a state-run occupational illness and injury hospital in Guangdong allowed employees of one NGO to provide legal advice to its patients, but later barred them from returning. "Employers are the hospital's customers," a senior official at this NGO concluded. Factory managers had told the hospital that if they didn't stop the NGO from advising workers on their rights, they would withhold payment or take their injured workers elsewhere.

The harassment limits the scope of what labor NGOs working in mainland China can do. "We are still working in a narrow space," says one Hong Kong labor advocate who asked that her name not be used for fear of retribution. "We still can continue, but we don't know when our center will be closed." Other Hong Kong NGOs refuse to identify their partners on the mainland for the same reason. Now is not a good time, they say.

Yet even as Beijing has increased its monitoring, it has also allowed labor advocacy groups to stay open and permitted international groups to continue funding Chinese labor organizations. It issues travel permits to allow labor activists from Hong Kong and the mainland to cross the border without hassle. Groups like China Labor Bulletin, an outspoken advocate of labor rights in the mainland, are allowed to publish reports that spell out clearly how the Chinese government is failing its workers. Chinese labor activists working in Guangdong can meet with foreign diplomats in China and travel abroad to study or speak at conferences. "It's good we are not sent to prison," one Hong Kong labor activist who works on the mainland said. "We are still here."

However, in its unwavering insistence on only one toothless union, Beijing is encouraging the very unrest it is trying to prevent. As the economy has developed, and labor disputes have inevitably arisen, workers have had no one to turn to. The government's neglect of workers' needs has created a vacuum that private labor advocates, who do not all share the government's passion for social stability above all else, have filled.

To quell the unrest and strengthen the government's control over labor, the ACFTU has been trying, with considerable success, to expand its membership. Foreign companies have long been targeted by the union as a fertile ground for organizing.

Under Chinese law, any enterprise with more than 25 employees may set up a union branch if the workers request one. But the intense competition between regions for foreign investment in China has not encouraged the establishment of unions, which many investors would rather avoid. Many export factories, especially those with investment from Taiwan or Hong Kong, have no union at all. As of mid-2006, only about 30 percent of foreign companies had ACFTU branches.[49]

Since 2003, the union has also been recruiting migrant workers, who had previously been excluded from joining.[50] It is training laid-off workers in cooperation with the International Labor Organization and the Ministry of Labor and Social Security, and opening centers that help workers find jobs and provide legal advice.[51] It is helping migrants recoup unpaid wages and setting up hotlines workers can call to complain about mistreatment. In 2006, the ACFTU even declared 18 migrant workers "Model Workers," up from only one the year before, in an effort to acknowledge their contribution.[52]

The latest recruitment drive of foreign companies netted notoriously antiunion Wal-Mart, an international coup. In March 2006, Hu Jintao, China's president, issued a directive that warned of instability among worker ranks and ordered greater unionization at foreign-invested firms. Around this time, the ACFTU set a goal to unionize 60 percent of foreign firms in 2006 and 80 percent in 2007. The ACFTU had already had its sights on Wal-Mart and other foreign companies years earlier, even threatening to sue if they didn't unionize.[53] This time, it enlisted the help of consultants from Beijing to help it crack Wal-Mart.

Starting with one man in the meat department at a Wal-Mart store in Quanzhou, in coastal Fujian province, the union organized 30 people and formed the first union in a Wal-Mart in China. Later that summer, Wal-Mart agreed with the ACFTU to unionize the rest of its stores in the mainland, along with its headquarters and a distribution center.[54] The union appears to have made strides in its relationship with the retailer: in the summer of 2008, after a campaign by the ACFTU, Wal-Mart agreed to sign collective labor contracts with employees at all of its stores.

The union has been opening branches around the country ever since, persuading Foxconn, the Taiwanese-owned manufacturer of the iPod and countless other consumer products, to establish a branch at its factory in Shenzhen. In the wake of a local media investigation that alleged it was paying employees in Guangdong less than minimum wage, McDonald's agreed to allow unions at some of its branches as well.

But skepticism of the ACFTU persists. Robin Munro, research director at China Labor Bulletin, believes the union has been tasked with easing labor unrest on top of its traditional role of enforcing labor discipline. But, he argues, "it's not been given the tools that would enable it to do either of these properly."[55]

Munro says that he wants to think the ACFTU will in the future represent Chinese workers. "But at the present stage," he says, "there isn't any real sign that the ACFTU is moving toward being a body that genuinely represents the interests of the workers and stands on their side."[56] Without a truly representative organization, Munro concludes, labor rights abuses will persist and protests will continue to escalate. "In other words, you're not going to get social stability if you're not going to allow these workers to have somebody representing their interests."

ON A SUNNY SUMMER AFTERNOON, Chen Wei, the student in Li Gang's personal development course who complained about his visit to the labor bureau, sits in a patch of shade in a Shenzhen park with several friends. It's Sunday, Chen's day off from the toy factory, and he is holding forth on his plans for the future.

At 25 years old, after five years and many more jobs in Pearl River Delta factories, Chen is a migrant worker ready to take his career in a new direction. "My current plan is first to study the labor law," he explains. Chen is lanky and narrow-waisted, with thinning hair and a thick Chongqing accent. "Then, if I have the chance, I'd like to get to know some buyers from other countries, like the United States, and set up a legal company."

Chen wants to be a trader, sourcing goods from the very factories that keep him on the line until close to midnight and illegally withhold his wages.

The son of a government official, Chen grew up in a suburb of Chongqing, one of the world's most populous cities, in southwest China. His intellect took him as far as the best high school in his town. But after his first year, a deterioration in Chen's family finances forced him to drop out. After the summer harvest, he boarded the train for Guangzhou alone, with one change of clothes, one book and $39.

For three years, Chen worked his way through the region, bouncing between cities and factories. He made bags. He made toys. Once, he was a manager, recruiting workers and setting their schedules. Another time, he worked as a quality inspector. He learned a few things along the way. He learned, for example, that factory managers prefer female staff because they are less likely to fight. He learned that foreign buyers sometimes don't pay factories for their orders. He learned how to file a complaint with the government.

Chen didn't tolerate mistreatment. Back at home, he had read his father's books on labor laws and other regulations. If a factory didn't pay him properly, he complained or quit. He shunned more controversial means like strikes. Instead, he used legal channels to voice his concern. Once, Chen called the city government to report that his employer, a toy manufacturer, had failed to pay his wages. He considered filing a request for arbitration with the toy maker, but balked at the nearly $8 application fee.

Li's organization gave Chen space to air his frustrations at the poor condition of the Chinese migrant worker. Through Li, Chen began to widen his circle of contacts. He met an American diplomat, to whom he complained about poor conditions at his factory. He met Chinese law students from Guangzhou. "They all talked about how to develop oneself," he remembers. Chen might have used his knowledge of the labor law to campaign for better treatment of fellow migrants. But instead, he concluded he needed to be his own boss. With his new international connections, sourcing goods seemed like a good place to start. Even Li, his mentor, had done this for a while before starting his NGO.

Chen maps out his vision. "If you're my client, and you'd like to make some kind of bag, we can make a plan for you and show you a pattern for the bag," he says. "If you're satisfied, we can deduct the cost of production from the price and calculate a profit margin to decide whether or not to sell to you. If we can sell it to you, we'll do it according to an agreement."

As well versed as he is in the labor law and its widespread abuse by factory owners, Chen believes that he would be able to buy from manufacturers that treat their workers fairly. A friend's wife works in a shoe factory that follows the labor law. Plus, as a buyer, he could put pressure on factories that operate illegally. "If a factory is deducting staff salaries and extending overtime and so forth, I will try to communicate with the boss and ask him to improve his treatment of his employees," Chen explains. "I can both help migrant workers and realize my own plan for the future. And I can make sure foreign businessmen are paying Chinese businessmen for their products on time."

Chen is preparing himself for the business world by examining his character for shortcomings that could hold back his career. He worries his Chongqing accent makes it hard for him to be understood. He is concerned that his friends tell him he interrupts others too often. Good communication skills are essential to success in business, he says.

CHEN AND LI MIGHT not seem like a threat to anyone. Both believe in making the Chinese system work for them, rather than overturning the existing order in pursuit of better conditions for workers. They are not revolutionaries.

But they and others like them are contributing to dramatic changes in the China price. Their increased awareness of their rights and intolerance of poor working conditions, however subtle they might seem by international standards, are helping set in motion a series of events that are already having a direct impact on the China price. Their change in attitude and their dwindling number could yet prove revolutionary. There is value in scarcity.

Workers like Chen and Li are partly responsible for the rising turnover that bedeviled Eugene Chan, the Wal-Mart supplier in chapter two. Annual turnover of 30 percent is now common among factories in the Pearl River Delta, according to Liu Kaiming, executive director of the Institute of Contemporary Observation, a Shenzhen labor research group.

Of course, China's economic expansion has allowed workers more choice. The one-child policy, and the constraints it is imposing on the supply of workers, has also helped. But as a result of these factors, some of these workers are distinctly more demanding than the generation that preceded them. They are forcing factory managers to provide air conditioning, better food, higher pay. Those that don't, suffer.

"Ten years ago, workers came to your factory and the first thing they asked was 'do we work overtime?' If yes, then they want to work. Now, they ask you, 'do you work overtime?' If yes, then they say, 'yes, I don't want to work for you,' " says one Taiwanese factory manager in Shenzhen. Despite raising salaries 37 percent the previous year, he is losing his workforce to factories that can afford air conditioning.

Another Taiwanese factory manager in Zhongshan echoes this view. "Every worker who comes in we have to pay a high minimum wage, even though they are not productive. After two to three years, they're qualified . . . then they leave."

One German factory manager has already felt the power of the second-generation migrant worker. A few years ago, a strike brought his electric cable factory in Dongguan to a standstill. Police and local officials descended on his office. Negotiations with the workers began. It was only then that the German manager learned the source of his employees' anger: They didn't like the food at the factory cafeteria. The manager hired an external catering company and began tasting the food himself every day. But the workers' demands continued. They wanted air conditioning on the production line because they were too hot. The manager, who says he cannot afford to cool the plant, agreed to pay them compensation for heat exposure when the temperatures were uncomfortably high.

Today, the manager is terrified of his employees. "The worker is king . . . I have 1,000 uniformed people who can press me into any kind of situation, which doesn't make sense," the manager says, referring to his staff. "I think the power of the worker will have consequences for China. They're losing control over the workers because they're giving the workers more rights."[57]

The reasons that factories began struggling to recruit and retain workers starting around 2002 are still a subject of debate among Chinese labor advocates, government officials and academics. Some argue that there is no shortage of unskilled workers in China, pointing to the estimated 100 million to 200 million unemployed and underemployed workers in the countryside as evidence. If there is a shortage, these people argue, it is of skilled workers. Others contend that the apparent shortage is a reflection of the poor working conditions in many factories, especially in Guangdong province, as a result of lax law enforcement.

The growth in the Chinese economy has given workers greater choice, these people argue, and workers are understandably moving where they will be better treated. Rising incomes in the countryside as a result of the cut in agricultural taxes have helped persuade rural workers to stay home. Coastal factories that pay above the local average and treat their workers fairly and according to the law have not struggled to find staff.

All of these explanations have merit; this is, after all, a complicated phenomenon involving hundreds of millions of people. But it is also true that younger workers, those born under the one-child policy, have demographics on their side. In addition, their increased awareness of the law and willingness to act on abuses, whether by leaving a bad factory or by challenging their employer through other means, has affected factories' ability to find staff.

Whatever the causes, factories' hiring difficulties have been among the factors driving Chinese cities to raise the legal minimum wage. By raising salaries, officials also hope to promote domestic consumption and eliminate one source of social unrest by narrowing the country's income gap.[58] As trade disputes have mounted, the government has strengthened its calls for the economy to move up the rungs of the value-added ladder, away from low-end manufacturing. Increasing workers' wages is one way to accelerate that transition.

Factories in coastal Guangdong and Fujian have started to move deeper inland to get closer to the supply of workers and take advantage of lower minimum wage rates there. Yue Yuen, the world's largest shoe maker, shifted some production to Jiangxi province, where labor and utility costs are 30 percent below those in Guangdong. Top Form International, the brassiere manufacturer, also moved to Jiangxi. Tak Shun Technology Group, a consumer electronics company, shifted production from coastal Fujian province inland to Henan, halving its labor costs.[59] Buyers began to look to Vietnam, India, Thailand and Indonesia, where labor costs were lower than in China.

The shift of manufacturing within China mirrored that of factories in the United States from North to South, and then to South

America and Asia, over more than a hundred years. But in China, it took only two decades—and one generation of migrant workers.

Chang Kai, a professor in the School of Labor and Human Resources at Renmin University in Beijing, has welcomed these shifts. He told me that the labor shortage raises questions about the sustainability of China's strategy of relying on cheap, unskilled labor for economic growth. "It is not a long term strategy for China to always compete on the low cost of its labor," he said. "For China to become a developed country, due to our plentiful labor supply, we needed to have low-cost labor for a certain period. . . . But it's just a phase. It's not feasible in the long term."

China needs to rely more on technology and innovation if it wants to compete in the long term, Professor Chang added. And its factories will need to continue to raise wages and improve working conditions. Otherwise, workers will become better organized and more violent. The development of a collective consciousness is inevitable, Professor Chang concluded.

Unless China makes sweeping changes to its family planning policy, this will only become more pronounced in coming years as the number of children per family continues to shrink. The number of women between 18 and 35 years old started falling in China in 2006.[60] Over the next 15 years, the number of 15-year-olds is expected to fall. Predictions vary, but the United Nations expects that China's working-age population will hit a peak in 2015 and start to fall.[61]

Today, China has a relatively high rate of workforce participation by young people between the ages of 15 and 24. As the economy develops and the number of people who can afford to continue in school rises, young Chinese are expected to delay their entry into the workforce, as has happened in other Asian countries over the last several decades. This, too, will put a strain on labor supply.[62] "Looking forward, China will lose its most competitive strength—

ample labor supply," Cai Fang, director of the Chinese Academy of Social Sciences' Population and Labor Economic Research Institute, has said.[63]

By introducing the one-child policy as it unleashed major economic reforms, China put its country on course for extraordinary social change. Where other countries have seen their fertility rates decline in line with economic development, China essentially pressed fast-forward. It is left with a rapidly aging population and a dwindling supply of young people.

Of course, as China continues to improve labor productivity, it will need fewer workers. Professor Chang believes these are positive changes for China, because they will force the country to compete at a higher level. "If your company has low-quality workers, is it competitive? From a human resources perspective, it's a question of how you improve your core competence. It can't be the case that the lower the quality of your workforce, the more competitive you are," he said. "Around the world, competitive companies don't have low labor costs. Because that would mean their labor quality was low. As a result, their level of innovation is high. The value added in their products is also very high."

Li agrees. "This kind of rights awareness will help create a reasonable competition" among factories, he says. "Modern enterprises need workers with independent ideas."

"We have shifted our focus from the labor law to community development," he told me at his office one spring afternoon in 2007. He was sitting at a table with two of his partners, a pudgy, cherubic man and a slight, quiet man in a black rock-and-roll T-shirt. None had a full set of fingers and hands. "We want to promote cooperation between workers and their bosses."

Across the street, factories had hung red banners advertising their need for "large quantities" of workers. Others had set up card tables on the side of the road, hoping to attract potential staff passing by. A banner hanging above the gate to Pressfield Knitting announced many openings for sewing machine operators and other jobs. Why did the factory need so many employees? "The wages are low," a factory employee standing outside the gate admitted. A monthly wage of several hundred renminbi, not including housing or food, was no longer enough to attract workers. Pressfield Knitting had several thousand workers, the man said. But it needed several thousand more.

Chapter 6

THE GIRLS OF ROOM 817

H IGH ABOVE THE TRAFFIC on a hazy Shenzhen morning, Li Luyuan stood at the edge of the factory roof, balanced between one life and another. She could see the concrete tops of other factories and the glass office buildings of Shennan Boulevard. She could hear the whoosh of cars speeding through the gray air.

Luyuan had spent almost every waking minute of the past year on the floors below, stitching sweaters for 12, 18 or more hours in a row. The year before that, she made parts of DVD players at the factory next door. The money she earned in these two buildings helped pay for a new house for her parents, more than 400 miles away in eastern Jiangxi province. There was even enough left over for a modest nest egg for herself.

Sometimes, on a break, Luyuan would climb up to this rooftop to rest. Someone had planted grass and a few shrubs up here, and butterflies hovered in the air. It was an urban sanctuary for a country girl.

This morning, she was here for the last time. When the clock struck eight, Luyuan would walk downstairs in her green polka-dot wedges, her borrowed white skirt and brown blouse, and tender her resignation. She had dressed for the occasion. She was getting out of the factories, she hoped, for good.

A few weeks before, Luyuan had found a job at a real estate agency across the street from the factory. Crossing the road meant taking a huge pay cut to work on commission in an industry she knew nothing about and losing her bed in the factory dormitory where she lived with her friends. She was leaving a sure thing for a future much less certain.

But Luyuan, who was 20, believed the risk was worth it. A junior high school dropout, she had made it out of manufacturing and into sales without ever leaving the block. "I wanted to find a job that I liked, and I did," she had said on the walk to the factory surrounded by her roommates that morning, letting out a big, open-mouthed laugh. Luyuan gathered her composure and headed downstairs.

FOR THE TWO YEARS she had lived in Shenzhen, Luyuan had been like any of the dozen girls in her factory dorm room. Most left home at 15 or 16, boarded a train or a bus with a slender wad of money tucked deep into their pockets and traveled a day or more to Guangdong. They were not only leaving the comfort of their homes and families; they were crossing the Rubicon between the old China and the new, from rural to urban, agricultural to industrial.

The girls had taken the baton in the relay race that began in eighteenth century Britain with the Industrial Revolution. They had edged out the women of Mexico's maquiladoras and Hong Kong's housing estates. They were the most affordable and productive workers the world had found, their value to the global supply chain evident in the tens of billions of dollars of foreign investment pouring into China every year. The girls were but a tiny portion of the tens of millions of migrants in Guangdong. Unlike other parts of China, where male migrants outnumber women, most in Guangdong province are women, their careful fingers and obedient natures more attractive to the managers of the region's export factories.

Shenzhen Rishen Cashmere Textile, the factory where they work, is part of the Ningxia St. Edenweiss International Enterprise Group, a Shenzhen Stock Exchange–listed company whose business lines also include building materials and real estate development. Ningxia St. Edenweiss has operations in Shenzhen, Shanghai, coal town Taiyuan and the western city of Xi'an. The group's cashmere products are sold in China, America, Japan and Europe.

Shenzhen Rishen sits in a nondescript industrial building on a leafy street in the city's Futian business district. Circa early 2005, the block also included a few cheap restaurants, a grocery store and some dirty, tiled dormitories.

Room 817 is located in a U-shaped, gray apartment block in a business park near the factory named Tianan Cyber Park, an optimistic name for a plot of land containing rows of tall, grimy industrial buildings and cheap dormitory blocks.

Luyuan stood in the courtyard and looked up at the facade of her building, which was dotted with laundry, wrinkled white T-shirts and blue factory jackets hung out to dry. To get to room 817, the girls entered through a doorway in the back of the building, a rectangle of dark dampness. The stairs were unlit, the landings on one side of the building open to the elements. The view from the landings expanded to a vista of opportunity: bright factory windows and glittering office towers, a members-only club housed in a glass dome, and a golf course.

Their room, like countless others in the same building and around southern China, was long and narrow. The floor was cold, gray tile, the light two strips of glaring fluorescent. As the girls entered the room, a tiny, dark closet with a porcelain-lined hole in the floor lay to their right. This was the toilet. To the left sat another closet-room with a shower nozzle, where the girls bathed. The room expanded slightly to accommodate six metal bunkbeds, three on each side. The bunks were so close together that when the girls placed a stool between the two rows of beds to make a table for a snack of lychees, the round pungently sweet fruit native to the region, they could almost reach the stool from beds on both sides of the room.

Many of the bed frames were hung with printed sheets, giving each girl a semblance of privacy. On the wall behind each bed, the girls had hung posters of Cantonese pop stars, lush landscapes, kittens in baskets. The mattresses were an inch think, the blankets piled at the end of the bed. In the winter, when temperatures would fall to 40 degrees, the girls would sleep two to a bed for warmth. Their modest wardrobes took up only half a foot at the end of each bed—shirts and jeans hung from every frame. Their shoes and worldly possessions fit under their beds.

At the far end of the room was a cement balcony fenced in by metal bars, where the girls put their laundry out to dry. There was a rusty industrial sink in one corner of the balcony. On the ledge above the sink, toothbrushes stuffed into plastic mugs jostled for space.

There was no kitchen in room 817, no air conditioner or heater, no dressers. Just a rusty fan and a cracked, green vinyl chair next to a broken mirror in the corner of the room, a phone balanced on top. The phone rang constantly at night when the girls were home, sending one of the girls flying toward it. These calls were their link to the world beyond the factory, to family and friends from home. The girls who could afford them had cell phones.

Every roommate had a story. Chen Qianyan—quiet, with a heart-shaped face—was married when she arrived in Guangdong. Her husband worked at a nearby clothing factory, but because his dorm was across town, the couple only saw each other once a week.

They had a little boy. He lived with Qianyan's parents in Guizhou, a poor, rural province in southwestern China. For most of her son's life, Qianyan had only seen him once a year.

One night in May 2005, Qianyan dug a photo out from under her bed. It was a picture of her son, six months old, lying on a red blanket at the local photography studio. Many of the girls have pictures like these, their relatives frozen unsmiling in front of a cheap wall hanging. The picture brought back memories. "When I called him last year, he wouldn't even come to the phone. I don't know why he wouldn't come," she said. "Whenever I go home, he stays away from me for the first few days and he won't show any affection for me and my husband. It takes several days for him to get over it."

Qianyan's four years in the Pearl River Delta had worn her down, physically and emotionally. Her weight had dropped from 128 pounds to 105 pounds, and she was more subdued, less prone to the exuberance of her younger roommates. She promised herself that when her son started elementary school, she would return home.

Jie Yuying was the only girl in the room from Guangdong. One of six children, Yuying had an easy sense of humor and a taste for the finer things: a string of fake pearls, new clothing. When she first arrived in the factories, she spoke only her native Cantonese, not the Mandarin, China's national language, that factory managers used with their employees. Her incomprehension made the managers' barked commands all the more terrifying. She remembers getting fined almost every day for violating rules when she started at a video disc factory. The food at the factories and the fast-food stalls in the industrial areas made her sick.

Zhang Juan, a Sichuan native, followed her older sister into the Pearl River Delta in her teens. Though a friend helped her find work quickly at a sawmill in Guangzhou, she lasted only three months there, smoothing out rough patches on wood with her hands on the night shift. The factory gave her cotton gloves, but her hands bled through them. Juan came to Shenzhen on her sister's advice. "When I was a little girl, I imagined Shenzhen was a prosperous city," she said. "When I got here, I realized I liked it better than anywhere else."

Meng was the newcomer, soft-featured and maternal, a talented cook. Meng grew up in a rural area outside the southwestern city of Chongqing without paved roads. Her house was a half hour's walk from the nearest bus stop and 50 minutes away from the market. School was an hour and a half away if she walked, 50 minutes if she ran. When the trek and the tuition became too onerous, Meng stopped attending school. She had made it through one semester of junior high.

Meng arrived in Guangdong in 2002. She found work at an office supply factory, then an artificial Christmas tree plant, and finally Shenzhen Rishen. She epitomized the second-generation migrant worker: Meng's parents lived in Guangzhou, where they worked in construction. Her younger sister, who was seven, attended school there at great expense because she lacked a local *hukou* or household registration. Their home outside Chongqing had been empty for years.

Luyuan was the smallest girl in the room, but her personality was the largest: She was the comic, the big mouth. Petite and bird-boned, she had a wide, jack-o'-lantern smile of crooked teeth and a physical sense of humor. When she was excited, as she often was, Luyuan liked to dart around the room, arms flapping, mouth running. Luyuan came from a large family of rice and watermelon farmers in the eastern province of Jiangxi.

Her mother's third child, Luyuan was born after China's family planning policy was introduced in 1978. Because her parents couldn't afford the fines they would have had to pay local authorities for violating the one-child rule, when Luyuan was three months old she was sent to live with her grandparents in a village a day's bus journey away from her hometown. Her grandparents sent her back to her parents when she turned seven so she could attend school. Luyuan returned to a crowded house without running water or a phone, where there was little to eat and no money for clothes.

Luyuan attended school until junior high, when she dropped out because her family couldn't afford the tuition. Luyuan didn't mind: She had never enjoyed school. When she was 15, her parents sent her away again. This time, she joined her older brother earning money for the family as a migrant worker in the factories of the Pearl River Delta. She was so short and baby-faced that no factory would hire her. "They'd ask me, how old are you, ten?" she remembered. She spoke with a thick Jiangxi twang.

When she returned the following year, Luyuan found work at the DVD component factory. A picture taken by a manager there shows a line of girls in matching white blouses sitting in blue plastic chairs at a table on the assembly line. Another picture shows Luyuan and other girls from the factory at Chinese New Year, when migrant workers who can afford the higher ticket prices return home for what is often their only vacation of the year. Luyuan and the other girls who couldn't afford the trip smile as they tuck into a meal of corn, red and green peppers and cabbage.

Other photographs show the girls from the DVD parts factory gathered around a cake piled with candles for someone's twentieth birthday. Huddled at the beach making the victory sign. And Luyuan, in a green swimsuit at the beach, raising her arms and cracking a wide grin as the surf rolls in around her. Before Luyuan moved next door to Shenzhen Rishen, she and her friends from the DVD parts factory exchanged phone numbers and promised to call each other in 2008 so they could watch the Beijing Olympics together.

The girls say that Shenzhen Rishen employed them all but two days a month, 11 or more hours a day during peak season. They say many had no insurance. All were paid by the piece, 17 cents a piece if they reached a monthly production quota, 16 cents if they didn't. When there were plenty of orders, the fastest among them earned almost $240 a month; the slower girls took home closer to $90 or $100.

During peak season in the second half of the year, the girls say they took their places at Shenzhen Rishen no later than 7:45 A.M. and didn't return home until midnight or later. While the managers there yelled less frequently than at those other factories where they'd worked, the girls say the managers still charged them 13 cents for every minute they were late and sometimes delayed paying their salaries for as long as a month. And a 14-hour day is a 14-hour day. An executive at Shenzhen Rishen reached by phone was unable to verify the working hours and salaries of the factory's employees.

Even wages inflated by overtime didn't go very far in the shiny new shopping malls sprouting on every corner in Shenzhen. Instead, the girls shopped at street markets, bargaining to buy stonewashed jeans, Hello Kitty slippers and flannel pajamas at discount. Their work made them experts in how to recognize a well-made sweater. Their wages made them ruthless bargainers.

Luyuan was a frugal shopper. Every few months, she sent about $120 home to her family, which they used to buy seeds for crops and pay for everyday expenses. When she could afford it, she would get her hair cut by different barbers for $1.25. "I always change hairdressers because I want to be more beautiful," she laughed.

In the off-season and on their rare days off, the girls sought out places that didn't cost money: parks and beaches. Or they just crowded onto one bed and watched the television they had saved to buy for $18. They liked soap operas the best, kung fu action movies almost as much. They may have lacked many things, but laughter was not one of them.

Their laughter was so loud that it riled their downstairs neighbors, also factory workers, who complained bitterly and glared at them when they passed in the street. Their laughter, boisterous and infectious, made up for the families, the houses, the lives they had left behind. It was their link to a more ordinary, less arduous adolescence.

Every girl nursed a private dream of a life outside the factories, of the civilized ease of office work or the independence of running a store. Almost all were certain their dreams were unattainable, given their junior-high-school educations. In a country where competition was so intense that even college graduates couldn't find work, who would hire girls who had stopped studying at 15?

Luyuan had been attending computer classes at the workers' center run by Liu Kaiming, the labor advocate who ran a research group called the Institute of Contemporary Observation. The classes lit a spark of ambition. Luyuan began to believe she was capable of more than just factory work. The year before she found herself on the roof of Shenzhen Rishen, Luyuan fantasized about opening a fast-food restaurant. Nothing fancy. Just a place where no one would boss her around.

AS THE GIRLS DREAMED of climbing out of labor-intensive manufacturing, so do government officials in Shenzhen and cities of the Pearl River Delta. They are trying to refashion these factory towns into high-tech, low-pollution, value-added modern metropolises.

In 1980, Shenzhen was still a fishing village with a population of 321,000, an inconsequential stop along the way to the Canton Fair in Guangzhou. Its designation as the country's first special economic zone that year transformed the city into a manufacturing center over the next two decades. First, it was a major production hub for toys and simple consumer goods. Later, the city began to attract more electronics manufacturing.

Today, Shenzhen is home to the world's fourth-largest port, China's second-largest stock exchange, the country's largest Internet company by market capitalization and its two largest telecommunications equipment makers, Huawei and ZTE. In 2006, it exported $136 billion worth of goods, a 34 percent increase from the year before. Shenzhen exports more than any other Chinese city.

Between 1990 and 2000, Shenzhen's population grew almost 15 percent every year, faster than any other city in China.[1] Shenzhen's official population is now about 12.4 million.

Liu Kaiming, executive director of the Institute for Contemporary Observation, a nongovernmental migrant workers' research and training center, estimates the population is closer to 18 million, because of the massive influx of undocumented migrants. Only a small minority of the population was born in the city, making Shenzhen China's greatest melting pot. Shenzhen's lingua franca is Mandarin, not the Cantonese native to Guangdong province.

These outsiders have generated enormous wealth: Since 1994, Shenzhen residents have sent remittances of $21 billion through the postal service.[2] Shenzhen's economy has grown faster than any other in China, expanding 28 percent on average every year since 1980.[3]

The growth is so fast that it has exceeded the city's ability to provide for its citizens. Public buses are overloaded during rush hour. The subway system covers only a portion of the wealthy residential and business districts and none of the needier industrial suburbs. The center of the city, where the girls of room 817 live, is evolving. Factories remain, but they are rapidly being replaced by or converted into office buildings.

From the air, Shenzhen erupts like a carnival of capitalism next to Hong Kong. Shun Hing Square, a 69-story office and apartment building, towers over the city's skyline. Residential tower blocks built by the city's hometown developer, Vanke, line the marshy border with the former British colony. Vanke's founder, Wang Shi, is China's Richard Branson, an intrepid businessman-adventurer whose expeditions include Everest and Antarctica.

The city's transformation can be seen most clearly in Shekou, one of the areas first developed for industry in the 1980s. Today it is one of the city's toniest residential districts. Its streets are lined with guarded gated communities, filled with modern villas and metal-and-glass high-rises with sleek stone balconies. Cranes hover over giant new luxury housing developments with names like The Hillside, New Era Apartment and Garden City. The only obvious reminders of the area's past are a few husks of aging factories and a handful of street names: Industrial Road Number One, Industrial Road Number Two.

As high-rise luxury has overtaken former industrial districts, factories have spilled out to suburbs like Bao'an, Longgang, Long-hua and Buji, taking their crowds of migrant workers with them. A few old factories in Shenzhen's city center have been turned into contemporary art galleries. A tiny handful, including Luyuan's, still remain in the city center.

Somehow, Shenzhen has managed to make this transition with a minimum of struggle. Like other Chinese cities, there are protests outside government offices, and occasionally someone will pop his head above the parapet to complain about the soaring property prices that are making housing unaffordable for ordinary people, or the government's development strategy. But most people come to Shenzhen to earn money. As a billboard in a wealthy district reads: EMPTY TALK ENDANGERS THE NATION, PRACTICAL WORK BRINGS PROSPERITY.

At night, Shenzhen's wide, palm-lined avenues light up like a birthday cake. Skyscrapers twinkle with neon and cast thin green laser beams out of their spires. Sons and daughters of senior Communist Party officials, known as "princelings," cruise the city in Mercedes sedans. Huawei's male employees tool around town in Buicks and Volvos. Their generous technology industry paychecks make them some of Shenzhen's most desirable bachelors.

When the sun sets, Shenzhen's legendary nightclubs fill with Hong Kong party kids who slip across the border to tap into the city's easy supply of drugs. The Luohu crossing at the Hong Kong–Shenzhen border is the world's busiest, with some 252,000 trips every day.[4] Aspiring Chinese entrepreneurs call for their bottles of Chivas Regal from behind the bar. Prostitutes from China, the Philippines and Russia ply their trade to customers from everywhere from Texas to Australia.

Life moves quickly in Shenzhen: Buildings shimmy up in months, assembled by an army of migrant men who live in their unfinished basements and watch communal televisions at local newspaper kiosks in the evening. It is said that in Shenzhen, buildings go up at the pace of one story every three days. In China, this pace is admiringly called "Shenzhen speed."

THE YEAR IN Shenzhen factories doesn't always start in January, or even necessarily after the Chinese New Year. It starts when the orders come in. Because sales in so many consumer industries—toys, clothing, electronics, even power tools—are tied to the Christmas shopping season, many factories close for the Chinese New Year, in January or February, and don't reopen until they have the orders to justify it. For some factories, the break lasts only a few days. For others, it lasts a month or more. Those can be difficult weeks and months for migrant workers, who return to the cities after the holiday well fed but cash poor. As American consumers check their bank account balances nervously after the holiday season, so do Chinese migrant workers, but for a different reason. Closed factories don't pay wages.

In early March, Shenzhen Rishen was still closed. Luyuan had returned the week before from Jiangxi, where she had spent the holiday watching television, hiking, setting off fireworks and praying at a local mountaintop temple. Her prayers were specific: She asked for more money.

One overcast morning, she rose early, pulled on jeans, a red shirt and hiking shoes and headed downstairs to buy vegetables for breakfast. Vegetables were getting more expensive, another sign of Shenzhen speed. When she returned to room 817, the lights were still off, and the few girls who were already back from the Chinese New Year holiday were sitting quietly on their beds, watching television. On the screen, a group of women in identical blue and white outfits was doing yoga. Many of the beds were still empty, stacked with suitcases, their inhabitants still thousands of miles away at home.

Luyuan and Meng set about preparing breakfast with the efficiency of professional chefs. Breakfast was more elaborate than usual, they explained, as they covered the bathroom sink with a board and placed an electric rice cooker on top, pouring oil inside. As she watched the oil warm, Meng explained that she had come to Shenzhen Rishen in June last year after working in the suburb of Longhua. The factories there weren't as nice as those in the center of the city where they work now, she said, not as clean.

Fang, Luyuan's cousin, carried some chopped mushrooms flecked with green leaves to the girls at the sink. A 17-year-old vocational school graduate, Fang had just arrived with Luyuan from Jiangxi to find a job in the city. Her degree made her a good prospect for factory work. Fang had been sharing a bed with Luyuan in room 817 since their arrival.

Luyuan stirred the mushrooms and leaves into the pot, added salt, tasted a mushroom. With the door to the room open, she could see the golf course spreading into the distance, the carpet of a wealthier person's life. A round of golf at the Shenzhen Golf Club cost $130 on a weekday, more than the girls' monthly salaries in the low season.

When the factory was open, the girls made only a simple rice porridge for breakfast. Today, they had time to prepare something more elaborate. The pair of chefs added a liberal amount of red pepper. Spicy food is a way of life in Chongqing and Jiangxi and a staple of the diet of room 817.

Food is central to Chinese culture—eaten out of shared dishes, it is both physical and emotional nourishment. China's size and geographical diversity have allowed distinct regional cuisines: Cantonese food is mild and rich in seafood, Sichuanese and Hunanese hot and spicy. Food has special meaning to migrant workers, who do little but work, sleep and eat, far from the flavors they grew up with. Fast-food stalls on the street, where workers queue to eat, are often dirty. The girls learn to eat fast and not dwell on how things taste.

When the dish was done, Luyuan unplugged the cooker and moved the board from over the sink to the center of the room, where she placed it on top of a red, upturned bucket. The girls huddled around the makeshift table for breakfast. Luyuan broached a familiar topic. Back home over the holidays, her family had introduced her to a man. He worked with his hands decorating houses. Like her roommates, she had classmates who stayed home, never leaving to become migrant workers, who were already married with children. Their lives revolved around housework and child care. If they didn't already have children, their mothers- and fathers-in-law were badgering them to have them. When the girls of room 817 returned home for the holidays, their families arranged meetings with prospective mates in the village. Choose one, they were told.

At 20, Luyuan was getting old to still be single in the countryside. In Shenzhen, she was considered too young for marriage. But Luyuan and Meng, who was 21, feared the responsibilities a husband would entail. They had enough responsibilities as it was at the factory. Even boyfriends were a burden. Give us a few years, they told their parents.

Not that they lacked for male attention. Luyuan was frequently

swatting away colleagues and friends who brought her gifts or declared their affections. She was happy to be friends, she told them
firmly, but she didn't need someone tying her down. Her family
lived by different rules. A girl her age should be thinking about settling down, they said. And so she learned to live with the tug of her
two lives—city and country, modern and traditional. New China
and old.

LATER THAT MORNING, the girls headed out to look at a bulletin
board spackled with ads for job openings. Like many of their colleagues, they were spending the remainder of the holiday looking
for better jobs. There were rumors that Shenzhen Rishen had lost
money the year before and might be laying off staff or moving out
of the city center to cut costs.

To reach the bulletin board, they picked their way past a line of
people distributing pink business cards. The cards carried telephone
numbers for companies that sold fake identity cards to migrant
workers who lacked the documents factories required, reminders of
the institutionalized discrimination of the *hukou* system. The girls,
who had enough documentation to get a low-level job, ignored
the cards.

Luyuan and Meng joined a crowd at the board. It was plastered
with help-wanted ads: ironing, quality control, cashier. Luyuan
pulled out a notebook and disappeared into the crowd to get a better look. She wrote down the details of jobs at four companies.
Luyuan had spent every day since she returned from Jiangxi looking for a new job. She made the rounds of factories that were hiring.
One made her take a math test. She failed. Another factory quizzed
her in English: "How old are you?" they asked. "What's your name?"
Luyuan failed that one, too.

Shenzhen speed was challenging one of the pillars of the China price by driving many of the labor-intensive jobs Luyuan and her roommates were qualified for out of the city. In place of those jobs, there were now positions at electronics factories, which usually required a high school degree.

The kind of factory work that had brought Luyuan to Shenzhen two years earlier was now disappearing before her eyes. Suddenly, it seemed, the economy was moving on without her, and retraining was financially beyond her reach. "Often, we don't meet the requirements. If we wanted to study design, we would need money for tuition," Meng said. "We need money to eat and live."

Between factory interviews over the last several days, Luyuan had also looked for vacancies in retail. Surprisingly, given the speed at which Shenzhen was growing, sales jobs she had seen advertised required a university degree and a Shenzhen *hukou*; Luyuan had a junior high school education and a Jiangxi *hukou*. Toy and clothing stores had turned her down on the spot because of her lack of experience. As Meng explained: "The places that have good working conditions have pretty tough requirements."

It wasn't just market forces—higher prices for labor, electricity and land—that were forcing low-end jobs out of the city. The government was doing its part to make sure they left. Despite their clear contribution to the city's celebrated growth rates, unskilled workers like Meng and Luyuan were not part of Shenzhen officials' vision of the city's future.

Academics at state-funded institutions were urging that certain people be excluded from the city. "This way," one told the *China Daily*, the Communist Party's mouthpiece, "the city's population growth will be better controlled and the overall quality of its residents improved." Another Chinese scholar urged the government to raise rent, food, transportation and utilities charges to get rid of the city's poor.[5]

Caught in the middle of these policies were people like Luyuan and Meng. Luyuan, like Shenzhen officials, wanted a life outside the factories, with their exhausting hours and monotonous work. "I really want to be a salesperson," she moaned.

Back at the dormitory later that morning, Luyuan spun a hula hoop around her waist. She read out a few of the jobs she had jotted down from the bulletin board: cashier, worker at an electronics factory, clerk at an electronics factory. The cashier position looked like her best shot. All they needed was someone with a junior high school education, a good temper and an outgoing personality.

Luyuan felt she had more to offer. She had, somewhere, acquired some knowledge of sales techniques. "To become a salesperson," she announced, "you've got to learn the psychology of the customer." Good salespeople, she said, are eloquent and crafty. They know just what to say to persuade people to buy things.

For once, Luyuan, the class clown, wasn't smiling. She was despondent. She worried that her failure to finish junior high school and continue on to high school had doomed her to a life of exhausting, underpaid factory work. She felt she was being discriminated against for her lack of a degree. "It's so unfair!" she wailed. "Nobody will give me the chance to sell tiny things, let alone cars or real estate." Her roommates sat and listened. Their ambitions were more modest. Meng, for one, just wanted a higher salary.

Luyuan said she had read in a newspaper article that some university graduates don't make good salespeople. "I don't have a good education, but it doesn't mean I can't do the job," she said. To prove it, she mimicked the tone of a saccharine saleslady. "Miss, what color are you looking for?" she asked an imaginary shopper.

"What color do you like?"

"If you like it, I'll sell it to you."

"You look good in that shirt."

"Why don't you take it?"

"How much is it? It's seventy renminbi," or about $9.20, she said.

THAT AFTERNOON, the girls set out from the dorm toward the restaurants and small businesses and their factory. Their neighborhood was changing at Shenzhen speed. They passed a basketball court that had recently opened. At night, healthy, muscular men—nothing like the reedy, pale-faced boys who worked in the factories—played aggressive games under bright stadium lights. A newly installed Papa John's pizzeria ("Better Ingredients. Better Pizza.") stood out from its industrial surroundings like a Michelin-starred restaurant.

Luyuan, in a dark mood, ducked into a bookshop with a help-wanted sign out front. They needed someone with a high school education. The girls continued to another new arrival in the area, a glass-fronted Hunanese restaurant with a row of palm trees planted outside. The restaurant was in the final stages of preparation before opening. The sign hanging out front, URGENTLY SEEKING EMPLOYEES, looked promising. Women with a junior high school education, 18 years or older, interested in the restaurant business, experienced staff preferred, it read. Food and accommodation provided. Salary to be discussed in person.

There is such a large gap between the wages of Shenzhen migrant workers and the cost of living that many low-end jobs, in manufacturing as well as services, provide housing. It is not uncommon for a hair salon, for example, to rent a room for its employees to share.

Inside the restaurant, a woman asked the girls if they had waitressing experience. They said they worked in a factory. Working here is harder than in a factory, the woman snapped. The girls kept their mouths shut. Another manager laid down the terms of employment: The regular working day was nine hours, with overtime every day. The monthly wage was $66. All employees were required to make a $26 deposit for the uniform.

Leaving the restaurant, the girls were unimpressed. It wasn't clear how many days off they would get every month. And nobody would tell them how many hours of overtime they would be working or whether they would get the $26 deposit for the uniform back. At least in the factory, they knew what to expect.

Down the road was a real estate agency, a glass-fronted cubbyhole dominated by a row of computer terminals. A help-wanted sign hung out front. Luyuan marched in, leaving her friends on the sidewalk. She was on a mission today. Luyuan sat down across from a manager at a table beside the row of computers. They spoke in hushed tones. A few minutes later, she was back on the sidewalk.

Only this time, Luyuan was smiling.

The real estate agency had made her an offer.

Luyuan repeated what the manager had told her. For the first month, she would work on probation: The agency would pay her the paltry wage of $39, not including food or accommodation. The next month, if she rented or sold $395 worth of real estate, her wage would rise to $79. Shift properties worth $1,316 and she could take home $132. Sell nothing for a month and she would be fired.

Even if she moved into the cheapest, dirtiest room in the redlight district across the highway, Luyuan would spend all of her first month's salary as a real estate agent on rent. And that was before she spent her first yuan on food.

But to a girl desperate for freedom, hunger was better than another year in a factory.

"I'm really happy," Luyuan said. "I've got my confidence back."

Later that day, Luyuan and the girls headed to Xiasha Park, a public park across the highway. Ringed by office and apartment buildings, the park contained a wide stretch of blacktop, a small running track, a public pool and a small gray brick Buddhist temple with a traditional Chinese tile roof. The girls wandered into the temple.

Inside, it was dark and smoky and cool. There were coils of incense and piles of apples. Pink lights glowed through the haze. Luyuan and Meng knelt down at tiny altars and prayed. Luyuan prayed for good health for her family. And she prayed that she had finally found a job she liked.

SELLING REAL ESTATE turned out to be a lot harder than sewing sweaters. As Shenzhen property prices rose rapidly—30 percent in 2006 alone[6]—real estate agencies opened thousands of branches around the city.

In every district in Shenzhen, agents stood on corners in matching black or navy suits and white shirts, squinting in the South China sun, distributing flyers of available properties. They sat hunched behind their miniature terminals, waiting for the phone to ring. On Luyuan's block alone sat three agencies, each with its own army of commissioned youth.

The explosion in the real estate business in Shenzhen and other large Chinese cities was so rapid that the central government, worried about a bubble, was trying to calm investment in the sector. It rolled out a new property sales tax and urged tighter enforcement of an existing capital gains tax on secondary property sales. Beijing urged banks to limit loans to the industry, issued rules to limit foreign investment in property and ordered local governments to encourage construction of affordable housing.

At the same time, Shenzhen was trying to manage its economic expansion more intelligently. In line with Beijing's directives on "Green GDP," the Shenzhen government was trying to improve the environment by discouraging investment by polluting factories and luring more energy-efficient, innovative, technology-dependent companies. The city was also trying to dispel its image as a thriving hub for intellectual property piracy.

Shenzhen officials were taking innovation so seriously they decided to make it the law. In March 2006, the government passed legislation requiring the government and private sector "to promote reform and innovation."[7]

In her first days on the job in March 2006, Luyuan wasn't allowed to do much of anything. Her boss discouraged her from doing any property deals until she learned more about the business, and that was fine with Luyuan. Confident as she was in her abilities as a saleswoman, she knew nothing about real estate.

Watching her colleagues, she learned she wasn't supposed to tell prospective clients in which building an apartment or office was located. She also had to tell clients the price was slightly higher than it actually was. Still, with so many real estate agencies in one city, there wasn't that much work to go around. One night not long after she started her new job, Luyuan confessed that the agency had had only three customers all day.

She was sitting on a miniature plastic stool in room 817, one leg folded over the other, hands in her lap, her head leaning against a bedpost. Luyuan was still living in the dorm because the factory remained closed, and she couldn't resign until it reopened. The television was tuned to a show of men singing. Yuying distributed oranges she had brought from home.

The other girls were getting ready for bed. Meng, just out of the shower and patting her cheeks dry, had changed into orange fleece pajamas for the night. Fang wore patched pajamas. Only Luyuan still wore her work clothes: light blue jeans, a gray shirt with gray and white striped sleeves and a white stand-up collar, white socks tucked into black pointy-toed pumps. The girls discussed the rumor that Shenzhen Rishen was moving away from the city center. Meng was thinking of quitting.

As she spoke, Luyuan's voice was quiet, her personality folded in onto itself. She was pensive, hardly recognizable as the boisterous girl from the sweater factory. A few days off the assembly line had made a deep impression. Luyuan had already resolved not to go back to the factory, whatever the consequences.

At the real estate agency, Luyuan made use of her fallow time to observe her new environment. The other agents were older than her colleagues at the factory, in their mid-twenties and almost exclusively male. In real estate, unlike the factories, companies preferred older agents because they had better social skills and gave the impression of competence. Years earlier, when she had first applied for factory work, Luyuan's youthful looks had disqualified her. Now, as she tried to propel herself into the service sector, Luyuan was once again the baby. She worried clients wouldn't trust her.

Luyuan's new colleagues didn't talk much, but she felt sure they would all become good friends. Most of the day, she and her colleagues sat in the agency's tiny office reading the newspaper, waiting for customers and wishing the phone would ring. When it did, the first person to pick it up got the business.

Alternately brutally competitive and boring, the job nonetheless thrilled Luyuan. Work that allowed you to sit down and read the paper hardly seemed like work at all. She marveled at how quickly her life had changed.

"At the factory, our social circle is limited and we don't communicate with anyone other than the people we live with," she said. Life was confined to the narrow, colorless strip between factory and dormitory. Now, her customers came from a mixture of backgrounds and income levels. And her days were no longer measured by the number of sweaters she sewed. "I like the freedom and the lack of restrictions," she said.

Luyuan's parents back home in Jiangxi and her older brother

Jialiang, who still lived in Shenzhen, were concerned about her decision to quit her steady job to sell real estate. "They told me to think hard about it," she said. Jialiang worried Luyuan wouldn't earn enough to support herself.

Married and in his thirties, Jialiang understood the differences between his little sister's and his parents' generations. Young Chinese moved on to something new if they didn't like their work; because that wasn't possible in his parents' generation, the concept was alien to them. But Jialiang, despite his doubts, stood by his sister's gamble. "She should do what she wants," he said.

THE REALITY OF LIFE outside the relative security of the factories sank in over the months that followed. In April, Luyuan resigned and moved out of the dorm and in with her cousin, Fang, who had found a job at an electronics factory nearby that provided her a bed in a dorm room. Eventually, Luyuan had to find her own place.

Luyuan's new apartment building was located across the highway from room 817, down a dark, pungent alley in the red-light district popular with mistresses of Hong Kong men. Working girls in her neighborhood charged $2.63 an hour, twice the price of a shampoo and shoulder massage.

Luyuan chose to live on a high floor because she believed the air was better there. She shared a dirty common area with the residents of six other rooms, their doors shut anonymously in a line. The grease-stained communal kitchen and bathroom with metered water taps disgusted her. The cardboard walls were so thin she could hear everything her neighbors said, every TV program they watched.

The girl who had always lived with others now lived alone in a room dominated by a rickety bunk bed. The brown door was falling off its hinges. Over the window, her brother had stuck a sign from a local store and hung a blue curtain to block the sun. She had a rice cooker, some eggs and her beloved hot peppers. Red ants had staked out their territory on her sack of uncooked rice. For this, she paid $39 a month, her entire first month's salary.

Luyuan was running on fumes. She had started her new career with her $132 nest egg from working at the factory and the $158 in unpaid wages Shenzhen Rishen paid her after she resigned. In mid-May she wired her parents $66 because they needed the money. She cut her own spending down to a minimum. Luyuan now spent 79 cents a day on food: 13 cents for a bun for breakfast, 40 cents for lunch and 26 cents for dinner. In a city where a cup of coffee can run to $3.29 and a trip to the grocery store at least as much, this was a financial high-wire act.

Luyuan had $25 to her name. Her remaining coins she stored in a clear plastic bear. Her poverty was painfully visible at work. Her boss had asked her not to dress so casually, to buy a suit like her colleagues or at least a skirt, but she couldn't afford one. The two suits the agency required cost $92.

Sometimes, Luyuan's thoughts wandered back to the factory, where life was less Darwinian. She spent her days walking the streets, looking at properties, familiarizing herself with the area. She snuck meager meals when she had a free moment; there was no more eating at regular times on the factory's schedule. She was losing weight.

But Luyuan felt liberated from the rigid and demanding schedule of industry. She was less tired at the end of the day. Sometimes, she ducked in to read books at the library in Liu Kaiming's workers' center during the day. And for the first time, she had a business card, which she kept perched atop her tiny terminal at the real estate agency.

Little of her old life remained. After Shenzhen Rishen reopened, the factory stayed in the same building in central Shenzhen but moved the girls out of room 817 and into an older dormitory outside Tianan Cyber Park. Their new home was a half hour's walk away from Luyuan's apartment on the other side of the highway, lengthening the distance between Luyuan and her old friends.

She got off work earlier than her former colleagues at the factory did, and it was easier to cross the highway and spend the evening alone in her new neighborhood than wait around for the girls to finish their overtime. She saw them less and less. Meng, her closest friend at Shenzhen Rishen, quit and found work at a factory outside the city center. She rarely came into town.

Luyuan was unaccustomed to having her evenings free and uncertain what to do with them. After work, she made a modest dinner at home and whiled away hours by herself in the book section of a grubby local department store reading books she couldn't afford to buy. She read up on poverty alleviation in rural areas and child psychology.

One sticky night in late May, Luyuan walked to Xiasha Park, where only a couple of months before she had prayed that she had found a job she liked. In the far corner, bright lights illuminated the blacktop where dozens of people danced to pop music that poured out through speakers into the evening air. The group, neighborhood men and women in basketball shorts and matching skirts and tops, moved to an unspoken choreography, flicking their heels, swinging their arms, spinning in unison. A crowd, some in their pajamas, gathered to watch.

Luyuan waded alone into the group of dancers, following their steps first hesitantly and then with more determination. Sweat beaded on her forehead as she lost herself in the music and the crowd, stepping and spinning and clapping in time with the others. For a moment, she looked relieved not to have to be on duty as an adult, to escape the loneliness of trying to make ends meet outside the gates of a Chinese factory.

IN JUNE, a man from one of the real estate agencies across the road called Luyuan on her cell phone. Could she come over and see him? She could. He had seen how she worked with clients and liked the way she closed deals quickly, he said. He offered her a job with a starting salary of $132 a month. Stunned, Luyuan accepted.

Gemdale Corporation, her new employer, was a large, Shenzhen-based real estate developer that also managed and sold properties. Listed on the Shanghai stock exchange, it had subsidiaries around the country. The office where Luyuan worked was slightly larger and staffed by a crew of jovial young men in white dress shirts and dark pants. On the wall, a sign in English next to a picture of I. M. Pei's glass pyramid at the Louvre read, YOUR APPRECIATION IS THE BEST MEDAL. Another, next to a picture of an arch, read, BUILD UP, YOUR OWN BUSINESS.

Two weeks into her new job, Luyuan's boss gave her a swelter-ing Sunday morning off. She called her old factory colleagues to check that they weren't working and set off to their new dormitory. She rarely saw them anymore.

As she walked, Luyuan giddily ticked off the terms of her new job. For every $592 in sales she brought in, she took home $53 in commission. She was earning $132 a month now, but she expected that would rise as high as $236, higher than her $197 peak season wage at the factory. Luyuan was eating more. She had raised her daily food budget to $1.31, half of which went to lunch with her colleagues, whom she adored. She was looking forward to moving into a nicer apartment.

For the remaining girls of room 817, not much had changed. Their new room was located a ten-minute walk from Luyuan's new office, on the fifth floor of a dormitory in a small business park. The hallway on their floor was dark, with water pooling in the corners and trash outside the doors.

The room was larger than room 817, the walls lined with bunk beds, a big fan hanging from the ceiling. There was no toilet or shower; the girls had to share a communal bathroom. Fire preven-tion regulations barred the girls from cooking in the dorm.

Ordering takeout, which the girls sometimes did in their old building, was also prohibited. Visitors had to register at the front gate to the industrial park, and the security guards there sometimes questioned the girls about where they worked. Yuying, the only girl from Guangdong province, missed room 817.

When Luyuan arrived around 11 A.M., the girls were still in their pajamas. Yuying was still lying behind her curtain on an upper bunk. A fan whirred on each girl's bed. Juan sat on her bed, next to her fan, enduring the heat. Luyuan sat down on a miniature plastic chair next to her bed. The gulf between Luyuan and her former colleagues was growing. Juan had gotten married earlier in the year to a truck driver from her hometown.

Luyuan belonged to another world now, a world where people wore suits and sat behind computers and talked about mortgages and speculators. "I think she's the most talented of all of us," Juan said admiringly of Luyuan. "I think she's the smartest."

Juan knew she could never do what Luyuan had done. In the service industry, you had to be nice to people all the time. That didn't sound like any fun at all.

Luyuan crossed the room to a scale next to Yuying's bed and weighed herself. Despite her higher food budget, Luyuan was still losing weight because she was on her feet showing properties all day. The girls argued whether the scale was accurate. She had to weigh more than the scale showed. Luyuan stretched the waistband of her pants like a character in a weight-loss advertisement.

The other girls were in a somber mood. There were hardly any orders at the factory, which meant salaries were low. There would be no party for Yuying's birthday the following week. "I don't have any money for food, much less to celebrate my birthday," she said gloomily, having climbed down drowsily out of bed. Working overtime, within limits, was better than not being paid at all, she said. More of their colleagues at Shenzhen Rishen were quitting. Those who remained were wilting in the heat. They had convinced the managers to keep the air conditioning on every day.

The former roommates, once the loudest girls in their dormitory, had little to say to each other now. Luyuan said her goodbyes and walked over to the noodle shop where she and her colleagues often ate. A month ago, she wouldn't have been able to afford a meal here. Now, she bought two steaming bowls of noodles with mushrooms and lettuce, one for herself, one for a friend.

Luyuan was thinking about buying an apartment in Shenzhen. She looked out the restaurant window at the skyscrapers, pondering the opportunities the city offered. Next to the agency where she used to work, a modern fusion restaurant was under construction. A Ferrari dealership had opened down the road.

Some things hadn't changed. Luyuan continued to resist anything that would tie her down. A colleague from her new company had asked her out on a date, but she told him she wasn't interested. We're so busy at work, she said, and after work, I'm too tired for a boyfriend. Can't we just be friends? Don't make up your mind so quickly, he told her. Take some time to decide. She told him she was already sure. The answer was no.

Back home in Jiangxi, another friend had gotten married and had a child, the latest reminder of the widening gap between her life and the one she would have had if she had never come to Shenzhen to work in the factories. "I can't believe that when I go home, someone is going to be calling me auntie," Luyuan marveled as she finished her noodles. For now, Luyuan had property to sell. She headed back to the office.

Six months later, Luyuan's cell phone rang. She took the call on her shiny black and red NEC phone on the balcony of her new apartment, speaking in the sharper tones of standard Mandarin. Working with customers and colleagues from around the country, Luyuan was losing her Jiangxi accent, shedding another link to her life back in the countryside.

It was a sunny Saturday afternoon, and Luyuan had gone into the office in the morning. She wore a navy blue suit now, with a white shirt, a blue and white tie and brown leather slip-on shoes. Her hair, once the object of barbers' whimsy, now hung stylishly below her shoulders. She had started wearing eye shadow and coloring in her eyebrows with quick, impatient strokes. She carried a yellow imitation Marc Jacobs purse.

In the fall, Luyuan had moved in with her manager and his girlfriend. Together, they shared a two-bedroom apartment above a hair salon not far from Xiasha Park. The apartment, which was larger than room 817, was sparsely furnished but immaculate, with a white tile floor, a forlorn but modern green couch, a glass coffee table and a giant Sanyo television placed on top of an office desk. Next to the couch was an ironing board and a broken fan. Two posters, one of horses running and another of a modern interior, hung on the walls. A balcony draped with drying towels ran the width of the living room.

Luyuan's room was narrow but easily fit a single wooden bed, her first nonbunk bed since she moved to Shenzhen. Her clothes, including a tracksuit, hung along the wall. Luyuan had started jogging after work.

The real estate market remained lively, despite attempts by Beijing to temper its explosive growth. Luyuan's favorite clients were the speculators who would buy a property only to flip it shortly afterward. Her agency made a commission on both transactions.

She enjoyed the competitive nature of Shenzhen real estate. If Luyuan and her colleagues didn't have the property a client was looking for, they would call other agencies, pretending to be buyers to get the telephone number of a property owner. Then they would call the owner directly to arrange the sale to their client.

Tactics like that helped Luyuan earn $790 in December, a wage beyond the imagination of anyone in her family. Most months, however, she earned closer to $263. If she sold nothing, she took home only $184. And it was understood that if her slow patch continued for a couple of months, Gemdale would fire her. Luyuan accepted the pressure as part of the job.

Luyuan was planning to spend some of her earnings on a trip home to see her grandmother over Chinese New Year. She was still thinking about buying her own place. Her roommates already owned one or two other apartments. "But it's a dream!" she said of her own plans, stretching her arms up joyfully over her head. A year ago, finding a job outside the factory had been only a dream.

Luyuan was as warm and talkative as before, but she had acquired more composure over the past half year. She was thinking about changing jobs again. Some former colleagues had set up a company to print business cards, and Luyuan was considering joining them. Business cards were a growth industry as Shenzhen converted itself from factory town to technology and services center.

Luyuan rarely saw her old roommates anymore. Meng was still in a suburb at another factory. Though those who remained at Shenzhen Rishen passed by her office on their way to work, their lives were different now. The girls were planning a reunion for January 1.

Sitting on the couch, Luyuan flipped through her photo album and found a picture of herself from a couple of years earlier. She was leaning on a new white car parked on a street. The photograph captured the kind of urban moment that would have seemed so fresh and exciting to Luyuan when she had first arrived in Shenzhen. Now its ordinariness was a reminder of how far she had come. "I thought I was such a grown-up," she said, pausing to look at the photograph. "I was 18, and I thought I was already all grown up."

Later that afternoon, Luyuan headed out to do some shopping. She was having her colleagues over for dinner that night. Her circle of friends from the real estate agency had introduced her to new habits. Lately, at dinner, she would sometimes have a glass of red wine, a Western indulgence she had picked up from her roommates. "I'll just have a little when I feel like it," she said, as she headed downstairs to the store. "It makes me really sleepy."

ON THE FIRST DAY of the new year, residents of Shenzhen pay homage to the man who made their good fortune possible. They pile into or Lotus Mountain Park, filing up the stairs that wind around the hill in an unbroken, panting stream. At the square at the top of the hill, with the city spreading like a skirt beneath them, they hold the cameras in their cell phones up to the statue of the man who put Shenzhen on the map: former Chinese leader Deng Xiaoping.

Deng set the wheels of Chinese economic reform in motion in 1978. His trip to Guangdong province in 1992, known as the Southern Tour, galvanized Shenzhen's role as China's original experimental city. Deng's picture still graces billboards in the special economic zone. The statue in the park, which depicts him walking, coat flapping out to the side, is a year-round tourist attraction. Rumor has it that local officials, in deference to his importance, refused to allow any of the buildings in the nearby civic center to be taller than the statue of Deng.

On January 1, 2007, most of the girls of room 817 couldn't attend the reunion they had planned. So Luyuan, her little sister Lujin, her suitor Little Zhao and her best friend Meng joined the pilgrimage to the top of Lotus Mountain. The day was bright and unseasonably warm, and the park was teeming with people. Men balanced babies on their shoulders. Children jumped rope. A group of musicians drew an audience.

Meng had three days off from the computer cable factory where she had been working in Longhua, an industrial suburb. Luyuan's 18-year-old sister Lujin, who had high cheekbones and full lips, had the day off from the nearby electronics factory where she had started working the previous year.

Little Zhao was a former colleague of Luyuan's who was starting a business card company. He was shy and soft-spoken, with a pencil-thin mustache, a too-big black suit and pointy black shoes. That morning, he had presented Luyuan with a huge bouquet of roses and other flowers wrapped in pink paper and a giant purple bow. Luyuan was embarrassed by the gift but otherwise unmoved.

At the top of the hill, the group elbowed their way into a spot in front of the statue and posed for pictures. The pictures show Luyuan, flanked by Meng and Little Zhao and Lujin, standing directly below Deng's legs. "China has too many people!" Luyuan exclaimed as she navigated her way away from the square. Crowds covered the hillside. The country should improve its population control policies, announced the illegally born third child of Jiangxi farmers. There were simply too many mouths to feed.

Luyuan was just getting warmed up. China was full of contradictions, she said, starting with the growing gap between rich and poor. The government should change the tax regime so "the rich pay taxes but the poor don't have to." It should educate poor farmers in the countryside on better agricultural techniques, she said.

On her path from factory worker to real estate agent, Luyuan had started spouting common refrains from the state-controlled newspapers. Maybe she had always felt this way, and now that she wasn't stitching sweaters she had more time to read the papers. Maybe her chats with her colleagues had galvanized her thinking. None of her arguments was remotely controversial in China: The insistence on the necessity of population control was a common government refrain, the plight of the rural poor a special focus of Chinese leaders. Luyuan's ideas were squarely in line with government thinking. They were also the intellectual underpinnings of a middle-class Chinese woman in the making.

Meng, too, worried about the income gap. Rich parents can buy their children advantage in China, while the children of poor parents, however intelligent, get left behind, she said as she threaded through the throngs of people on the hill. She passed a young boy in his school uniform, his identity papers laid out before him on the pavement, pleading with passersby for tuition money. Meng sympathized: She counted herself among China's poorest, though her income at the computer cable factory put her well above the most destitute.

Meng's current employer was South Korean and insisted on strict observance of the labor law. She appreciated the extra free time. But she still wasn't satisfied. She wanted to learn new things, not just how to assemble another product. Meng was planning to quit the computer cable factory. Maybe the following year, she would return to Chongqing and study to be a beautician.

She told her little sister to study hard so she could attend university and give herself more options beyond factory work. "I don't want her to have to live this migrant worker's lifestyle."

Chapter 7

ACCOUNTS
AND ACCOUNTABILITY

IN THEIR SPARE TIME, staff at a shoe factory in Zhongshan in Guangdong province, visit the on-site library and borrow Chinese translations of *War and Peace*, *Oprah Winfrey Speaks* and *Confessions of a Venture Capitalist: Inside the High-Stakes World of Start-up Financing.*

They take dance classes under a spinning disco ball and play games of ping-pong at the factory's union office. Female employees who return to work after childbirth take breast-feeding breaks and use an on-site nursery. There is even an annual Christmas party with balloons and pictures of Santa. The factory's 7,000 employees have time for these activities because they work a strict 60-hour, five-and-a-half-day week and earn at least the local minimum wage.

Owned by Taiwanese holding company Pou Chen, the world's largest athletic shoe manufacturer, the factory would seem to offer an unbeatable combination to its customers. It provides competitive prices as a result of its economies of scale and, especially important in an industry historically plagued by bad press, relatively good working conditions.

In response to demands from its customers, Pou Chen, whose shoemaking subsidiary is a Hong Kong–listed company called Yue Yuen Industrial, has evolved to become one of the more socially responsible manufacturers in China. Shoe brands can be fairly comfortable working with the factory's manager, a man named Allen Wu.

The reverse is not always true.

Between 2005 and 2006, the Zhongshan government introduced double-digit increases in the minimum wage, substantially raising Wu's costs. In 2005 alone, authorities pushed through a 28 percent increase to $75 a month. But Timberland's buying department refused to agree to a price hike to reflect his higher costs, Wu says. At the same time, Timberland executives responsible for enforcing the company's labor and environmental standards expected the factory to pay the local minimum wage.

Wu was at his wits' end. Meeting over Sunday golf games and meals out at restaurants to avoid attracting attention, he and the managers of two other major Timberland suppliers agreed on a plan: They would each go to Timberland and ask the brand to raise the prices it was paying for the shoes they were making. They would add that if Timberland refused, they would have to be more selective with the orders they accepted from the company.

It was a brave decision: Brands have the upper hand in relationships with their suppliers, and in the competitive world of athletic shoemaking, this kind of bargaining is rare.

In late 2006, according to Wu, Timberland caved. The New Hampshire brand agreed to split with its suppliers the cost of the increase in the minimum wage, equivalent to about 12 cents to 15 cents more per pair. Timberland confirms that it raised the price it paid Wu's company after its annual supplier conference that year, though it does not say whether the increase was related to the higher minimum wage.

Timberland and Wu were arguing over pennies. But what seems

like small change at the factory becomes dollars by the time it reaches a store shelf. While the ratios vary by shoe and brand, the template is roughly the same. If a manufacturer sells a shoe to a brand for $20, the brand then sells it to a retailer for $50. The retailer then puts the shoe on its shelves with a price tag of $100. Sometimes, the markup is even greater. One successful brand sells shoes for $30 that it buys for $3.

That multiplier effect means that a $1 difference at the factory can translate into a $3 or $4 difference in the retail price. Or, put another way, 20 cents to 30 cents can translate into $1 at retail. That may not seem like a lot, but to a factory, 20 cents per shoe is a big deal.

"Even though they share the costs," Wu told me months later, "it's two years too late." We were sitting in his office on the ground floor of the factory, a local Timberland representative at my side. Unlike other factory managers' offices I had visited in China, which were almost invariably filled with product samples and piles of paper, Wu's was exquisitely neat. There were no teetering stacks of documents, no piles of Skype and Bluetooth headsets. Just a big, orderly desk, a clean expanse of floor and a sofa and chairs arranged around a coffee table.

The decision by global shoe brands to force their suppliers around the world to follow a single set of rules over working conditions dictates how Wu runs his business in ways that don't always make sense to him.

Wu refused an order from Timberland because, in order to ship on time, he would have had to work his employees longer than the 60-hour limit. The brand's social compliance team monitors his working hours, but its buying team makes the decisions about how much to pay for shoes. And the buying team, Wu said, "only look at price."

Wu is essentially the mayor and single employer in a small town: the factory. Like many factories in China, it has all the problems of

a small town—including crime, illness, emotional problems and litter. While workers follow the factory's rules about keeping their
dormitory rooms immaculately neat, they sometimes drop trash on
the factory grounds. Wu has tried various strategies to keep the litter under control, but nothing seems to work. He wanted to impose
fines for littering, but his customers wouldn't allow it. Because
some factory managers impose fines as a way of saving on payroll
costs and keeping workers in line, some Western brands have out-
lawed the use of fines at their suppliers.

Wu understood his customers' desire to protect his employees'
rights. But the brands wanted something for nothing, he said, and
that wasn't fair. "The Americans had about one hundred years" to
reach a level of socioeconomic development where they had the
luxury to protect employee rights, he said. "How can they expect
China to get there within fifteen or twenty years?

"The reason why the shoe industry moved from the UK to the
U.S. to Japan, then Korea, then Taiwan and then to China is because
it was chasing cheap labor," Wu continued. "If you're looking for the
same working environment as developed countries, then you have
to pay for it." In other words, you have to pay more than just the
China price.

THE FRAUGHT RELATIONSHIP between Wu and Timberland, like
that of factory owner Eugene Chan and Wal-Mart in chapter two,
is the product of a malfunctioning auditing system. Without a
doubt, the presence of social compliance inspectors in China since
the 1990s has increased awareness of the perils of using child or
slave labor and of workplace hazards. But the existence of shadow
factories like Chan's and the widespread falsification of records allows sweatshop conditions, including excessive working hours and
illegally low wages, to persist.

Multinationals are learning less about their Chinese suppliers even as they make greater efforts to know more. Through recalls and product-safety scares consumers are already paying the price of this lack of knowledge about what's really going on in Chinese factories. And the framework that many brands and retailers use to safeguard their reputations is not encouraging significant improvement in the conditions for Chinese workers.

The idea that brands and retailers are responsible for the working conditions in their supply chains overseas is less than two decades old. The system of monitoring that has sprung up to support that idea is equally adolescent.

In the early 1990s, NGOs and unions in the United States and Europe began stepping up the pressure on Western multinationals that sourced overseas. Starting with apparel and footwear brands, and using the media to communicate its message, the network of groups that became known as the antisweatshop movement persuaded multinationals that they were responsible for the working conditions in their supply chains abroad.

In 1991, Levi Strauss became the first company in the world to introduce a code of conduct for its suppliers. The jeans brand had a reputation for affiliating with socially progressive causes.

Based in part on International Labor Organization principles, Levi Strauss's code barred suppliers from using child or forced labor. It also prevented discrimination against employees on the basis of gender, race or ethnicity. And it encouraged freedom of association and collective bargaining, among other requirements, including ones detailing acceptable working hours, wages and benefits, health and safety and the environment. While it matched Levi's socially aware corporate ethos, the code arguably also served to protect the company's reputation from association with sweatshops.[1] Levi's denies this. The code, the company said, "was conceived and implemented to ensure the people making our products in contract factories were being treated with dignity and respect, and working under safe and healthy working conditions. The concern was originally raised by employees who questioned whether workers in contract factories enjoyed the same or similar working conditions as workers in our owned-and-operated facilities."[2]

Regardless of its motivation, the move marked a turning point in the relationship between companies that source goods overseas and their customers. While there were strong traditions of consumer and labor rights activism in America, consumers either had been unaware of abuses in foreign factories or had been willing to tolerate the occasional story that linked Western brands to sweatshops abroad. These stories might not have made customers feel good, but the prevailing sentiment was that those were issues best resolved by the countries where the sweatshops were located.

"The watershed," said Gare Smith, a former Levi's vice president who is now chairman of the corporate social responsibility practice at the law firm Foley Hoag, was "when consumers became unwilling to accept the violation of worker rights in other countries. There are certain inalienable rights that consumers and shareholders want to ensure the brands they associate with are respecting."[3]

In 1992, Nike came under pressure in what would become one of the antisweatshop movement's most publicized cases. Reports in various newspapers and magazines began to appear about the working conditions at its suppliers. *Harper's* magazine published an article documenting labor abuses by Nike contractors in Indonesia, including the memorable fact that the local labor costs for a Nike shoe that retailed for $80 were only 12 cents. The *Oregonian*, Portland's leading daily, published a damning three-part series on Nike's labor abuses in Indonesia.

Nike initially rejected the allegations, arguing that because it didn't own the factories that were making its shoes, it could hardly control their working conditions.[4] "Exploitation? I don't think so," John Woodman, Nike's general manager in Indonesia, was quoted as saying in February that year. "Yes, they are low wages. But we've come in here and given jobs to thousands of people who wouldn't be working otherwise."[5]

"People argued that we were taking advantage of the poor Japanese workers 20 years ago," Phil Knight, Nike's founder, told another reporter. "Now Japan makes no Nikes and imports $100 million of them."[6]

Not long after Levi's introduced its code, Sears, Roebuck and Co., under pressure from the Amalgamated Clothing and Textile Workers Union, announced that it would not import products made by Chinese prisoners. Suppliers would need to agree in writing not to have goods made in prison. The retailer said it would get lists of prison labor sites and of its suppliers in China and would start unannounced inspections of its Chinese suppliers.[7]

Then, in late 1992, a *Dateline NBC* segment alleged that Wal-Mart was using child labor in Bangladesh and that it was misleading customers about where its products were made by selling goods labeled as having been made in China, Korea and Bangladesh under banners hanging from the ceiling reading MADE IN THE USA.[8] In the same program, the NBC correspondent showed David Glass, then Wal-Mart's chief executive, pictures of children who had died in a fire at a factory in Bangladesh less than a year before Wal-Mart shifted some orders there. "Yeah," Glass responded, "there are tragic things that happen all over the world."[9]

Wal-Mart, which today claims it was unfair for NBC to have even raised the issue, investigated the factory in Bangladesh. Before the program aired, Wal-Mart also published a press release. In it, the retailer apologized for the MADE IN THE USA banners but denied the other accusations.[10]

After the broadcast, Franklin Research & Development, a socially responsible investment firm that owned shares in Wal-Mart and is now known as Trillium Asset Management, suggested that Wal-Mart introduce a code of conduct barring the use of prison or child labor.[11] Franklin helped the company draw up a code of conduct that required vendors to follow local laws and pay their employees "wages and benefits . . . consistent with prevailing local standards."[12]

The code, announced at the bottom of a press release about charity fundraising in 1993, was loosely worded and limited in scope. Wal-Mart, it said, would "favor" vendors whose employees worked less than 60 hours a week. Workers "should" get at least a day off every week.[13] The code initially applied only to vendors in China and Bangladesh, according to Wal-Mart executives.

In the wake of Wal-Mart's code, others followed. Nike drafted a code of conduct for suppliers. So did Reebok, Gap, Liz Claiborne, Disney and clothing brand VF. The codes barred the use of child labor, slave labor and discrimination in the workplace. They set standards for wages and other working conditions. Some, but not all, encouraged freedom of association and collective bargaining.

These codes were primarily intended to protect brands and retailers from reputational damage and to improve their image for potential new hires and customers. "Generally, the motivation behind the codes was legal and reputational risk management," said Gare Smith, the former Levi's executive who is now a lawyer at Foley Hoag. "I'd say about eighty to eighty-five percent of the time legal and reputational risk management was the motivational driver, and about fifteen to twenty percent of the time brand enhancement was the motivating driver. Of course, some companies, like Levi's, were also driven by a sense of decency, and simply wanted to do the right thing."[14]

In drafting these codes, multinationals essentially created an industry from scratch. There were no protocols, no specialists in code-of-conduct compliance. The companies with new codes employed no one with the training to inspect factories overseas. Under these circumstances, companies took different approaches to enforcing their codes. Some hired staff to monitor factories. Others relied on their contractors to police themselves, sending them questionnaires about compliance. Still others asked their quality-control staff, who were trained to inspect products for defects and to look for underage labor, locked exit doors and other safety hazards.

After Reebok presented its code to overseas suppliers in 1993, the athletic shoe and clothing brand distributed a questionnaire. Doug Cahn, who oversaw one part of the footwear and apparel group's human rights program for 15 years, remembers receiving a call not long afterward from the company's vice president in charge of production based in Hong Kong.

"And he said, 'Doug, we're getting those forms back . . . but I don't have a lot of confidence that the information we're getting is accurate,'" Cahn recalled. Cahn, who had never audited a factory, convinced two colleagues who had experience in footwear factories to join him on a trip around Asia to inspect the factories themselves.

Some companies admitted they were ill equipped to spot code violations. "When you go into a factory, it's very difficult to make a judgement whether someone is twelve or fourteen," Kenneth Russo, then vice president for sourcing at JCPenney, told journalist Bob Ortega in Ortega's book, *In Sam We Trust*, published in 1998. The company's inspectors were trained to do quality assurance, not determine the age or treatment of workers; they "don't ask unless it's a blatant issue."[15]

Russo added that with business in more than 50 countries and thousands of factories, "To be alert and aware of all the issues we're faced with around the world, well, it's just very difficult."[16] An executive from Wal-Mart also told Ortega that while the company had inspectors visiting factories, it also depended on its vendors— precisely the companies whose profits depended on making sure these problems never surfaced—to follow the codes and police their own behavior.[17]

As brands began to expand and amend their codes, they added requirements that limited weekly working hours to 60. They asked that factories pay at least the local legal minimum wage, and that proper safety equipment be installed. The audit became a set-piece process featuring a factory tour, document inspection and worker interviews.

The antisweatshop movement's greatest moment didn't come until the late 1990s. In 1995, Charles Kernaghan, a New Yorker who ran the National Labor Committee Education Fund in Support of Worker and Human Rights in Central America, was in Honduras looking for factories making clothing for Gap. While he was there, Kernaghan received a tag from a factory bearing the brand Kathie Lee.[18]

Kathie Lee was the eponymous brand created by Kathie Lee Gifford, the bubbly female half of the wildly popular *Live with Regis and Kathie Lee* television talk show. The Kathie Lee line, which pledged to donate a portion of its proceeds to children's charities, was sold in Wal-Mart. Kernaghan researched the Honduras factory that produced for Kathie Lee, documenting the use of child labor as well as low wages, forced overtime and other issues.

He took his findings to Gifford, who took them to Wal-Mart. Not satisfied with their response, Kernaghan mentioned his discoveries about the Kathie Lee line during a hearing before the Democratic members of the House Committee on Labor. On her talk show, Gifford responded, angrily, tearfully, with a threat to sue. The display made the former beauty pageant queen a national laughingstock.

Gifford hired a publicist and began to dig herself out of the scandal, promising inspections of the factories that produced her label. Then another sweatshop producing Kathie Lee clothes emerged, this time in New York City. Kernaghan arranged a press conference for Kathy Diaz, an underpaid, overworked former child worker from the Honduras factory that had produced the Kathie Lee line. Gifford met Diaz. She looked on approvingly as George

Pataki, governor of New York, signed a law barring the sale or distribution of clothing made in sweatshops.[19]

Gifford's humiliation and rehabilitation helped focus the attention of both the public and companies sourcing their production overseas on sweatshops. At the initiative of the Clinton administration, Gifford joined clothing companies, NGOs and union representatives to discuss a code of conduct for the entire clothing industry. This group, which became known as the Apparel Industry Partnership (AIP), was a forum for unions, consumer advocates, nongovernmental organizations, retailers and importers to discuss ways to improve working conditions at suppliers.

While not without controversy, the AIP created a milestone for the antisweatshop movement. In 1997, the group released one of the first "multistakeholder" codes—that is, codes of conduct that had input from different groups with an interest in sweatshops, including brands as well as NGOs. The code included clauses about freedom of association and collective bargaining. The AIP also included a mandate to inform consumers about its findings. Later, the AIP became the Fair Labor Association (FLA), which sets standards for auditing, certifies auditors and reports on these audits. Its membership includes some of the biggest brands in the business.

"Up to that point we were fat, dumb and happy, sourcing our goods, figuring that local governments were taking care of all the ills in those countries," remembers Ron Martin, director of compliance at VF, the group that sells brands including Lee and Wrangler jeans, North Face and Jansport. "We weren't doing anything blatantly, it was just that there was no concern—concern hadn't been raised."

Other multistakeholder groups and codes proliferated. The Council on Economic Priorities, a public interest research group founded by a former stock analyst, Alice Tepper Marlin, created another labor standard, SA8000. Tepper Marlin created Social Accountability International (SAI) to accredit auditors who would then inspect factories that wanted to be certified according to the SA8000 standard. In the UK, where pressure was mounting on the clothing and food industries, NGOs, union representatives and companies created the Ethical Trading Initiative, which in turn drafted its own code of conduct. The Clean Clothes Campaign in Europe also wrote a code of conduct based on International Labor Organization principles.

Industry-wide codes for contracted manufacturing also came into vogue. The American Apparel Manufacturers Association drew up its own code, Worldwide Responsible Apparel Production or WRAP. The International Council of Toy Industries created one. So did electronics companies.

Students even drafted their own code. Unions had helped bring the antisweatshop movement to university campuses, igniting a power base that is still very influential in the antisweatshop movement today.[20] Universities sell clothes, hats and other gear that are often made for U.S. brands overseas by contractors. As the media coverage of sweatshops intensified, students began to question brands about the goods they produced for their universities.

Students formed United Students Against Sweatshops, which pressed the Collegiate Licensing Company, agent to 160 universities, to implement a tougher code of conduct for its suppliers.[21] USAS also demanded that the companies that produced their schools' goods disclose lists of the factories they used—a demand that the licensees initially rejected. This ultimately became a requirement at more than 150 universities.[22] USAS, unsatisfied with the Fair Labor Association, formed a rival pressure group known as the Worker Rights Consortium.

As brands began to audit their suppliers, these pressure groups increasingly demanded that third-party groups be allowed to monitor factories, instead of only the brands themselves. Brands, the NGOs argued, couldn't be trusted as reliable sources of information about working conditions in their factories. Contracting out to third-party auditors would provide a more reliable picture.

In 1998, Nike bowed to this pressure. Conceding that "the Nike product has become synonymous with slave wages, forced over-time, and arbitrary abuse," founder Phil Knight announced new ini-tatives to resuscitate the company's ailing reputation in a speech at the National Press Club in Washington, D.C. Knight introduced minimum ages for contract workers to ensure that children would not be producing the company's goods. Air quality standards would be improved at overseas suppliers, and the company would switch from chemical solvents to water-based adhesives in its shoe produc-tion. Independent third-party monitors would be given access to Nike's suppliers. Third-party monitors became the new benchmark in social compliance. Gap, the original target of Kernaghan's inves-tigation in Honduras, had agreed to allow external monitoring of its subcontractors back in 1995. Liz Claiborne allowed monitors into a supplier in El Salvador in 1999.[23]

The original third-party monitors were accounting firms. Price-waterhouseCoopers (PwC) and Ernst & Young, which were already preparing annual audit reports for many of the brands that had adopted codes of conduct and had global networks, began auditing factories. By 1999, PwC was doing thousands of audits a year for companies like Disney, Nike, Wal-Mart and Gap. It was the largest private labor and environmental monitor in the world.[24] Accoun-tancy KPMG joined forces with UK retailer the Body Shop to con-duct social audits.

Eventually, accounting groups lost out to companies with better knowledge of factories: the much lower-profile firms that had qui-etly been doing product testing, quality assurance and certification for multinationals for years. Today, these firms, including Bureau Veritas, CSCC, Intertek and SGS, dominate the multimillion-dollar auditing industry. Other companies that do factory monitoring include Global Social Compliance, a spin-off from PwC, the American nonprofit Verité and TÜV Rheinland.

No one audits the auditors. Most prefer to stay out of the media, citing client confidentiality. CSCC, also known as the Cal Safety Compliance Corporation, started out providing safety training to contract manufacturers in California. In 1992, after the U.S. Department of Labor began requiring local manufacturers to monitor the wages and hours of their suppliers, some of CSCC's existing clients asked the firm to help with this new kind of monitoring. With help from a former Department of Labor official it hired, CSCC drafted a model for monitoring contracted factories. It claims to have been the first third-party company to offer these services.

SGS was founded in 1878 as a grain shipment inspection house in Rouen, France. Bureau Veritas was founded in Antwerp in 1828 by three men who hoped to help insurers assess ships and their equipment. Today, from its headquarters in Paris, BV provides a huge variety of testing, certification, inspection and consulting services. Both SGS and BV declined to discuss their social compliance auditing activities in China.

Today, multinationals use a variety of approaches to auditing their supply chains. Larger companies with more developed social compliance programs have a team of internal auditors but use multiple third-party auditors as well. They might also belong to one of the industry associations, such as the FLA, which will do its own inspections. Smaller companies may have an internal team or rely entirely on third-party auditors. And some don't audit at all.

THE GLOBAL BOOM IN factory monitoring hit China in the late 1990s. Timberland began auditing its mainland suppliers around 1999. The Gap began auditing after 1996. Reebok had full-time auditors in China starting in 1997. Wal-Mart suppliers in China have been audited since 1993. At that time, Wal-Mart relied on its exclusive agent, Pacific Resources Export Limited or PREL, to conduct audits. In 1997, Wal-Mart expanded its auditing program to include factories producing in-house brands and all suppliers in Egypt, Pakistan, India and Nicaragua. PREL used third-party auditing companies Global Social Compliance and Intertek to audit these suppliers until 2002.

That year, Wal-Mart acquired PREL and opened a sourcing office in Shenzhen, across the border from Hong Kong, to assert more control over the quality of the products it was buying and the working conditions in the factories where they were made. The retailer absorbed PREL's social compliance team and hired additional auditors.

Since then, Wal-Mart has audited all of the factories that supply it directly. Like other retailers, Wal-Mart divides the goods it buys into two categories: those that are sourced directly and those that it purchases indirectly. Goods that are purchased directly are bought by a Wal-Mart department known as Global Procurement. Wal-Mart audits these factories itself.[25] The remainder are purchased by external importers, sold to Wal-Mart and considered indirect sourcing. Goods purchased indirectly that fall into what Wal-Mart considers high-risk categories—products that are stitched or have a high labor content—are audited by third-party auditing firms. These categories are shoes, clothing, sporting goods, toys and accessories.

Factories that make some of Wal-Mart's "private label" or proprietary brands, including Mainstays, George and HomeTrends, are also audited. In 2003, Wal-Mart introduced a color-coded system based on a stoplight to grade suppliers' performance under the code. Today, the system has several colors: Green is a pass with no or only minor violations, yellow indicates what the retailer calls "medium-risk" violations, such as missing pay slips; orange covers "high risk" violations, including failure to pay the legal minimum wage or overtime, falsifying documents or having employees work after they have punched out for the day. Orange-age is for factories with one or two underage workers. Red is reserved for the most serious infractions, including the use of underage or forced labor.

Factories with four orange ratings within two years are barred from working with Wal-Mart for one year and their existing orders canceled, unless the goods are already on a boat steaming toward a store. Red factories are permanently banned from producing for Wal-Mart.

The company, like others, frequently updates its compliance program. In 2006, Wal-Mart and its third-party auditors audited 8,773 factories, including 6,757 factories that supply the retailer directly and 2,116 that supply importers or produce the goods locally.

The challenges Wal-Mart has encountered auditing its suppliers in China are no different from those met by other multinationals sourcing there. But its insistence on "everyday low prices" highlights the effect of the competing, if not conflicting, demands companies now place on their Chinese suppliers as a result of the auditing programs.

Two former Wal-Mart auditors agreed to discuss their experiences with me because of their concerns about the challenges in the auditing industry in China, on the condition that their real names not be used. They felt acutely the inherent tension of their role. Social compliance auditors are often caught between the interests of the multinationals and the factories they inspect. Sometimes, auditors are the only people workers can turn to for help during a labor dispute. Many describe receiving calls, often in the middle of the night, from employees of their company's suppliers asking the auditors to confront their bosses about poor treatment.

When Wal-Mart staff first started conducting its audits of factories in China in 2002, the former auditors said, it was immediately apparent how difficult it would be for suppliers to comply. "The factories did not take it as seriously as we did, because it was impossible to comply," said Max, one of the auditors. "If they were very strict, you'd have to close all the factories. You can't do that. It's a fact that not all suppliers or all factories can comply with Chinese laws."

As the auditing continued, factory managers' next response was to hide incriminating information. The auditors began to notice that as they toured the factory floor, supervisors were yanking production and overtime records off their desks and stuffing them into drawers. Then factories began to falsify payroll records and time-cards.

Initially, the auditors spotted the deception easily, because employees would confess their actual working hours in interviews. But then workers started lying. "From the U.S., the instructions were very clear: If you find falsified records, then give a red," Max recalls. Evidence of their deception was rapidly disappearing, however, as factory managers became more adept at disguising their real hours, wages and working conditions.

Max and his colleague wrestled with the contradictions in their roles. On the one hand, their job was to defend the retailer against the antisweatshop movement's attacks by removing code violators from the supply chain. On the other hand, it was rare to find a factory that could honestly meet all of Wal-Mart's requirements on both price and social compliance. Even today, only 5.4 percent of Wal-Mart factories worldwide are good enough to earn a green rating.[26] If they repeatedly failed the factories, the plants would lose the business.

If the auditors enforced the code to the letter, "it's very possible that these factories would suffer. They want to get orders and these workers want to get money," Max said. "Some owners or vendors, they actually provided pretty good living conditions for the workers. But still, if you did a very strict audit according to the rules, they still couldn't pass."

The way these auditors saw it, Wal-Mart's auditing system put the factories in a catch-22: If factory managers were honest and complied with all of the ethical standards, their costs would rise and they would likely lose the retailer's business. But if they didn't comply, they would never get the business anyway. Falsification allowed the factories to give Wal-Mart the China price and the impression of compliance.

The auditing system had other perverse effects as well. Managers I spoke to said they wanted to avoid a green rating, because it was widely believed among Chinese suppliers that Wal-Mart did more unannounced audits of factories with green ratings, although the official Wal-Mart policy is to reaudit after two years. Better to skate by on a series of yellows and oranges, the managers I spoke to concluded. "Being legal and following all the rules can cause you problems," the manager of one Wal-Mart supplier told me.

Ben and Max, the auditors, also worried that the rapidity with which Wal-Mart moved its orders from factory to factory, for either business or social compliance reasons, was costing the company dearly. The auditors would train a factory to comply with the code, and then Wal-Mart would move its order to another factory. The auditors would then need to train and educate managers at the new factory.

The retailer that offers "everyday low prices" would need to make significant changes in the way it does business to address the problems falsification presents, said Max. "I always try to ask myself, what would I do in [Wal-Mart chief executive] Lee Scott's position, and even I can't figure out how to do this."

WAL-MART SUPPLIERS are not the only Chinese factories forging their documents to pass audits. Falsification affects every single company that buys consumer goods from China and enforces a code of conduct on its suppliers. Auditors estimate that between 50 percent and 90 percent of Chinese plants doctor at least some of their documents. Daniella Gould, former director for North America and East Asia for the labor and environmental consultancy Impactt, has noted that "audit fraud in China has escalated. Impactt's experience shows that a majority of factories cook their books to some extent."[27]

"It was almost to the point where we could make certain assumptions . . . if a factory had not been subject to a remedial program to address this issue by a major brand or retailer previously . . . we could act on the assumption that falsification was taking place," recalls Doug Cahn, who oversaw Reebok's human rights program for 15 years.[28]

In its 2005 Human Rights Report, Reebok included a first-person account by Sherry Yuan, who monitored the group's apparel and footwear factories in China. She wrote:

> *The most common problem I face in my job has to do with records being falsified to cover up excess overtime and improper payment of wages. This issue comes up in almost every new factory because they think that brands will be happy with a piece of paper with the right figures on it. They believe that brands don't care about actual conditions. Sadly this is the case with some brands, but not with Reebok, who takes this issue very seriously.[29]*

Of course, Chinese factories are not the only ones lying. Mark Hui, a compliance executive at clothing brand VF, estimates that between 50 percent and 60 percent of factories in Vietnam and Bangladesh and approximately 30 percent of factories in India falsify their records. Auret van Heerden, president of the FLA, says he has seen fake books in Central America.

Nor are Chinese factories the first to cook the books and coach their workers to fool inspectors. American cotton mills at the turn of the twentieth century forged certificates and kept two sets of accounts—"one for the inspector, another for the countinghouse." Muckraking journalist Edwin Markham wrote in 1906 that "even the children are taught to lie about their age, and their tongues are ever ready with the glib rehearsal. Some mills keep a look-out for the inspector, and at the danger signal the children scurry like rats to hide in attics, to crouch in cellars, behind bales of cotton, under heaps of old machinery."[30]

Today, the difference between China and the rest of the world, in the production of fake factory records as in the manufacture of other things, is scale and skill. Chinese factories have turned the forgery of documents into an art form. Fake timecards, with carefully varied punch-in and punch-out times and worker signatures, are virtually indistinguishable from the genuine article.

These techniques are honed by China's ranks of "falsification engineers," consultants who teach companies how to outsmart auditors. The nature of the work ensures that falsification engineers keep a low profile—after all, they are showing Chinese factories how to hide illegal overtime and underpayment of wages. But their presence is widely known among factory managers, labor advocates and auditors. In the game of cat and mouse that auditing has become in China, these engineers are a mouse's best friend.

HUANG XIAOBING'S OFFICIAL JOB is quality inspector, ensuring that the goods factories make meet buyers' quality standards. But he also teaches factory managers how to make records that pass social compliance audits. Huang is a falsification engineer.

"You are the mice, what you must learn is how to escape being caught by the cats," Huang told a group of factory managers from around China at a seminar, according to a December 2005 report by Chinese newspaper *Southern Weekend*. "You win the game if you can cover your issues and problems from the inspectors." At the seminar, Huang recommends that factories apply for a waiver from the local government to allow their employees to work longer hours than the legal maximum—a common way of evading the law in China. Many multinationals have no choice but to accept these waivers.

Huang cautions the participants in the seminar, primarily factory managers, that international brands and retailers will take particular interest in their younger workers. They should also keep a tight leash on female migrant workers around the age of 40, who Huang says are particularly prone to blab to auditors about actual working conditions, perhaps because they are less timid than their younger colleagues. "Be careful of those troublemakers," he warns.[31]

When I contacted him by telephone, Huang first pretended he was someone else, then pretended he spoke no Mandarin Chinese. He eventually conceded that he was in fact Huang, but was reluctant to meet to discuss his business. With the help of a Chinese friend, I prepared a short list of flattering reasons: Only he knew what was really happening in factories, only he could tell me the truth. Huang was nonplussed. "What's in it for me?" he asked.

The Web site for Huang's company is vaguely worded, most likely to discourage scrutiny. Shanghai Chaowang Consulting's Web site is similarly innocuous: It claims the company is a "consulting firm specialized in social responsibility and ISO quality management systems."[32] But the same company's advertisement on the China Dada sourcing Web site poses a series of compelling questions:[33]

"Have you ever faced a surprise factory visit and provided pay and work records full of holes?"

"Do you know your factory won't pass an audit? Are you in the export business but worried about audits?"

The ad goes on to explain that the company can provide software that will alter records for wages, working hours and benefits to give the impression of full compliance with buyers' requirements. "After several years of modification," the advertisement claims, the software "can now help you easily resolve problems when Wal-Mart comes. We have more than 500 clients, from Zhejiang, Jiangsu, Shanghai, Shandong, etc. With our software, a factory with more than 3,000 workers can produce data for one month in 30 minutes. It not only saves your labor and cost from it but also helps you pass their audits and get orders from the United States and Europe."[34]

It's unclear to what degree Chinese factories' skills in falsification are due to these kinds of consultants, and how much is down to individual ingenuity. What is clear is that the ethos of evasion has spread through the supply chain.

In an October 2003 memo addressed to "all departments and work places" at a factory in Huizhou city, Guangdong that was supplying Liz Claiborne, management warns employees that the brand would be auditing the factory the following Tuesday. The memo, obtained by a Hong Kong NGO, orders training for all workers to prepare for the audit and provides a list of questions that the auditors are likely to ask, with the correct answers. "How many days are you working per month? Answer: 26 days," the document reads. "How many overtime hours are you working per week or per month? Answer: 2 OT hours per night from Monday to Friday." "What is your general impression about the factory? Answer: Good."[35]

The memo reads: "Each department can make adjustment in training workers. But workers should not be allowed to let the buyers know that we have given prior training to workers based on the specifics of the workers' interview."

One Hong Kong–owned toy factory in China assigned workers to rub falsified time cards in dirt to make them seem genuine, according to Parry Leung, formerly a researcher with the Hong Kong

Christian Industrial Committee, a now-defunct NGO. The manager of a large garment factory in Guangdong province told me he assigned a team of six employees to create a paper trail of fake documents for his foreign customers. Some of these workers punched fake time cards. One manager was charged with creating matching payroll records on the computer. The factory, in other words, was devoting management resources that could have been used on human resources to doctoring records. The two sets of time cards were identical, except for their content. The fake time card showed a monthly wage of $111 while the real card indicated the employee was paid $187 to reflect the longer working hours. "This is a perfect match for their requirement," the factory manager told me, reviewing his staff's handiwork.

Like any lie, Chinese factory managers' forgery creates stress. The garment factory manager admitted that though his staff trains a portion of the workforce every week in how to respond to auditors' questions, employees were harder to control than documents. When auditors interviewed his employees to cross-check what they had found in the payroll records, "I just stand outside and pray to God, 'I know I have done something wrong, but please protect me,'" he said.

THE EPIDEMIC OF FALSIFICATION has much more serious side effects than stress. Deception on this scale means that almost a decade after they began auditing factories in China at a cumulative cost of perhaps billions of dollars, multinationals are learning less about the actual working conditions in their suppliers and more about the skills of factory managers in hiding those facts. It means that consumers buying Chinese-made products have no way of knowing for certain under what conditions they were produced. Falsification weakens the flame of consumer pressure by convincing people that what they are buying was made under good conditions.

The veneer of compliance is luring consumers into believing that U.S. retailers and brands are working with their Chinese suppliers to ensure that ethical minimums are met. Under the cloak of this assurance, all manner of lies, evasions and fraud are being conducted—which further increases the already steep cost of the China price for the Chinese people.

The fact that so many factories are lying about their working hours and wages raises questions about their honesty in other areas, including chemicals and raw materials used in production. What else are Chinese factories hiding?

In the realm of working conditions, at least, factories are hiding gross violations not only of multinationals' codes of conduct, but also of Chinese law. One compliance executive at a company that sources widely from China found that the worst-paid employees at his suppliers were making less than one renminbi an hour; workers were earning hourly salaries a third lower than the minimum wage.

A compliance manager interviewed by *BusinessWeek* said that only 20 percent of Chinese factories follow wage regulations and only 5 percent comply with working-hour rules.[36] Liu Kaiming, executive director of the Shenzhen labor research group the Institute of Contemporary Observation, takes a similar view. He believes that 30 percent of factories in Guangdong don't pay even the minimum wage, and 50 percent don't pay overtime wages.

"No one in China, no one, even the best performers that we have, is compliant with the law in China," says one compliance manager from a large apparel group. Gap's social responsibility report for 2005, which is admirably forthright, shows that between 25 percent and 50 percent of its factories in Asia do not fully comply with local laws.

When the Association for Sustainable & Responsible Investment in Asia (ASrIA) and U.S. investor group Environmental Health Network met with companies, investors and supply chain specialists in Asia in November 2006 about the issue of toxic chemicals in manufacturing, they found "chronic mislabeling of bulk chemicals in China," according to Melissa Brown, ASrIA's executive director. In a report about its findings, ASrIA wrote, "it is common for suppliers to substitute locally available chemicals for the specified international standard chemicals on the view that the end consumers will not be able to detect the difference."[37]

Paul Midler, president of outsourcing and supply chain management group China Advantage, has watched Chinese manufacturers try to raise their profit margins by gradually lowering the quality of materials they use without telling their customers.

At the root of the falsification problem is the tension between companies' social compliance auditing programs and their buying behavior. At many companies, the drive for cheaper products conflicts with the drive for products made under better conditions. "Many of the merchandisers and sourcing teams from all the retailers, they start from the retail price and they work it backwards," explains the head of compliance at a U.S. clothing and shoe brand. "It may be fifteen cents they need to produce it. That production cost that they are backing up to is not enough to support minimum wage and the mandated benefits."[38] The executive uses the example of a very cheap shirt of the type that would be sold in a discount retailer. "Let's back it up all the way back to the factory," she says. "If you were able to do that, I'm sure we are going to end up in a factory that is not paying minimum wage."

Chinese factories' skill at falsification has become a competitive advantage. In a world where so many are cheating to keep costs down, telling the truth becomes a handicap. "Companies will be rewarded that in fact are not the best on price or quality, but are the best on corruption," says Sam Porteous, managing director for Asia at Navigant Consulting, a corporate advisory firm. "The whole idea of social compliance is weakened because you've got a whole system that's ineffective."[39]

Factory managers in other countries told one former China-based auditor that China's skill at falsifying puts them at a disadvantage. "Time and time again, when I give out my business card, the factory owners all over the world say, 'You know, we just don't understand China, we just don't understand how the factories operate. What is wrong with just doing things by the books?'"

THE ANSWER TO THAT question involves a complicated set of factors, rooted in the way that China and global supply chains have developed. At the heart of the falsification problem is a lack of law enforcement by Chinese officials. Although China's laws on wages and hours are good, they are poorly enforced, particularly in regions that want to attract and retain foreign investment. Officials, whose careers depend in large part on generating economic growth, often put investors' interests ahead of those of workers.

China's reluctance to enforce its own laws leaves the job to multinationals, who are businesses with shareholders and customers, not policemen or human rights organizations. China has essentially outsourced its own labor inspection to the likes of Wal-Mart, Gap, and Adidas. But the companies themselves, and to a certain extent their shareholders and customers, are also partly to blame. The expectation of simultaneous price declines and improvement in working conditions has put undue pressure on Chinese suppliers and compelled them to cheat.

The first problem is that there are too many different codes of conduct, with too many different approaches to enforcement. The explosion in the number of groups sourcing from China and the proliferation of codes have forced factories to comply with several different standards. While most codes are now very similar, multinationals' approaches to enforcement vary enormously. Some companies will allow a factory to get away with much more than others, allowing them to work 72 hours a week compared to only 60. Falsification is one way factories cope with the differences in multinationals' expectations.

At the same time, factory managers, tired of running around to satisfy different customers' requirements when they could have been running their business, have begun to suffer what is known in the compliance industry as "audit fatigue." Multiple audits have become, in the words of one former auditor of Chinese factories, "a gross duplication of effort and money and time."

The second problem is the business model. Many multinationals rely on ever-larger supply chains, making it difficult, if not impossible, for them to accurately diagnose problems and incentivize change in individual factories.

Wal-Mart buys from more than 8,000 plants around the world.[40] VF purchases from 1,500 suppliers. Kingfisher, the UK group that owns B&Q, the home furnishings retailer, relies on thousands of vendors. Within these giant pools of suppliers, companies often move orders from one factory to another to take advantage of lower prices, better quality or faster delivery times. "A lot of factories you're in and out of in one season. Maybe you only run one order through there," says Ron Martin, compliance director at VF. "So as far as spending a whole lot of time—you want to make sure, as I said, that there's nothing really serious going on there, that people aren't being absued—but you don't want to spend too much time, money and effort with a factory that you're not going to be in more than one order or one season."[41] Likewise, factory managers don't want to spend time, money and effort to accommodate demands for social compliance from a customer that will only place one order.

Partly because of this tendency, one customer often only represents a small portion of a factory's output. An apparel factory might supply Adidas, Phillips–Van Heusen, Gap and the Limited in the same year. A single brand might account for 5 percent or less of a factory's capacity. That kind of business relationship limits the leverage companies have to improve conditions in Chinese factories. "If you're under five percent, you've got a pretty long row to hoe," says VF's Martin. "If you're fifteen or twenty percent or more, then you can probably get them to paint the factory pink."

Some buyers have stretched their payment schedules so they don't pay the factory until long after it has shipped the goods. A cash-strapped factory might not be able to pay its workers until the buyer's check arrives. "Almost every small and medium-sized company that we talk to has a cash flow problem," says one industry consultant. "And so when the auditors come and say, 'Well, have you paid wages?' of course they lie. Because they know they're going to lose the contract if they say 'oh, we haven't paid our wages for two months.' "

In its 2004 social compliance report, Gap conceded that "buyers like us can have a negative impact on working conditions through inefficient purchasing practices or unreasonable demands."[42]

Local conditions can also make it easier to lie than to tell the truth. Frequent power outages, which have been common in industrialized areas in coastal China in recent years, can make it more difficult for factories to meet buyers' delivery schedules within the legal limits. Often, factories lack a properly trained human resources manager and therefore are ill equipped to respond to buyers' demands for shorter hours. And, as Eugene Chan, the Wal-Mart supplier in chapter two, argued, many migrant laborers would prefer to work longer hours than multinationals' codes of conduct specify in order to increase their pay.

But perhaps the most significant factor driving the truth about factory conditions underground is the pressure on price. In some highly competitive, labor-intensive products, such as shoes and clothing, prices are in free fall. Retail prices for footwear dropped 3.5 percent between 1998 and 2006, despite a 23.7 percent increase in overall retail prices over the same period, according to the

American Apparel and Footwear Association.[43] But the downward trend also extends to electronics. Prices of flat-panel televisions fell 40 percent on average in 2006, in part because of discount wars between retailers.[44]

The pressure on price has convinced some auditors that multinationals benefit from, if not tacitly encourage, falsification. "I think . . . both parties sort of complicitly wink and nod at each other and sort of know what's going on," says a former auditor. "The companies claim to be appalled by the falsification of records, but at the same time know that that is the way they can manufacture cheaply while still claiming they are compliant with the laws."

A quality control manager at a U.S. importer says, "Technically, we will tell [factories] how to comply with the law the right way first. But of course a lot of them aren't willing to pay more to their workers. So eventually, from their point of view, I won't tell them how to cheat on audits, but I will tell them the experience of other factories." That is, he will tell them to falsify. The executive feels compelled to do this because "that's the real world. We have to face these kinds of things. We have no choice. We have to ship our goods."

Some of the problem can be traced to the scarcity of good auditors. Even a decade after audits began on a large scale, the industry still suffers from a personnel problem. Aside from SA8000, the social compliance industry has not yet developed a standard professional qualification on which everyone—companies, unions, NGOs—can agree. There are no certified public auditors of factories.

In China, where so many of the world's audits now occur, this fact is particularly glaring. "There are auditors out there whose only credential is being able to write a report in English," says Stephen Frost, director of CSR Asia, a Hong Kong corporate social responsibility consultancy. "There are people who are doing auditing whose skill for getting the job is that they did English literature at Beijing Normal University, not environmental health and safety or Chinese safety standards. Where are all those people? They don't bloody exist."[45]

CSCC, the third-party auditing group, says that a decade ago, "no one knew that a job like 'social compliance auditor' even existed. Now, we see applications from people who have past social compliance auditing experience and some are even approved auditors for the various social standards certification programs out there."[46] It adds that it also trains all of its auditors itself.

Wages in China's auditing industry, as in the factories it monitors, can be low. One veteran inspector says auditors working in mainland China for a brand or retailer can make as little as $263 to $395 per month. Third-party auditors earn more, according to this person: between $658 and $1,316 a month. Although other auditors say wages are often higher than this and rising, turnover is high.

Low salaries and high turnover increase the opportunity for corruption. Some auditors routinely use bribes and other graft to increase their salaries. At one third-party auditing firm, auditors used to pad their estimates for their daily transport costs until the company caught on. And despite the fact that many multinationals sourcing in China require auditors to fail factories that offer to bribe auditors, managers will often try to influence the result of an inspection with a gift. Elaborate lunches at local restaurants, also frowned upon by many buyers and auditing firms, are common— they stall the auditors and may even keep some sweet. But lunches are a minor indulgence compared with the other treats on offer: One former third-party auditor recalls that the managers of factories she was auditing would find the hotel where she was staying and quietly pay her bill. Or they would offer money, folded into an envelope. One senior executive at a third-party auditing firm describes how a factory manager, his bribe refused, opened the door of his auditors' taxi as they were leaving and threw the money at them.

"More than ninety percent of code-of-conduct compliance auditors, when a person from a Chinese factory gives them something under the table, will tell the factory, 'your report will be okay,' accept the bribe and pass the factory," says a veteran auditor for Western brands. Bribes range from $500 to $4,000, depending on the size of the factory, he says.[47] Obviously, bribes make a mockery of the auditing process: They show factories that a multinational or third-party auditing firm isn't serious about compliance and will allow all manner of infractions to pass unnoticed.

Wal-Mart, one of the only companies that has commented on this issue publicly, has admitted that it has had to fire several employees in China in recent years for requesting or accepting bribes during an audit. It says that it investigates every report of unethical behavior and fires the employee if it finds the allegations are correct. "Wal-Mart believes in conducting business in an open environment based on ethics and integrity," reads a company flyer distributed to suppliers. "By this we mean that all our business transactions should be straightforward and transparent. **No money or other favors should be asked [sic] by our associates nor provided by our business partners.**" The flyer includes a Chinese toll-free number that connects to Wal-Mart's global ethics office, where there are Mandarin speakers on call.

But palms don't always need to be greased. As the number of social compliance audits has mushroomed in China, brands and retailers have started shifting the cost of auditing to their suppliers. Some companies require factories to pay for every audit. Others insist on payment only for follow-up audits, after an earlier inspection has uncovered violations. But the trend is clear. One auditor estimates that factories now pay for 70 percent to 80 percent of the audits in China. As multinationals pressure their suppliers for lower prices on the goods they produce, suppliers are pressing third-party auditing firms for lower prices as well. Sales staff at a leading third-party auditing firm, says a former employee, "get calls from these factory staff who just want a quote, who say, 'Give it to me straight, how much?' They're not interested in the sales pitch, they're like, 'How much is it going to be?' They're calling around, and really what they care about is the price."

Social compliance audits that include consulting services can cost $10,000 for a thorough inspection. But at least one company has offered audits in southern China for less than $300, according to industry consultants. Big auditing companies charge as little as $700 per audit. At prices like this, quality is necessarily compromised.

"In many companies, I think we're seeing people forced to price audits at such a low level that you can't really be sure that the audits are doing what really should be done," says Sam Porteous of Navigant Consulting.[48] CSCC contends that it refuses to do business with clients asking for prices "that would compromise the quality of the service we provide."

Cost pressures and surging demand are making some social compliance audits in China shorter. In some cases, audits that once took two days may now take one. Some auditors for external monitoring companies race through as many as six factories in a week. Auditors might see two factories in one day. In a year, an auditor might visit 200 factories.

Auditors, like the factory employees they are supposed to be monitoring, are under pressure to get through their work quickly. Unsurprisingly, some miss a lot of what is actually going on. "I tell auditors that I cannot tell them the truth in relation to some of their questions. They smile and move on to something else," the manager of a garment factory in Dongguan told CSR Asia, the Hong Kong consultancy. Of course, not all auditing firms or brands work this way.

Compliance, of course, also costs money. According to one estimate, following the local law would raise production costs between 10 and 77 percent.[49] An internal survey by Reebok in 2001 found that full compliance with its code of conduct—including investment in protective gear, fire safety and eye washing equipment, hiring social compliance managers and paying all workers in the factory the legal minimum wage—raised the FOB (free on board) price, or the cost of a shoe when it is sitting on the container ship, by $1. That may seem like a minor increase, but the FOB price for a simple canvas shoe can be as low as $5.

The pressure on price can pit a company's compliance department against its buying department. Buyers look for a combination of best quality and fastest delivery time at the lowest cost. But factories that meet these requirements are not always the most socially responsible.

In an ideal world, multinationals' buying and social compliance departments would work closely together to develop long-term relationships with factories that satisfy demands on price, quality and delivery times as well as on working conditions. In reality, that happens relatively rarely. In a twist that may surprise some consumers, exceptions to this rule include companies like Nike, Gap and Adidas, where the sourcing and compliance teams work more closely together. In many other companies, sourcing executives bring in business; compliance officials are often in the position of turning it down.

A compliance executive at a well-known American brand complains that his division suffers because it is a cost, not a profit, center. The buying team, he says, ignores his e-mails. A former auditor at a large U.S. footwear brand complains that senior buying executives at his previous employer would go over his head to tell factory managers they didn't have to comply with certain elements of the code. The head of compliance at a clothing brand concludes: "The sourcing group and the compliance group could almost be on different planets."

Ironically, the result of all of these factors is that auditing has made the truth about what is happening in many Chinese factories a secret. Multinationals sourcing in China have helped to create and perpetuate this response through the demands they place on factories and the way they purchase goods. "There are better incentives to cheat," says the FLA's president, Auret van Heerden, "than to conform."[50]

"My overall assesment," says Dara O'Rourke, associate professor of environmental and labor policy at the University of California at Berkeley, who has been a vocal critic of certain aspects of the auditing industry, "is that the system is set up to basically only look at symptoms, not root casues, and then to incentivize the factories to cover up the problems. You've got the absolutely perverse system where everyone is incentivized to cover up the problems."[51]

FOR ALL ITS FLAWS, social compliance auditing has served an important purpose: It has alerted multinationals to the scale of the problems in their supply chains. The fact that falsification is widely known among companies today is a direct result of their auditors' diligence.

In response to what they are finding, many companies are trying to meet more regularly with suppliers to educate them about their expectations. Wal-Mart, like other retailers and brands, conducts regular sessions with factories that repeatedly fail to meet its standards.

Without the retailer's knowledge, I observed one of Wal-Mart's training sessions to see how it communicates with its suppliers. What I saw offers one clue to why the retailer, and others like it, might have trouble getting their factories to comply.

Shortly before nine on a summer morning, the conference room of a Shenzhen hotel filled with men and women in casual business clothes, khaki pants and short-sleeved shirts. They took their seats

in the rows of cheap metal chairs on the gold and red flowery carpet, talking quietly among themselves. At that hour, especially for
people who had made the hour-and-a-half-long journey across the
border from Hong Kong, the room was an intensely bright, unwel-
coming place to be. The walls were upholstered with a fabric printed
with gold and blue roses. At the front of the room were big, white
screens. There was no spread of coffee and Danishes at the back of
the room, just more chairs.

Suddenly, a cry rang out. "Give me a W!"

"W!" the crowd answered with all the enthusiasm the early
hour allowed. A few fists pumped the air.

"Give me an A!"

"A!"

The world's largest retailer's trademark cheer was not new to
this group, representatives of about 250 of Wal-Mart's thousands of
suppliers in China. The men and women in the room had been
doing business with the American giant for at least two years. In
that time, they had accumulated enough violations of Wal-Mart's
code of conduct to endanger their future business with the retailer.
Their misbehavior had earned them a seat at this training session.
Wal-Mart calls it orange school. But really, it's summer school for
bad factories.

"What is the impact of non-compliance?" a Wal-Mart executive, a Chinese man, asked the room rhetorically in English through
a microphone. "Only short-term business relationship can be
maintained."

The impact on Wal-Mart of badly behaving factories, he continued in a professorial tone, is unwelcome media coverage. American
unions spend millions every year to monitor Wal-Mart. Journalists
or others mention the retailer more than 500 times a day. "So you
should know that Wal-Mart is always under the spotlight of the
media," the man said.

The participants, many of whom had attended orange school

before, knew all about the threat of exposure. Among them was a representative from an importer that supplied Wal-Mart and sometimes resorted to showing factories how to falsify. He and his colleagues were repeat offenders. It was annoying to have these problems, but this was just part of doing business with Wal-Mart.

Wal-Mart employees distributed quizzes to the audience. The quiz consisted of 10 multiple-choice questions in English and Chinese about Wal-Mart's compliance program. The questions ranged from the straightforward ("Who is responsible for compliance issues?") to the complex ("A factory received 3 successive Orange assessments during the period Jan-Oct 2005. On the 4th Audit in Feb 2006, it was assessed as Yellow. On the next audit in June 2006, the factory received an Orange assessment again. What would be the consequences?").

At the end was a nongraded, open-ended question: "How do you rate China's factory [sic] today?" Participants were told to evaluate factories from one to five, five being the best. The room fell silent as the suppliers leaned over their laps, circling their answers. They handed them back to Wal-Mart employees for grading.

"Last time they had to do the quiz again, because so many people failed," the importer whispered. "Most attendees got less than half of the questions correct."

Then the morning's lecture began. Another Wal-Mart executive took the floor and launched into a PowerPoint presentation explaining the retailer's complex system for monitoring and punishing its supplier base. She explained the goals of Wal-Mart's ethical standards team: to educate its suppliers about the local law and Wal-Mart's requirements; to check that factories are meeting these requirements; and to encourage changes that will result in improvements in working conditions.

She reminded them that child labor was a no-no and would lead to an immediate red, that four orange ratings would cause a factory to be banned from supplying Wal-Mart for a year. All of the vendors in the room were on their second or third orange. "We don't want to see you again" at the school for bad factories, the woman told the audience, with a smile. Some of the participants laughed.

Then, using PowerPoint slides, she walked the class through each color on Wal-Mart's ethical standards stoplight. It was a long and complicated explanation involving the types of infractions that would lead to each color rating, the number of days between audits at each color rating and the status of orders made at that factory depending on the color. She paid special attention to the retailer's policy on child labor, for which she stressed it had "zero tolerance." If Wal-Mart found one or two underage workers, the company would give the factory 30 days to remove them. After 30 days, the auditors would return, and if they found underage workers again, the factory would be given a red rating. If no evidence of child labor was found, the factory would get an orange rating.

While simpler than it used to be, Wal-Mart's auditing system is still bewilderingly complex. The ethical standards manuals it provides suppliers are thick documents that list the rules and consequences for violating them. Suppliers say these rules change, and it's easy to slip up. "You need to have somebody working very closely with Wal-Mart because they change their requirements very frequently," the importer told me.

At the end of the presentation, the Wal-Mart executive put a slide up that read: "Having good ethical standards in place leads to greater productivity" and "You should be compliant because it's the right thing to do, not because you have to."

When the quiz results were announced, it became clear that few people understood the system. Less than half the class passed, meaning they answered half or more of the questions correctly. The class broke into peals of laughter. Unamused, Wal-Mart executives distributed fresh copies of the same quiz, just as the importer had predicted they would.

While the second batch of quizzes was being graded, the Wal-Mart executives called for questions. One supplier, a Western man, said he was confused: Were the maximum weekly working hours Wal-Mart would allow 60 or 72? (Answer: 60 hours or below will lead to a green rating; between 60 and 72 hours earns a yellow rating, 72 hours and above is an orange.)

Another supplier asked what the difference was between having two and three underage workers. Wal-Mart's policy on child labor, like other retailer's, is strict. But Wal-Mart is also trying to give suppliers the chance to correct their mistakes. Their efforts can leave some suppliers confused. "The difference between one or two child laborers and three is absolutely different," the Wal-Mart executive replied. "If there are three or more child laborers in your factory, then we will give you a red for child labor."

Others were annoyed that Wal-Mart had not uploaded changes to its compliance procedures on Retail Link, the proprietary computer system it uses to communicate within the company and with suppliers. "Wal-Mart demands us as a supplier to submit some kind of information in some kind of speed," one supplier said. "But when we ask for some kind of information, it's quite difficult" to get it from Wal-Mart. The frustration in the room was tangible. Some suppliers threw up their hands in disgust when a Wal-Mart executive promised to put the updated information on Retail Link.

The announcement of the second round of quiz results lightened the mood. The morning's lesson had gone in one ear and out the other. After more than an hour of instruction, only 47 percent of students in the school for bad factories were able to answer at least half the questions correctly, only 5 percent more than when the group arrived.

The meeting finished before lunch, and there was no suggestion that Wal-Mart would be serving any. The suppliers filed out of the room, eager to get back to the business of making and selling things.

There was scant mention of the practical business benefits of working within the code of conduct (beyond being able to keep producing for Wal-Mart) and no discussion of the business reasons why these suppliers were performing so poorly on the audits. Wal-Mart gave its suppliers no information about the management skills they might use in order to comply or the variety of legitimate consulting services available to factories in China.

Less than half the students at orange school could even retain the specifics of the retailer's sourcing guidelines while they were still in the room. Despite Wal-Mart executives' attempts to explain the system, there were so many possible permutations that the rules were lost on many. If this was an attempt at remediation, it seemed to have failed.

Later, Beth Keck, director of international corporate affairs at the retailer, told me: "We feel like we're doing a really good job of providing the opportunity for them to have the knowledge, but it goes on both sides as well. They have to put some effort in as well to be knowledgeable."

THE PROBLEM BETWEEN Chinese factories and their Western customers runs deeper than a lack of knowledge of standards. Widespread falsification of records in China has raised questions about the efficacy of factory monitoring and the consequences of multinationals' escalating demands on their suppliers.

The reality is that a decade of monitoring by multinationals has not led to substantial improvement in working conditions in Chinese factories. Falsification and the use of shadow factories allow underpayment of wages, excessive overtime and unsafe conditions to persist.

Jill Tucker, who was for eight years the director of human rights for Reebok in Asia but who has since left the auditing industry, said the most significant change she saw was greater worker awareness of the law and their rights. But while this is indeed a major change, it has not necessarily forced factories to raise their standards. Fire safety also improved as a result of auditing. "There were many micro-level improvements, but many of them were not sustainable," she said. "Fire safety is something that is noncontroversial and factories are happy to address, so you're going to see fewer of the horrendous fires and loss of life that you saw in the early 1990s and before."

If auditing is encouraging only superficial improvements in working conditions, and factories are just hiding their violations in order to get on with business, then what should companies be doing instead? Some compliance executives believe part of the solution is to convince factories to come clean. It's impossible to make improvements in working conditions when you're being lied to, these people contend.

Many companies are auditing more aggressively. Auditors from these companies view themselves as part detective, part consultant. One of these auditors, a former employee of a leading shoe brand, remembers that he and his colleagues would arrive quietly at the factory the evening before the official audit. They would interview motorcycle drivers—who serve as affordable alternatives to taxis in southern China's industrial towns—about the times of day they saw hordes of young girls pouring in and out of the factory gates. During the audit the following day, they would check the factory's overtime records against what they had learned about the plant's actual working hours from the motorcycle drivers.

Then they would sit down at the factory office's computers to look for the real working hours data, which sometimes, this auditor said, was hidden behind a layer of falsified data in the same file. They would pore over food service records and interview cafeteria staff. Factories often forget to coach these employees.

One U.S. company has started a type of amnesty program, where factories agree to confess their true working conditions without penalty from the company, as long as they sign up to a series of incremental improvements. Although the program is admirably progressive, the company will not discuss the program with the media for fear that it would be exposed as knowingly sourcing from bad factories. A UK retailer has introduced a three strikes policy for factories that falsify documents. Wal-Mart says it started sending two auditors on every audit in 2006, partly to spot any discrepancies in the information gathered during the audit. It has raised the proportion of unannounced audits to 25 percent in order to combat falsification.

But as audits have become more aggressive, some observers believe goodwill has been lost. More aggressive audits "have created a profound sense of mistrust between [brands] and suppliers," wrote Daniella Gould, then the director of North America and East Asia at Impactt, a CSR consultancy, in 2005. "Factory managers feel they are passive victims in an unfair process that's imposed on them, without taking into account what's achievable. When trust breaks down between supplier and customer, it becomes very hard to initiate any improvements."[52]

To avoid this antagonism, some social compliance executives have also started to move away from traditional auditing and start discussing the root causes of factories' inability to comply with codes of conduct. Without understanding why factories fail audits, these people contend, they can't help them comply.

Since the session of orange school described above, Wal-Mart has begun meeting with small groups of suppliers around the world on a quarterly basis to discuss the root causes of their problems complying with the code. Given the sheer number of suppliers Wal-Mart sources from, this sounds like a small step in the right direction. Even Rajan Kamalanathan, vice president for ethical standards, admits that these initiatives have not yet led to any improvement. "We continue to work with the factories to get them to stop what they're doing and be open and honest with the information they're providing us. And that's going to take a little bit of time to resolve," he says.[53]

Other executives advocate greater cooperation among brands in order to reduce "audit fatigue" and encourage adherence to a single standard, evenly enforced. Levi Strauss is leading a drive to collaborate on factory audits, in hopes of reducing the duplication of effort when several brands are conducting audits of the same factory. It says it is working with 17 brands in more than 100 shared factories to do joint monitoring and share monitoring results as well as draw up remediation plans and conduct training together. Disney and McDonald's are cooperating on a project at 10 factories in China that aims to address the causes of code violations and develop a system of preventing and resolving them at the factory level.

Carrefour, Metro, Tesco and Wal-Mart, along with Migros of Switzerland, are drafting a unified code of conduct for their suppliers of both food and nonfood products through an initiative sponsored by CIES, an association of food stores and suppliers, called the Global Social Compliance Program.

Some companies are pooling audit results through databases to prevent factories from presenting different information about their conditions to different buyers. One of these databases, the Fair Factories Clearinghouse, was created by Doug Cahn, formerly of Reebok, and the shoemaker's chief information officer, Peter Burrows. The system, which is based on Reebok's in-house database of factory audits, went live in spring 2006. Reebok, Timberland, L. L. Bean and VF are among the companies that have signed up for the database. Other companies have signed up for Sedex, the Suppliers Ethical Data Exchange, another database that pools information about factories' working conditions online. The London-based group counts Burberry, John Lewis, Li & Fung, Marks & Spencer and the Body Shop among its members. "Pooling audit results through a shared platform won't prevent factories from presenting inaccurate information about conditions," says Cahn. "But it will enhance the leverage that buyers have to enforce standards."

ANOTHER SOLUTION is to choose a set of suppliers and work closely with them to improve compliance. Back in 2001, Adidas, the athletic shoe and clothing brand, realized that traditional auditing was not enough. "The failing of the compliance programs tends to be that people get better and better at finding problems but they don't get better and better and better at solving the problems," Bill Anderson, the company's head of social and environmental affairs in Asia, told me several years later.

"Because there's such a long history now of the nature of the way compliance works, and because of this cat-and-mouse game that's been created, the first thing you actually need is a trust relationship to build," he continued. "And it doesn't exist, in the sense that you're the big buyer and they're the little supplier, and you know, it's easier to fool you than it is to trust in you."

It took a few years to implement, but starting in 2004, the brand began a program of what it called "strategic compliance" with its largest suppliers and the ones that it had selected as long-term partners. It hoped to build more long-term, trusting relationships with these factories, including about 100 in Asia. The best-performing factories in this program would receive more orders.

During audits of these plants, Adidas began to spend most of its time isolating the most pressing problems and showing management how to prevent and manage these issues on its own. Adidas allowed me to observe one of these audits at Dongguan Kuan Ho, a ball factory, in late 2006. Inside the giant white and blue factory in the industrial city of Dongguan, the workers were divided into groups by the type of ball they made.

One group manned ancient-looking sewing machines. Another unit, entirely young and female, sat in neat rows on benches, stitching orange volleyballs for Wilson. Another team in blue and maroon uniforms nearby used long metal prongs to sew the thick white stitches on American footballs, a surprisingly violent and energetic process. The football was strapped to a board with what looked like Ace bandages, a quaint pairing for a ball used in an injury-prone sport. Using the prong, the women yanked the lace through the holes. The air was filled with the whirring of machines and the concentration of 6,500 pairs of eyes.

Meanwhile, in the factory's large conference room overlooking a tiny golf course, a group of executives from Adidas and Kuan Ho sat facing each other at a giant table. The executives were casually dressed, in polo shirts and loose-fitting pants. Each flipped through a binder of notes.

On a whiteboard at the front of the room, someone had drawn a line with branches fashioned at angles, like a Christmas tree lying on its side. At the end of each branch was a word—"policy," "channels," "procedure," "training." At the top of the tree someone had written the word "communication."

This was the second day of a two-day audit. During the audit, Adidas executives had examined the factory's facilities and records and then settled on a core issue that they felt the plant's management should address. The issue was laid out on a graph like the one at the front of the room, as part of a process Adidas called root cause analysis.

The day I visited, the Adidas team had chosen to focus on faulty electrical wiring they had found during their tour of the factory. "We're not going to check each thing each time," Barry Tang, Adidas's social and environmental affairs manager for North Asia, told the Kuan Ho managers assembled around the conference table. "Now we're going to speak to you about one high-risk item."

Anderson told me that the biggest benefit of this program is the change in Kuan Ho executives' attitude. Occupational health and working hours, which had been a chronic problem, had improved. Still, he wrote in an e-mail after I visited the factory, "the reality for any social compliance team is that whether using traditional auditing/action plan approaches, or new and novel ones, you simply cannot capture and address all issues."

ANDERSON IS unusually frank about the challenges of compliance. At many retailers and brands, a culture of secrecy shields the corporate social responsibility programs from outside scrutiny. A deep-rooted fear of reputational damage or legal challenge prevents many compliance executives from admitting in public what is really going on in their supply chains. This reticence stunts the development of social and environmental compliance, and keeps Chinese factories' working conditions a secret.

To name a few examples:

• Disney refuses to disclose how many factories it currently uses, in China or elsewhere. It declined to answer my questions about the company's social compliance program, referring me instead to its Web site and articles in the press.[54] The company's Web site, which a spokeswoman described to me in an e-mail as "fairly comprehensive," at that point featured the company's code of conduct and an overview of its collaborative project with McDonald's at 10 factories in China. But it offered consumers and investors no information about the progress the company had made in enforcing its code of conduct. Disney customers had to take it on faith that the brand's code was being effectively enforced.[55]

• In its 2007 corporate responsibility report, retailer Target explained at length its community giving and diversity programs. These initiatives doubtless made a valuable contribution to society. And yet the supplier section of the report outlined Target's policy on factory audits without mentioning how well its vendors were performing according to its standard. Whereas the community giving section was rich in detail about issues like the amount of funds spent on certain projects, the global vendor section read more like a policy statement, a laundry list of expectations, than an account of the actual conditions in the supply chain.[56]

• Kohl's, another retailer, did provide a paragraph on the performance of its suppliers against its code in its 2006 corporate responsibility report, noting that 57 percent of manufacturing facilities were in compliance, a surprisingly high figure considering the prevailing conditions in Chinese factories.[57] But the retailer provided no information in the report about where its suppliers were, except to note that it had cumulatively performed 10,200 monitoring visits of more than 3,000 facilities in 73 countries.[58]

• Home Depot devoted just a page on its Web site to its social and environmental compliance program. It provided no useful information about the working conditions or even the geographic location of its suppliers.[59]

To be fair, at least these companies publicly acknowledge social compliance as an issue. Many other groups can't even do that. Still, more than a decade after the antisweatshop movement began to pressure brands and retailers, these companies' lack of disclosure constrasts with the more open approach adopted by companies like Reebok, Adidas, Nike, VF, Gap, Timberland and Wal-Mart. These groups regularly publish the results of what they're finding in their suppliers and how well their compliance programs are working to improve conditions. Often, more honest companies will come clean and say that certain issues, like excessive overtime or underpayment of wages, continue to dog them in certain regions. Some of these companies do acknowledge the limitations of monitoring and discuss the connection between good working conditions and the company's business objectives.

But the lack of transparency in many other companies' disclosure about the conditions in their supply chain is striking. What are these companies not telling us, and why?

The efforts toward corporate responsibility at many companies that use overseas contractors are stalled in a reactionary phase. The fear of public exposure—the original impetus for the compliance programs back in the 1990s—is still too often the primary motivator, as opposed to improving working conditions in a way that sincerely benefits the business of both buyer and supplier. "Auditing is politics," says an industry consultant. "Brand X hires audit company Y to audit its supply chain. The last thing brand X wants is 99 percent of its audit reports coming back with serious remediation required. Actually, no one wants that. The factory doesn't want that. The auditor doesn't want that because that's more work per audit. And the brand doesn't want that because it's just too difficult to deal with."

The consultant continues: "What a lot of brands want, what a lot of retailers want, is a piece of paper that goes into a database that show graphically at the end of the year 65 percent of our companies are in 80 percent compliance or 90 percent compliance or whatever. And that keeps everyone off their backs."

Another auditor agrees. "Some clients told us frankly that the inspection was just a gesture. They didn't want us to audit seriously, they didn't want to see many problems." The fact is that companies are buying from China to save money and satisfy customers' demand for ever-cheaper products. Factories' inability to comply with codes of conduct is, in part, a response to this desire. So is the falsification of records. It gives multinationals what they want in terms of both price and a paper trail that proves compliance.

"If you look at the marketplace, the exacerbation of this underpayment issue and whatever impact it's having is driven by the consuming public that wants low-cost goods and is looking to retailers to provide them," says Doug Cahn, the former Reebok executive who helped create the Fair Factories Clearinghouse. "Is there culpability here on the part of Wall Street or the investment community that accepts the paradigm that exacerbates or promotes this kind of behavior? I think the answer is yes. They're not the only motivator. I do think there's a fair amount of truth to the argument that Wall Street, through its natural proclivities, has expanded all of this and has contributed to the problem."[60]

The expectations that investors place on retailers and brands for continuing revenue and profit growth fuel problems in supply chains. If investors expect companies to return greater value to shareholders by squeezing suppliers to the extent that factory managers are forced to lie, substitute shoddy materials and mistreat workers to survive, they should also be prepared to accept part of the blame for the consequences of that pressure: quality and safety problems, increasing pollution and persistent sweatshop conditions.

IF COMPANIES AND CONSUMERS really want to know where the goods they buy come from, if they want to know that these products were made under safe and legal conditions, social compliance has to move beyond reputational and legal risk management to become part of corporate strategy.

"The moral imperative only gets you so far, and unfortunately, it's not far enough," says Jill Tucker, the former Reebok executive. "When compliance is an island and the exclusive job of the auditors, it's bound to fail. Compliance needs to be integrated into the company's overall business strategy." Today, compliance is often relegated to a noncore activity, out of sight and mind of a company's senior executives. CSR is "not considered value-added," says a compliance executive at a European retailer and brand.

Michael E. Porter, the strategy guru, and Mark R. Kramer, managing director of a nonprofit consulting firm, make a strong case for linking CSR to business aims.[61] In an article in *Harvard Business Review*, they argue that many companies' efforts in CSR are not as productive as they could be because they are based on a fundamental misperception that business and society have opposing interests, and they take a generic, rather than a company-specific, view of a company's social responsibilities.[62]

Porter and Kramer contend that some of the arguments for CSR—including the idea that it's the right thing to do, or that communities give companies a "license to operate," or that it's necessary to manage reputational risks—fall short because they don't help companies determine which social initatives are best aligned with the company's strategy. The result, they argue, is often "a hodge-podge of uncoordinated CSR and philanthropic activities disconnected from the company's strategy that neither make any meaningful social impact nor strengthen the firm's long-term competitiveness."[63]

Companies' social initatives should create value for the company and society, they write, arguing for "strategic CSR." Management should be involved in identifying and evaluating social issues in the context of how they relate to the business and its competitiveness. Rather than measuring whether stakeholders are happy, they should measure their CSR initiatives' social impact. "The focus," Porter and Kramer conclude, "must move away from an emphasis on image to an emphasis on substance."[64]

On substance, many companies' compliance programs still come up short. Despite their public commitment to improving factory conditions, many, if not most, companies still do not give more business to plants that actually comply with the code of conduct. "For many of the brands, we've been in a situation where we haven't been able to connect social compliance with business. We haven't been able to reward compliant factories with additional business," laments a senior compliance executive at a leading American brand. "At the end of the day, it's all down to making money from our point of view."

For these companies, the belittling of social compliance to a reputational risk-management function denies the value compliance teams can bring to a company's sourcing operation. The way a factory manages its workforce, handles chemicals and views safety—just a few of the insights auditors gain—are key indicators of that supplier's reliability and product quality. Factories that treat their workers well are more likely to be able to consistently generate high-quality goods.

Academics have found that U.S. multinationals have focused too much on cutting costs out of the supply chain to the detriment of their relationships with suppliers. Hau L. Lee, the Thoma Professor of Operations, Information, and Technology at the Stanford Graduate School of Business, has argued that companies must "develop collaborative relationships with suppliers" as well as customers.[65] "Companies must give up the efficiency mind-set, which is counterproductive; be prepared to keep changing networks; and, instead of looking out for their best interests alone, take responsibility for the entire chain," Lee has written.[66]

In the world of social compliance, consumers are a powerful constituency. Many brands and retailers design their social and environmental compliance programs and their level of transparency according to the expectations of outside groups, including consumers. Continually lower prices are good for consumers in the short run, but they necessitate social and environmental shortcuts that could end up harming consumers down the line.

The case of the toxic wheat gluten made in China and mixed into American dog food is a good illustration. So is the growing cloud of pollution from Asia on the west coast of the United States. Given the scale of deception about wages and working conditions by Chinese manufacturers, it is safe to say that there are plenty of other harmful consequences of cost-saving efforts by Chinese factories that have yet to be seen.

Wal-Mart, a company known for its meticulous collection of data, says it has no idea whether its customers care enough about social compliance to pay more for products that are made in factories that pass all of its ethical standards. During my interview with Wal-Mart for this book, I asked the company whether its customers were willing to pay more for goods that were guaranteed to have come from a factory on which it has bestowed a green rating, meaning the factory has only low-risk ethical violations. After a long pause, Beth Keck, director for international corporate affairs, replied, "I think you'd have to ask our customers." And then she burst into laughter. "It's hard for us to answer. We're kind of sitting here shaking our heads."

Rajan Kamalanathan, vice president for ethical standards, added, "You know, if you do a survey, I'm sure customers will say yes. But it's something that we don't know. We don't really know the answer. Maybe you should pose that question to them."

In fact, it's well known that at least some consumers are willing to pay more. Surveys taken since the 1990s have shown that a majority of consumers were concerned about sweatshops and say that they would be willing to pay more for goods that were made under better conditions.

Studies conducted by Marymount University in 1995 and 1996 indicated that 86 percent of those surveyed would pay an extra dollar for a $20 piece of clothing that was guaranteed to have been made under good conditions.[67] A later study showed that consumers were willing to pay about 28 percent more for a $10 product and 15 percent more for a $100 product made under good conditions.[68]

Of course, people often say one thing and do another. To study consumer behavior, researchers from the University of Michigan put two stacks of identical white athletic socks next to each other in a department store in a working-class neighborhood in the greater Detroit area in 2002. They labeled one stack as having been made under good working conditions ("Good Working Conditions means/ no child labor/no sweatshops/safe workplaces"); the other stack had no such labels or signs, implying that the socks hadn't been made under good conditions.[69]

Socks in the "good working conditions" stack were originally the same price as or more expensive than the unlabeled stack, but during the experiment both stacks were discounted to the same price to sell a larger volume. When the prices were the same, half of shoppers chose from the "good conditions" stack, and half chose from the unlabeled stack. But when the researchers raised the price of the "good working conditions" socks, only about 30 percent of shoppers chose them. When the price of the good socks was raised 30 percent, only 11 percent of shoppers bought them. [70]

The researchers concluded that while most people did prefer cheaper socks, about a quarter of consumers surveyed were willing to pay more. This conclusion could support a few ideas. One is that consumers are skeptical and aren't sure whether they can believe the claim that the socks were made under good conditions. Another possibility is that more affluent consumers have the luxury to take working conditions into account in their shopping.

There is evidence that this niche of "conscience consumers" is growing. Fair Trade products, which are certified to have satisfied certain social, ethical and environmental requirements, are increasingly popular. Product Red, the brand created by U2 singer Bono and backed by American Express, Gap, Giorgio Armani and Converse, which is owned by Nike, is one indication. A portion of the proceeds from the sale of Red products, which include an American Express card, Converse shoes and Gap clothing, go to fight AIDS in Africa. American Express thinks the number of conscience consumers in the UK will rise from 1.5 million in 2006 to 4 million by 2009.[71]

Still, social compliance executives at other multinationals say they need a better indication from consumers that they care about these issues in order to persuade management, which often views CSR as what one former compliance executive called an "irritant." "If I could walk into my chief operating officer's office and say, 'Look, there is proof that the consumers are stopping buying from certain brands based on their ethical sourcing practices,' " says the head of corporate compliance for a large U.S. apparel brand, "then they would pay attention."

The most powerful thing consumers can do is ask questions. If you buy from or invest in a retailer or company that sources from overseas, ask them a few simple questions: What evidence do you have to prove that conditions at your overseas suppliers have improved since you started working with them? How are you creating incentives for your suppliers to improve their working conditions? How does this benefit me as a shareholder? If the retailer or brand buys from licensees or importers, are these companies left to monitor factories themselves or is there supervision by the brand?

An auditor at a prominent European brand suggests consumers ask brands whether their buyers are incentivized to consider working conditions as part of their decision about the factories they buy from. How often do social and environmental compliance managers report to the chief executive? How often does the chief executive visit the factories (including the worker dormitories) in developing countries that supply the company?

One former auditor for big international brands urges consumers to take one particularly cheap product to the retailer or brand and demand to know where it was made. Consumers should ask not only for the factory name and location, but also for the legal minimum wage in that area and the average wage of workers in that factory. If the minimum and average wage in the factory are the same, he says, something is wrong. Factories that only follow the minimum wage generally have other problems.

Knowing more about companies' answers to these questions can help consumers make buying decisions they feel good about. Factories and multinationals aren't convinced that you care. "I just want to know if people are talking about this, if people really feel this is important," says Wu, the manager of the factory that supplies Timberland and other brands. If so, "then you have to pay five dollars more, you have to pay ten dollars more."

"You have to show it," Wu adds. "If you really care, then you have to pay for it."

Chapter 8

THE NEW MODEL FACTORY

THE FACTORY CAFETERIA HUMMED with the energy of a high school dance. Squeezed into rows of red picnic tables, two hundred young employees chatted, fidgeted and played with their mobile phones. Their gossip echoed off the walls.

At 10:30 A.M., a sturdy man in a gray shirt and pants appeared at the front of the cafeteria, microphone in hand. Abruptly, the din faded. The workers, the man announced, were here to elect a committee of their colleagues. Committee members would act as employees' representatives in negotiations with management to ensure their rights were protected. The result, he said, would be better "competitiveness and solidarity for the company."

The man, an employee named Yang Hui, was setting in motion an extraordinary process. Elections are a foreign concept in Communist China. Labor organizations independent of the government-sponsored All-China Federation of Trade Unions are at best controversial. At worst, they are threats to the regime. This election had nothing to do with the ACFTU. Even more unusually, the election was happening at management's behest for the third year in a row.

Two years ago, when the workers here elected representatives for the first time, they chose Yang. To prepare for his role, Yang was trained in presentation and negotiation skills. He traveled to other factories to speak about the importance of empowering workers through representative committees. His wife, Liu Haiyin, could hardly believe the changes in him. "He could never talk like that before," Liu, who was sitting at one of the picnic tables, marveled as her husband delivered his speech.

Yang handed the mic to Liu Li, a slender girl with close-set eyes and long hair from Sichuan province. Liu Li had been elected in the first and second polls. Now, she was up for a third term. She addressed her colleagues confidently, as someone comfortable on the campaign trail. Liu Li listed the the committee's achievements over the past year. It had organized training for workers in AIDS prevention and helped raise funds for the care of the sick son of one employee, "expressing the love of every worker and the warmth of the company as a big family." Representatives worked with management to arrange transportation for employees traveling home for the holidays. They persuaded the factory, which makes coats and other sportswear, to increase subsidies for the education of employees' children.

The committee was composed of 14 workers, one from each of the production teams on the factory floor. Today, half of the factory's staff would elect half of the leaders. The remaining representatives would be elected the next day.

One by one, candidates for seats on the committee rose from within the crowd and said a few words. Most were too shy to say much, but their colleagues enjoyed watching them try.

The audience dissolved into giggles as Liu Nanfang, a tall man with a big nose, approached the front of the room. "Good morning, I'm from Jiangxi," he said, referring to his home province in eastern China. He paused. The crowd laughed harder. He thanked his production team for their support and fled to his seat, where he leaned his head on one arm, an embarrassed grin on his face.

Yang Hui, who was both the election's emcee and a candidate, said: "If I'm lucky enough to be elected this time, I will work hard and achieve more success. In 2006 we did a fairly good job. I hope to gain your consistent support and trust."

When the ballots and pens were distributed, the workers made their choices and deposited their votes in red containers to be counted. In democratic countries like America and the UK, where elections are the stuff of watercooler conversation, casting a vote for a company representative is an ordinary event. Not so in a Chinese factory. Li Haiyin, a 28-year-old employee from southwestern Sichuan province, was thrilled at the chance to cast her ballot. "If you have a problem, you can ask your representative for help," she said. "It's good for us and it benefits the factory."

Later, Zhang Yisheng, the factory manager, took the microphone. "I'm encouraged and comforted every time I watch these elections, seeing the representatives become more mature," he told the workers as their votes were being counted. The room fell silent. "We have adopted suggestions from our workers. We are gradually making progress. I hope you can pay attention to our committee and help the representatives you chose in order to achieve a harmonious company, a harmonious factory and a harmonious workshop. We can work happily in a harmonious workplace. Thank you."

Precisely an hour after the elections began, they were over. Yang Hui, Liu Haiyin, Liu Li and their colleagues filed obediently back to their places on the shop floor. Not a moment was wasted. Within minutes, maintenance workers had arrived to take down the banners in the cafeteria that promoted the election. Cooks in white jackets began stacking metal plates for the lunch rush.

On the shop floor, Liu Nanfang, the shy man who had elicited

peals of laughter only minutes before, was too busy sewing pockets
to discuss his candidacy. The time for electoral politics had passed.
There was work to be done.

DURING THE FIRST THREE decades after 1949, factory workers in
China enjoyed special status as the builders of modern industry in
a young socialist nation and participants in socialist struggle.

In the 30 years after economic reforms began, labor, particularly in foreign-invested and private firms, became commoditized.
With scant law enforcement, a countrywide bias toward economic
growth and cities flush with labor, there was little incentive beyond
individual conscience to treat workers well, encourage their personal development or keep them healthy. That attitude has helped
propel China to become the fastest-growing economy in the world.
But it is not indefinitely sustainable. Nor will it improve the country's competitiveness as it climbs to higher rungs of the value-added
ladder. In fact, cheap, overworked labor could hinder China's development. Despite the widespread labor shortages that have affected
coastal China in the last few years, most factory managers still don't
see things from this perspective. But a small group of managers do.
Their efforts suggest that it is possible for Chinese factories to treat
their employees well and still make a profit.

Zhang Yisheng is one of those managers. In 1998, he was a senior manager at Chai Da Manufacturing, a privately owned jacket
and clothing factory in Guangzhou. Timberland, the U.S. shoe and
clothing brand, was his largest customer. That year, the brand notified him that it would soon start doing audits of its suppliers in
China according to its code of conduct.

A manufacturing veteran, Zhang had been dealing with international buyers for years. But this talk of codes of conduct and
corporate social responsibility was something new. It struck him as
a Western idea, the luxury of a rich society. But Zhang's factory, like

most factories, wasn't paying the full legal wage or providing complete benefits. Following Timberland's code meant, at least initially, that Zhang and his fellow managers would bring less home to their families.

"The hardest thing was the big drop in profits," Zhang recalls. Wiry-thin with high, sculptured cheekbones, Zhang keeps his jet black hair in a military flattop. In conversation, he has the demeanor of an orator, using dramatic pauses, traditional Chinese idioms and theatrical gestures to get his point across. "Before, we didn't need to pay overtime. Now, normal overtime you had to pay 50 percent more. For overtime on Sunday, it was double. Public holidays, three times. This was one area of difficulty for us. It was an increase in costs. It was an extreme increase."

The demands were more than Zhang could handle. Like many other Chinese factory managers, he concluded that in order to pass Timberland's inspections, he had to cheat. Timberland spotted the forgery of his records.

Zhang wasn't surprised. "Cantonese people have an expression: A fake is a fake. If you have 10 bottles and only eight caps, there will always be two bottles without caps," he said. Timberland warned him that it would not tolerate falsfication. The factory needed to focus on figuring out ways to comply with the code, or forget about doing business with the U.S. brand.

In 2000, Zhang resolved to stop cheating and try to pass Timberland's audits. He started shutting off lights and locking doors to the factory during lunch and after the day shift finished, to prevent employees from sneaking in to do extra overtime. He forced production team leaders to limit employees' hours. He told workers that if they wanted to keep working at Chai Da, they had better start wearing protective gloves and masks. "I don't talk about the law, I just talk about what's good for you," he said later of his approach to workers who didn't want to follow the new rules.

The process was painful. "Before, a manager could earn a lot of money, but [after codes of conduct were introduced] he had to take the money out of his pocket for social compliance. And at the same time, the owner of the factory had to look into changing his management style," he said.

In China's fiercely competitive, labor-intensive industries, the decision to follow the law eliminates advantages that one's law-breaking rivals enjoy. It adds new costs—insurance, maternity benefits, air conditioning—to a factory's overhead. It demands more sophisticated management to improve efficiency, so that orders are completed on time, within the legal overtime limits. In short, it takes a different kind of manager. In many labor-intensive factories in China, going out of your way to take your employees' welfare into account, banking on this being the right thing to do, is still progressive.

But the revolution at Chai Da had only just begun. A few years after it rolled out its compliance program in China, Timberland realized that audits, or what it calls "assessments," weren't sufficient to improve working conditions in its supply chain. The team concluded that any substantial, sustainable change would have to involve greater participation from workers.

Timberland had been speaking with Social Accountability International (SAI), a New York–based nonprofit human rights group that tries to improve workplace conditions around the world. SAI was best known for its SA8000 social compliance standard, which was based on United Nations and International Labor Organization standards.

But the group also trained employees, managers and auditors on improving working conditions. The SA8000 standard requires that workers be free to form or join trade unions and bargain collectively. If that is not possible, SA8000 mandates the creation of an alternative channel for workers to group together and bargain with management. SAI was looking for factories in China where it might train workers to communicate more effectively with their bosses.

Chai Da wasn't interested in SA8000 certification, but Timberland and SAI thought Zhang might be interested in training for his workers. Like other factory managers in the region, Zhang had been struggling with rising turnover. He couldn't understand why, even after he had gone to great lengths to make his factory compliant with Timberland's code of conduct, so many of his employees were leaving. Even if workers preferred longer hours to earn more money, surely they must have appreciated the better conditions. Zhang accepted SAI's offer of training at no cost to the factory.

The experiment began in April 2004. Trainers from SAI, including some former workers from other factories, sat down with groups of Chai Da employees on the shop floor. Conscious of the Chinese government's sensitivity to the issue of human rights, they kept the discussion focused on legal rights. SAI explained that according to Chinese law and the country's commitments to the International Labor Organization, they were entitled to a certain wage, working hours and treatment by their boss.

At first, the workers were "puzzled," Martin Ma, SAI's China program director, who oversaw the project, recalls. Rights were an alien concept. "You know, 'what are you talking about?'"

In the next session, SAI's trainers showed the workers how to calculate their legal hourly wage based on the local minimum wage so that they could determine whether they were being paid properly. They asked the workers to write down where Chai Da fell short of international and Chinese standards for working conditions. The workers responded with a torrent of complaints about low wages, bad food in the cafeteria and high temperatures on the shop floor in the summer.

In the third session, SAI told the workers they had several options in how to handle their complaints about the factory. Among the choices they presented were a branch of the ACFTU, a female workers' consultation committee, a health and safety committee and a general workers' committee elected by the employees. Chai Da's employees chose a workers' committee.

Zhang approved of their decision. He felt his workers needed an organization to represent their interests. As the head of the union branch at his previous employer, he had firsthand experience with the ACFTU. The union lacked the grassroots connections of its counterparts in the United States and Europe. It wasn't even clear to him whether his employees, all migrants who were technically still farmers in legal terms, would be allowed into the state-backed union.

But an election sounded like a drain on productivity. Zhang worried that the voting would take his staff away from the production line for too long. To allay his concerns, SAI designed the election to be managed efficiently.

On November 30, 2004, each of the 14 production teams on the shop floor nominated at least two candidates. Their campaigns consisted of a series of speeches by the candidates. Some had prepared brief remarks. Others, as in the third election, were too excited to say much of anything. "They had simply no experience in electing anything," Ma remembers.

After the election, SAI representatives returned periodically to the factory to train the new worker representatives in negotiation and presentation skills. Among this group was Yang Hui, the employee who would go on to emcee the third election. These were people who had grown up on farms and had come to the city to become one of hundreds on a production line. Now, they had a new identity. They were leaders, people with responsibility for their fellow workers. The ACFTU, as it exists today, does not offer the same opportunity.

ZHANG COMES FROM A generation of Chinese who have lived through wrenching changes in their country. The oldest son of military parents, Zhang grew up in Guangzhou. While his family's People's Liberation Army connection conferred certain privileges, like housing, luxuries were rare. "In those days, owning a fan was like owning a Mercedes Benz," Zhang remembered. During the Cultural Revolution, Zhang was sent to a labor school in the countryside to be "reeducated." There, he studied Mao Zedong's teachings and worked on a farm.

In 1972, Zhang was sent to southwestern Sichuan province, where he studied rare metals, with a focus on uranium refining. He spent several years there and in Beijing studying, until he was sent into the mountains somewhere in China to work. Despite his volubility on almost every other topic, Zhang won't discuss what he did in the mountains.

After three years, Zhang left. By then, it was the mid-1980s, and Deng Xiaoping's reforms were bringing big changes to the economy. A friend who was getting into the shoe business invited Zhang to join him. The government-owned factory they joined imported an entire shoe assembly line from Italy.

But nobody knew how to use the machines. So Zhang and 13 other Chinese employees spent three months in Italy, sampling the local cuisine and learning how to make shoes. When he returned, Zhang stayed at the company for a decade. Then, again at a friend's invitation, he moved to another factory. This one, which was privately owned and became known as Chai Da, had secured a contract to make jackets and cotton sportswear for Timberland.

In 2000, Chai Da moved to Kaiping, a quiet city of about 700,000 people two hours south of Guangzhou. Unlike most cities in Guangdong, Kaiping retains an old-world charm. On the outskirts of town, farmers still work the fields in conical hats and rolled-up pants.

Kaiping is best known for two things: its *diaolou*, or fortified watchtowers, which residents built starting in the Qing dynasty to defend against marauders from rival clans and which are now a United Nations Educational, Scientific and Cultural Organization world heritage site, and its criminals. In 2002, Kaiping shot to fame when former bank managers from the local branch of the Bank of China were accused of embezzling $482 million between 1992 and 2001. Following a well-worn path for corrupt Chinese officials, three of them fled overseas.[1] They were eventually caught and thrown in jail in the United States.

Today, at least half of Kaiping's traffic is motorbikes and bicycles, piloted by men and women in soup bowl helmets. The apartment buildings are less dazzlingly modern-looking than in Shenzhen: Squat and made of tile and concrete, there are plants and laundry peeking through metal grilles around their balconies. On the narrow lanes between these buildings, women sell watermelons laid in neat lines on tarpaulins and elderly men recline, hands on knees, staring at the human traffic. Kaiping moves at a gentle pace.

Kaiping is primarily an industrial town, a major production center for faucets and textiles. Set on a quiet spot on the banks of the Cang River, Chai Da resembles countless other factories in the region: one story tall, with a sloping roof and giant doors to allow supplies in and product out. Between the factory buildings is a landscaped path wide enough to accommodate a container truck.

Inside, however, the factory runs on different rules from its neighbors. Since the creation of the workers' committee, turnover at Chai Da has fallen. Some workers who had left the factory have returned. At the factory next door to Chai Da, much of the workforce left one Chinese New Year and never returned.

Zhang now discusses the factory's cost structure with the workers' committee. He consults the committee about whether and

when to assign overtime, a highly unusual practice in an industry
that has historically depended on employees' willingness to toil
ceaselessly without complaint. It's hard to tell how confrontational
their meetings are, but it's clear that the committee has improved
the quality of life of the workers.

The workers' committee has organized sports competitions and
a party each spring. After the tsunami devastated huge swaths of
coastline in Southeast Asia in December 2004, the workers' committee at Chai Da raised more than $180 for the victims of the
disaster.

The committee has brought other benefits, some subtle and
others more obvious. Since the committee's inception, working
hours have declined but productivity has risen. More workers return now after the Chinese New Year holiday, which suggests they
are happier in their jobs than they were before. It also means Zhang
doesn't have to train new employees and quality remains more consistent throughout the year. Employees have stopped scrawling
graffiti on the walls of factory bathrooms—what Zhang called the
factory's "toilet culture." Workers who once destroyed pieces of
clothing they were working on to protest a manager's unfair treatment now complain to their representatives instead.

Zhang has continued to organize training sessions for his employees, teaching them about parts of the labor law they didn't
understand, first aid, fire safety, HIV/AIDS prevention and even
human resources management. Zhang keeps scrapbooks of these
training sessions and displays them like the proud father of an unusual family. Inside are pictures of a worker putting out a fire in a
metal can, her colleagues watching her in a circle behind; a man
running with a fire hose; a woman pretending to perform CPR on
a factory manager; workers standing in a line on the factory floor
holding fire extinguishers. There are pictures of candidates making
speeches for the workers' committee election and employees lined
up to cast their votes.

Zhang has also changed his management style. Rather than relying on Timberland alone, he has sought out multiple customers, so that he has leverage in his negotiations with them. If his factory is busy with other orders, he can argue for a higher price. He has also started turning down orders if he knows he can't make them within a 60-hour workweek. Because he has to pay his workers one and a half times their normal wage for weekday overtime, he accepts an order only if his profit would be high enough to cover the additional cost.

"Efficient work is limited to eleven hours a day," Zhang said, sitting in the glass-walled conference room at his factory. Behind him, the production line whirred with activity. "Efficiency declines as working hours increase, and we have to pay extra for it. It's obvious we don't want them to work overtime, since it would result in a vicious cycle, which is not only inefficient but also can lead to accidents."

In the cutthroat Pearl River Delta, turning down orders because they would require overtime work is heresy. "Factories that don't pay overtime salary tend to accept more orders because they can earn more without incurring any extra costs," he continued. "But if they pay overtime, they won't let workers work overtime because the benefit from the orders won't cover the extra expense of overtime pay."

Zhang makes a conscious effort to hire men in the belief that having a more balanced workforce is more stimulating for the employees. "Why do we recruit boys? Because I offer them a fair environment where they don't want to do anything bad," he said. Zhang's workforce is also older than most others in the region, partly because employees are staying longer.

He keeps detailed statistics about his employees, believing that the better he understands them, the easier it will be to communicate with them. Forty-eight to 52: the ratio of male to female workers. Fifty-five percent: the percentage of workers between the ages of 18 and 25. One-third: the portion of the computers used by his workers on a Sunday at an Internet cafe near the factory. Eighty percent: the proportion of employees with mobile phones. Workers "have the right to voice their thoughts. They're not just accepting orders from their leaders. They are respected here," Zhang told me.

On a summer afternoon in 2006, Zhang took a turn through the shop floor, past mountains of stuffing and piles of puffy Timberland jackets with fur collars, rows of sewing machines humming to the command of his employees. The air was steamy and thick: May to September is peak production time for winter jackets.

As he walked past, Zhang did not inspire his employees to hunch over their work, trembling like caged animals, as I'd seen happen when the boss passed through the production floor at other factories. Zhang joked with one female worker, calling her by name, and his jokes prompted another to dissolve in giggles. Zhang knows almost all of his employees' names and where they are from, and sometimes even whether they have a new boyfriend.

But what was most striking was that Zhang's workers were not afraid of him. In an industry fueled by fear—fear of not meeting the buyer's deadlines, fear of not getting paid, fear of being fined for going to the bathroom—its absence came as a surprise.

LIU LI, the workers' committee representative who spoke so confidently at the election, didn't seem like the type to scare easily. She arrived in Kaiping in 2003 into the embrace of family: Two of her brothers and an aunt and uncle were already living there. As she stepped off the bus, $13 and one suitcase to her name, a woman walked by carrying a tiny silver purse. The bag was the most fashionable thing Liu had ever seen. One glimpse of city life was enough to stoke her material appetite.

Liu worked briefly cleaning a construction site and at a garment factory. She took a course on sewing machine operation. But mostly she hung out at her aunt and uncle's house. As much as she would have liked to be earning her own money, Liu was willing to wait for the right job.

One day after her eighteenth birthday, a friend of her aunt's who worked at Chai Da came over after work. She described the factory's good conditions: plenty of time off and reasonable pay. Liu applied and, despite her dismal performance on a sewing test, got the job. At Chai Dai, she earned more than $132 a month, which she saved, rather than sending it home to her family in the countryside. After work and on their days off, she and her friends window shopped and dined at cheap local restaurants. In the spring of 2005, she was elected her production team's representative on the workers' committee.

That autumn, though, Liu decided it wasn't enough. She wanted more money than she could make during Chai Da's restrictive hours. Liu resigned and found work in another garment factory in the nearby city of Jiangmen. There, employees worked through lunch to earn more money.

But the frantic pace didn't suit Liu. She returned to Chai Da and got her old job back. She was even reelected as a worker representative. "I prefer this kind of factory, where you can rest," she said, sitting in the conference room at Chai Da. Liu had a self-assurance uncommon among Chinese factory workers when called into their boss's office. Working long hours, people made more money but got sick easily, she said. Here, her salary may have been lower but her more reasonable schedule meant she rarely fell ill. That wasn't the only benefit. At other factories, management could ignore workers' needs. But here, she said, "if you represent a production team, the managers take you seriously."

And the silver purse that had caught her eye when she first arrived? It was sold everywhere these days, she said. At just over $5, she could easily afford one.

ZHANG'S EXPERIENCE and wit make him a natural on the Chinese corporate social responsibility speaking circuit that emerged along with the surge in factory monitoring in the early 2000s. Zhang has become a regular presenter at conferences organized by the Institute for Contemporary Observation, the Shenzhen-based research and outreach group. Zhang's employees' donation to the Southeast Asian tsunami victims even earned the factory a mention in the international media. None of this, however, has lessened the pressure he feels from his customers and competitors.

Treating your workers well costs money. Zhang has extended full benefits to all his workers. He also pays 20 percent of the cost of employee meals in the canteen, or almost $4 per worker, every month. He gives another $4 a month to punctual workers. Workers who hit a daily production target get a $13 monthly bonus, and those who work to plan get a $6.58 bonus. He pays married couples who live outside the dormitory a rent subsidy. He hires a bus to ferry workers to the train station in Dongguan at Chinese New Year.

All together, Zhang calculates that he is paying an additional $53, on average, per worker every month, on top of their regular salary. That is $53 most of his competitors aren't spending.

Though Zhang wouldn't say exactly how much, his prices are higher than his competitors because of his expenditures on worker benefits. "Ninety-nine point nine percent of factories cannot do what we do," Zhang said. "We've been doing this long enough that we can survive. But we feel it's unfair that factories that don't fulfill their responsibility also survive. And so we're under pressure."

At the same time, as a manager trying to do right by his employees, he wonders where his responsibilities end. Are air conditioners a human right? What if installing air conditioners and then paying for the electricity they use becomes the tipping point that pushes him out of business?

Costs are rising across the board. Beijing's decision to revaluate the renminbi in July 2005, and the successive loosening of the trading band around the currency, have hurt his bottom line. Power shortages are driving up the price of electricity. Local officials are pushing up the minimum wage 20 percent a year. "In the Pearl River Delta region, the average salary in a legal factory like ours has reached $120 to $150. But factories in Vietnam that make the same products, their salary is $60 to $90. Timberland will move where the costs are low," he said.

Zhang understands why. He has been to the United States and seen how little clothing sold for there. He knows American shoppers, like Chinese shoppers, want bargains. He knows Western brands have to source from abroad, where costs are cheaper than in domestic factories, to survive their own tough competition at home. "Everyone wants as much as possible for as little money as possible," he said.

But that doesn't make it any easier to stomach buyers' tough negotiations. He has tried to raise his prices, but his customers won't accept it. Even a factory that has gone to great lengths to listen to its workers, to treat them fairly, to provide a safe working environment—even a factory like this could lose orders in a heartbeat to a cheaper competitor. Zhang has heard of buyers switching their orders to countries like India, Bangladesh, Thailand and Vietnam to avoid China's rising labor costs. These developments worry him.

One night in summer 2007, Zhang took an executive from a German retailer and two German journalists to dinner at his favorite restaurant, a modest local eatery that kept both televisions and air conditioners running at full blast. "Both buyers and factories should have social responsibility," he said, when the conversation turned to the relationship between multinationals and their Chinese suppliers. The Germans tucked into the sweet buns, fried shrimp and pigeon, awaiting interpretation from Zhang's young female assistant. Zhang continued: Buyers should leave more on the table for factories that follow the law. He wanted a "win-win" situation, where factories earned a reasonable profit and so did buyers.

Zhang had been thinking about moving Chai Da deeper inland in China to lower his costs, but the infrastructure wasn't there yet. Guangdong's greatest advantage was its range of suppliers of everything a manufacturer could need—the so-called cluster effect. Inland provinces had no clusters. If a machine broke down or he ran out of thread, his production line would be down for too long before help arrived.

As an interim measure, Zhang's boss, the owner of the factory, had hit on another strategy to improve its bottom line: develop its own brand. Working with designers from Austria, the company developed snowboarding pants and jackets that could undercut top brands on price, but that would still leave room for a healthy profit for Chai Da. They were thinking of expanding into women's fashion. If Chai Dai couldn't beat the brands, it was going to join them. "The market," Zhang said, "doesn't believe in tears."

HALFWAY ACROSS THE COUNTRY in a province outside Shanghai, another clothing factory manager was finding a way to make a profit without having to create his own brand. Yin Guoxin structured the manufacturing company he runs, Chenfeng, on the belief that treating his workers well would be good for his bottom line.

Chenfeng employs more than 11,000 people in two factories producing clothing for some of the biggest brands in the business: Adidas, Liz Claiborne, Eddie Bauer, Jones New York, Uniqlo of Japan. Its newer factory is located an hour and a half's drive outside of Shanghai, on Chenfeng Road. Housed in several solid gray stone fortresses with green mirrored windows, the plant would not be out of place in an American business park. Inside, the assembly lines are immaculate and brightly lit, imbued with an air of calm and order absent at other Chinese factories. The shop floor is fully air conditioned and stocked with new machines.

Yin, who is in his forties but looks at least a decade younger, started his career as a shop floor worker stitching pants in the early 1980s. Paid by the pair, he realized that when he was motivated, he worked more efficiently. And he noticed that if he and the other members of his production team each specialized in certain tasks, they would finish more pairs of pants.

Years later, he traveled to Sanya, the resort town on the southern Chinese island of Hainan, for a reunion. Late one night, he walked into a Western restaurant looking for dinner. The waiter there encouraged him to leave because, he told him, the food wasn't very good and there were hardly any customers.

In the waiter's sabotage, Yin saw a business lesson. "I told my staff these kind of people are terrorists within the company who want it to go bankrupt," Yin said. "If you treat the money you spend on your staff as costs, you might end up with workers like that."

This, he argued when we met in the summer of 2006, was Chinese factories' Achilles' heel. "The price of Chinese products is low because of their bad reputation," he said. "It's a vicious cycle: You treat workers as a cost, and to make things cheaper you need to cut costs and the price falls." Treat workers better, incur fewer costs of turnover, make better products and you could charge more for your product.

When he took over operation of Chenfeng, Yin looked for ways to inspire his employees, to make them passionate about their work. He invested heavily in worker dormitories. Managers also started a competition to encourage workers to design clothes themselves.

Yin paid for every employee's ticket home on Chinese holidays. He invited academics and labor specialists to train his managers in the labor law, insurance benefits and corporate social responsibility. Managers then trained employees in the same issues, so they knew their rights. He spent at least $62 on welfare benefits for each employee every month.

Instead of trying to find ways to reduce his outlay on payroll, Yin set targets to raise wages by increasing the piece rate. In 2005, the average wage was $158. In 2006, he aimed to raise the wage to $171; in 2007, to $197. Mindful of international buyers' codes of conduct, he tried to limit the factory's weekly working hours to 60.

He offered other services to buyers as well, including fabric sourcing and design advice. Chenfeng's turnover was only 1 percent to 2 percent a month, an extremely low figure for a Chinese factory. Like Zhang, he found better worker retention meant that he had more productive employees and more reliable quality, since his staff were familiar with their work.

Yin was choosy about his customers. He declined to do business with people who he felt were only interested in securing the lowest price possible. He has refused to do business with Wal-Mart or even to allow executives from the retailer into his factory. Mary Zhou, a Shanghai-based manager for social and environmental affairs at Adidas who has worked with Chenfeng, says Yin accepts only the best orders. "They only focus on high-level products," she told me. Zhou added that Chenfeng's products are still competitively priced. Yin wouldn't say how much more expensive his products were than his rivals'.

Yin's strategy followed textbook business principles: Motivate employees to perform, deliver consistent product, focus on quality and efficiency and add value for the customer. These should be the gospel for a country whose manufacturing prowess has inspired fear in factory towns around the world. But in China's labor-

intensive manufacturing sector, Yin was a pioneer. His factory attracted visitors from around the world.

"It's not about the bottom line for him," said one of these visitors, a compliance executive from a large American company that
buys from Chenfeng. "He understands that this strategy can give
him a competitive advantage. He understands that these issues are
at the core of his success." In February 2006, the Fair Labor Association, the organization that monitors conditions in factories, quietly approved Chenfeng as its first participating supplier. At the
time, all the other members were large international brands.

Yin may have been picky about his customers, but he still chafed
at the contradictory requirements of some of their auditing programs. One customer insisted his fire exit signs be blue, another
required them to be red. The best sign, Yin told them, was the one
his workers could find in an emergency.

At other times, his customers' demands for a 60-hour workweek have conflicted with his employees' desire to spend a few
days at home with their family every month. An employee might
ask to work more overtime before her vacation, so she wouldn't
have to sacrifice her salary to see her family. But Chenfeng's customers would argue for strict limits to working hours, regardless of
the situation.

In these cases, Yin, who admitted that he had in the past forged
documents to pass compliance audits, turned the widespread falsification problem to his advantage. He used the threat of falsification as a bargaining chip. "My goal is to meet the demands of my
employees," he said. "Whenever customers ask me to correct this, I
tell them that there's nothing I can do. If I have to correct it, I'll
have to cheat."

Yin was not perfect. One compliance executive who deals with
Chenfeng says the factory still exceeds China's legal working hours,
although not by much.

Other workers declined insurance coverage, fearing they would not be able to recoup the money they paid into the government system if they moved to another region. Under the Chinese welfare system, insured workers were designated a hospital near the factory for their health care. Yin worried that if, for example, a pregnant worker traveled to her hometown to have her baby at a hospital near her family, her insurance plan would not cover her medical expenses.

Yin was aware that his sensitivities to workers' needs put him in the minority among factory managers in China. He saw how some of his competitors spent their earnings on golf games and luxury cars for themselves instead of building better dormitories for their workers. But he also blamed a system that he argued had been created by uneven or nonexistent law enforcement by the Chinese government.

"Companies don't obey the regulations, and the government doesn't supervise and enforce the implementation of the law," he said. "Those who want to obey the law may find that they are less competitive in the market, so they will give up obeying the law. If you don't pay insurance for workers but I do, my costs will be higher than yours. If you delay paying salaries, you can use the money to run your factory, but if I pay regularly, I lose this opportunity."

This was unfair competition, which allowed Western companies to buy goods at prices so low they could only be produced under illegal conditions. "The government should create a platform for fair competition, otherwise problems will occur," Yin said. "If Wal-Mart asks for something for five renminbi, you can't do it but others can because they're illegal. If the government allows illegal activities, there is no fair competition.

"The government should create a platform of fair competition where companies compete with each other legally and fairly," he argued. Unusually for a factory manager, Yin actually has a say in political affairs: He has been a member of the National People's Congress, China's legislature, for a decade.

Yin also had advice for companies buying from China. Factories and brands should "treat each other as partners," he said. Buyers should choose their suppliers carefully. They "should respect [their] suppliers instead of treating them simply as manufacturers that they can choose as they like and switch among them at all time. If they think like that, they will lose money."

CHINESE GOVERNMENT POLICY toward industry, like its policy in other areas, is created through compromise among many ministries and agencies, each with its own constituency, culture and set of vested interests. Despite massive streamlining to reduce the size and improve the efficiency of the government bureaucracy, the extraordinarily rapid economic and social development of China since the 1980s has outpaced the development of government institutions. And although the government is becoming more transparent, its policymaking is not always open to outsiders, including the Chinese public. Speculation about this process in Beijing keeps a cottage industry of academics and researchers employed in think tanks and universities around the world.

The lines of institutional command, if not the substance of policy debates, are clear. Overarching responsibility for industrial policy lies with the State Council, China's cabinet, and the powerful National Development and Reform Commission, which sits under its wing. The NDRC sets economic and social policy: It does everything from approving large construction projects to drafting plans for specific sectors of the economy to overseeing agricultural development. Many other ministries are involved in industrial policy as well. Broadly speaking, the Ministry of Finance sets taxation policies; the Ministry of Commerce makes trade policy; the Ministry of

Land and Resources oversees the conversion of farmland to industrial plots; the State Environmental Protection Administration tries to lean on polluting industries; the State-Owned Assets Supervision and Administration Commission supervises key state-owned enterprises. The Ministry of Labor and Social Security drafts labor policies and oversees the social insurance scheme; the Ministry of Health's duties include occupational health. The State Administration of Work Safety looks after occupational safety.

Each of these organizations brings its own priorities to the table, complicating the policymaking process. In a July 2007 article, Drew Thompson, director of China studies and Starr Senior Fellow at the Nixon Center in Washington, D.C., listed 16 different government bodies that were represented on a committee to review the health care system.[2]

Among the problems with the diffusion of responsibility across multiple ministries is that issues can fall through the cracks, even at the very top. Infighting among government bodies, in China as elsewhere, can delay decisions. Cooperation by ministries that have overlapping jurisdiction in a particular area can be strained.

Although Beijing drafts policy, it has traditionally left enforcement of policy to local governments. Local officials sort through the policies handed down to them and decide how stringently to enforce them, depending on their area's particular situation. Because local governments rely heavily on the revenues they generate through taxes and other fees, there is little incentive for them to implement policies that would threaten that income stream. China has "a political economy where political power has been monetized to a high level because of the partially reformed economy with a completely unreformed political system," says Jason Kindopp, former leader of the China team at the Eurasia Group, a political risk advisory firm. "The political economy is highly decentralized and highly competitive among local provinces. These two things account for a lot of the dysfunctionality."[3]

As in other countries, it often takes a crisis to alert central government officials to the scale of a problem. The outbreak of Severe Acute Respiratory Syndrome, or SARS, in 2003, which forced the government to become more transparent and responsive to public health threats, and the more recent revelations that China was exporting food that contained harmful chemicals, which prompted an effort to upgrade regulations, were two such cases.

China is also realizing the downside of its historical reliance on local governments to enforce policy and is trying to bring more power back to the center. "The $64,000 question is, will the Hu and Wen administration be able to marshal enough political resources to achieve their policy objectives?" says Kindopp.[4] One question is whether Beijing can move away from a system where local governments compete to have the least stringent law enforcement and rack up economic growth, to one where the laws are enforced more evenly and social and environmental objectives gain greater priority.

The government is starting to take a stand on these issues. Beijing is stepping up its environmental protection efforts. It is strengthening legal protection of workers. There is also talk of the need for corporate social responsibility. These efforts are politically motivated, either to quell domestic unrest, to counter international critics or to dispel trade disputes. But they have not all received the warm welcome abroad that some Chinese leaders had been expecting.

In spring 2006, the central government released draft legislation on labor contracts for public comment. The law proposed the most extensive changes to China's labor rules in more than a decade, substantially strengthening legal protection for workers. Among the new policies the draft proposed were giving a larger role to the ACFTU in approving company decisions, imposing a standard probationary period for new hires and limiting the damages employers could seek from a worker who changed jobs in an industry with proprietary information.

The labor contract law was part of the drive by Hu Jintao, China's president, and premier Wen Jiabao to create a "harmonious society." The concept is an attempt to steer the country's focus away from encouraging rapid economic growth and toward lessening its negative side effects, including corruption, a widening income gap, rising popular unrest, pollution and a social safety net full of holes.

But harmonious labor relations meant different things to different people. The legislation set off an intense debate. In the month after it was released, the draft attracted almost 192,000 comments, more than any other law in China's recent history except the constitution. Most of these comments came from workers. But there were also suggestions from state-owned companies, unions and multinationals.

The American Chamber of Commerce in Shanghai, the US-China Business Council (USCBC) and the European Union Chamber of Commerce in China, which represent the interests of their multinational members, all voiced concerns to the Chinese government. AmCham Shanghai's concerns reportedly filled 42 pages.[5] In its statement, the USCBC, whose members include Microsoft, Coca-Cola, General Motors and Wal-Mart, warned that the law could "reduce employment opportunities for PRC workers and negatively impact the PRC's competitiveness and appeal as a destination for foreign investment."[6] The foreign business chambers touched a nerve. Their comments were interpreted by the media to imply that the draft law would make them think twice about investing in China.

Their concerns, which were picked up by the international press, marked an important milestone. China—and its manufacturing sector—had become so important to the global economy that its labor laws were the subject of an international debate played out on the pages of the New York Times.

Foreign business groups' reservations may have been partly a reflection of the same frustration factory managers Zhang and Yin felt about uneven law enforcement. Western investors that directly employ people in China (rather than simply outsource manufacturing) say they face more pressure to comply with the law than do private Chinese companies. Some investors speculate that this might be because Western investors lack the government connections that some local investors can rely on to evade enforcement.

Labor advocates inside and outside China were unsympathetic. They accused the chambers of hypocrisy. Since the antisweatshop movement of the 1990s, U.S. and European companies had been public champions of strong labor protection. Now, they were publicly critiquing legislation that would raise Chinese labor standards.

Global Labor Strategies, a project created by not-for-profit foundation Global Movement Strategies, published a report that accused the groups of trying to hold Chinese labor standards down, contradicting their own policies. It wrote: "US based corporations have repeatedly argued that they are raising human and labor rights standards abroad. . . . But US based corporations are trying to block legislation designed to improve the remuneration, treatment, health and safety, and other standards of Chinese workers."[7]

In December 2006, a second draft of the law was presented to the National People's Congress, China's legislature. The draft addressed the concerns of the foreign business chambers, amending a requirement on the maximum length of a probationary period for new hires and making clear which company rules required employee input to be changed.[8]

And yet the finger pointing continued. The following spring, Liu Cheng, law professor at Shanghai Normal University, toured the United States, speaking to Congress, workers, unions and labor groups about the law. He was introduced as an adviser to the government on the labor law and argued in its favor.

In April 2007, the USCBC sought to clarify its position. In a statement, the group said it felt it had been misrepresented by Global Labor Strategies and the media. It pointed out that it had not opposed the law, merely criticized it, and that while "substandard" working conditions might happen in local companies and those owned by investors from other countries, they rarely occurred in enterprises directly owned by U.S. companies. "US companies are part of the solution, not the problem," the business group said in a statement on its Web site. "US companies tend to bring their global employment and EHS practices and standards to their facilities in China. In most cases, these practices and standards exceed local law. US companies generally act as models for the improvement of employment and EHS standards in China."[9]

The same month, the United Steelworkers, the largest industrial union in North America, came out in support of the proposed legislation. Leo Gerard, the union's president, called the American Chamber's efforts an "immoral campaign to undermine Chinese workers' rights." AmCham denied that it had lobbied against the legislation.[10]

Finally, in June, after brick kilns in Shanxi province were revealed to be using slave and child labor, the National People's Congress approved the legislation, introducing a raft of new requirements for employers. The Law of the People's Republic of China on Employment Contracts included a requirement that companies discuss any rules or regulations that would have an immediate impact on employees with their representatives or with employees themselves. If employees disapproved, the rule would need to be "improved" after further consultation. It also required companies that wanted to lay off more than 20 employees to inform the union and listen to its views. An earlier draft had required companies to obtain union approval.

The law also addressed common abuses in the manufacturing sector. It barred employers from firing an employee who had or was suspected of having an occupational disease. And it prohibited the confiscation of identification cards, which is common among export factories.[11] It was, in short, a dramatic strengthening of China's protection of labor.

Although other measures that foreign investors had criticized remained in the law, the legislature went out of its way to allay their concerns in a way unimaginable in a country with a strong legal system. "If there is some bias in the application of the law, it would be in favor of foreign investors because local governments have great tolerance for foreign investors in order to attract and retain investment," the Associated Press quoted Xin Chunying, deputy chairwoman of the law committee of the NPC's Standing Committee, as saying. "Even if they (companies) violate labor law, they (officials) are still hesitant to resist them."[12] In other words, if you violate the law, we'll probably look the other way.

THE DEBATE OVER the labor contract law came at a time when Chinese exports were already a hot topic internationally. The country's surging shipments abroad were prompting governments around the world to clamp down on Chinese-made products, from furniture to shoes to towels. China's poor labor and environmental protection record continued to make headlines overseas as well: One day it was accusations that iPods were made under bad conditions, another day it was toys, another day clothing.

Some Chinese companies, government bodies and industry associations hit on corporate social responsibility (CSR) as one way to fight back. Promoting CSR, itself a Western concept, was a way to counter international criticism of the country's labor and environmental practices. The textile and clothing industries took the lead.

In the early 2000s, concerns began to mount about what would happen to global textiles and clothing production after the Multi-

Fiber Arrangement (MFA), the agreement that had governed the global trade in textiles and apparel since the 1970s, expired in 2005. In 2003, China accounted for 17 percent of global trade in textiles and apparel. In 2004, the World Trade Organization said that the country's share could rise to more than 50 percent.[13]

The MFA had established a system of quotas for production of certain items that effectively distributed clothing manufacturing around the world. When these quotas were lifted, buyers were expected to swiftly shift production to China, making it the dominant clothing producer in the world. Other countries that had been granted quotas to produce clothing under the MFA were concerned about losing business to China. American manufacturers, fearing further job losses, had started to complain. In November 2003, the U.S. government imposed a quota on imports of Chinese bras, dressing gowns and knitted fabrics. It was only the beginning of a global showdown on Chinese-made textiles.

The China National Textile and Apparel Council (CNTAC) was on the front lines of this dispute. Formerly the Chinese government's Ministry of Textiles, CNTAC is an umbrella organization that represents the interests of Chinese textile and apparel makers. The import quotas and antidumping duties were creating challenges for CNTAC's members. At the same time, as part of the anti-sweatshop movement, Chinese clothing manufacturers were also under increasing pressure from foreign buyers and NGOs to improve working conditions.

"The Chinese textile industry faces a challenge from the global market, especially on three issues—first is antidumping, second is intellectual property and third is corporate social responsibility," Xie Fang, a CNTAC official, told me when we met. "China has to face it and cope with it."

CNTAC knew that China's competitive advantage in textiles was partly a reflection of its lower costs of labor, land and raw materials. But it also knew that few of its members were following

Chinese law on working hours, that most employed workers without contracts, that local governments were complicit in helping manufacturers violate the law. "We have to understand that the Chinese law, especially the labor law and regulations concerning working hours, are pretty much beyond the reality of China's industrial situation," said Fang Xilin, another CNTAC official. "Many factory managers tell me there is no way they can follow the law and survive. What we can do is try to find a way to minimize the gap between the legislation and the practice," he added.

CNTAC decided to kill two birds with one stone by introducing its own code of conduct or, as it preferred to call it, a "management system," to help Chinese manufacturers comply with the law. It called the code CSC9000T.

The organization hoped that CSC9000T, released in May 2005, would help deflect concerns about China's apparel factories from the antisweatshop movement and encourage manufacturers to raise prices. That would help defuse trade disputes and accusations of dumping by Chinese companies. A manufacturer is considered to be dumping if it exports goods for less than the cost of production or the dominant price in its home market and causes what is commonly called "material injury" to the industry in the export market.

CSC9000T covers the same ground as international codes of conduct: no child or forced labor, fair wages and welfare benefits, no discrimination, harrassment or abuse, occupational health and safety, labor contracts and trade unions and collective bargaining. But unlike many codes, CSC9000T is voluntary. It has no audits that factories pass or fail, no certification system that gives factories a stamp of approval. CNTAC was unimpressed with the auditing in China. "We could say that the auditing factory system doesn't make very good results in China," Xie said.

Intead of monitoring factories against a fixed code, CSC9000T shows managers how they could improve the conditions in their factories and increase profitability. Treating workers better, CNTAC argued, would improve employee loyalty, reduce turnover and boost efficiency.

Of course, following CSC9000T would increase a factory's costs, Xie admitted, but not enough to make China less competitive. Perhaps the improvements in working conditions would add one dollar to the price of a pair of pants, he supposed. "With one dollar, you can do a lot of stuff in CSR and make a lot of improvement in factories," Xie concluded. While this is true, one dollar at the factory gate is a significant difference.

Still, having better conditions might give China's textile factories greater bargaining power with international buyers, Xie said. In 2006, CNTAC rolled out a pilot of CSC9000T with 10 factories, including an evaluation of the factory's situation and training in the system and in specific issues.

Despite its admirable aims, CSC9000T was not much more than a gesture. CNTAC only assigned a handful of employees to work on the system and a budget of about $395,000 for the pilot, according to Xie and Fang. The aim was to train external organizations, such as third-party auditing firms, in the system and, after the pilot, to shift responsibility for implementing it to them. CNTAC was already working with SGS and TÜV Rheinland, a German auditing firm.

Nor was it clear how enthusiastically the Chinese government supported the standard. CNTAC said it had been working closely with the Ministry of Commerce and the National Development and Reform Commission as well as the ACFTU, but not the Ministry of Labor and Social Security, the natural partner for such an initiative. But the labor ministry had not opposed CSC9000T and in fact had attended meetings with CNTAC, Xie said. "In China, this kind of support is good enough," he added.

Since then, individual companies and government institutions have also started making symbolic efforts to promote CSR. Chinese companies have started publishing reports on their CSR activities.

The Shenzhen Bureau of Labor and Social Security and the Shenzhen Stock Exchange, China's second-largest stock market, have issued instructions for companies on CSR. The stock exchange's instructions include a number of suggestions on labor and the environment. Like CSC9000T, they discourage the use of forced labor and excessive overtime and encourage the implementation of good health and safety practices, social benefits and paid leave.[14]

The state-controlled media report more frequently not only on CSR, but also on the conflicting Western demands for low prices and good working conditions. "Customers want it cheap, workers pay heavy price," read one headline in the *China Daily*, the government mouthpiece. The piece neglected to mention China's poor law enforcement as one of the reasons factories struggled to meet buyers' demands.

Some observers, however, are making the connection. "In China we need to regulate social responsibility strictly," Zheng Gongcheng, a professor at Beijing's Renmin University, told the *South China Morning Post*. "China has a surplus of labor, and it is too easy for companies to tread roughshod over their employees. We need to bring CSR into the legislative arena. We need new laws and better enforcement."[15]

Some companies in the Pearl River Delta are trying to position themselves as socially responsible manufacturers. After Foxconn, the Taiwanese contract manufacturer that assembles the iPod for Apple in China, was accused of having sweatshop conditions, the group opened its factory to journalists to show them new facilities it had built for workers.[16] Following its own investigation, Apple reported that many of the allegations about Foxconn were unfounded. However, it did discover that employees worked longer than the 60 hours its code of conduct requires about 35 percent of the time and worked more than six days in a row 25 percent of the time.[17] Esquel, a leading manufacturer of premium cotton shirts that supplies Banana Republic, Polo Ralph Lauren, Burberry and Tommy Hilfiger, among others, also touts its socially responsible initatives.

But it does seem odd to make social responsibility the priority in a country where even the most basic laws on labor and the environment are still routinely broken. "You can only start talking about CSR when you hit compliance and move beyond," says Stephen Frost, director of CSR Asia, the Hong Kong–based consultancy. He says that despite the increased attention to these issues in China in recent years, most companies' CSR programs are stalled. "CSR is bogged down in philanthropy and public relations. And actually I think to some degree we're going backwards," Frost adds.[18]

Some social compliance executives doubt whether CSR is the right way to approach these issues in a country with as widespread law enforcement problems as China. Conferences on CSR in China, which have proliferated in the last few years, rarely focus on the core issues facing multinationals and their suppliers. One I attended in Hong Kong in early 2006 featured executives from disparate industries making self-congratulatory presentations about their community relations programs. Less than an hour away in southern China, thousands of factories were underpaying and overworking their employees.

Not all of the industry's programs are like this, of course. But plenty are. "You go to these CSR conferences and it's so frustrating because there are a whole bunch of people talking about philanthropy," says one compliance executive at a European company who is a regular speaker at CSR seminars. "These are real business decisions!"

Ultimately, the only way to lessen the social and environmental cost of the China price is for the Chinese government to do more.

The labor contract law and, to a lesser extent, the promotion of CSR, are steps in the right direction. But more policies are not the answer. Enforcement of laws is.

At least one local government is starting to become more picky about whom it gives permission to invest. Shenzhen officials turned away one Italian businessman who was looking to open a leather tannery on the grounds that his factory was too polluting. He finally settled in Xiaolan, a district in the city of Zhongshan in the province's less developed west. Even there, to get approval from government officials to invest, he had to spend $200,000 on a water treatment system to ensure that he didn't discharge toxic chemicals into the water supply.

"They're readjusting things," he told me, referring to the Chinese government. "They do things properly. I'm talking about safety, issues linked to the environment."

The manager of a small clothing factory in Foshan in western Guangdong that produced for the domestic Chinese market said local authorities came to inspect the factory more often than they used to. The officials have asked the manager to open the windows and improve fire safety procedures.

One wealthy district in Shenzhen has started conducting due diligence on potential investors in the area to screen out factory managers who may be fleeing labor disputes in another jurisdiction. "They don't want any bad stories" in the press, said a person familiar with the district's plans. Of course, this person admits, some investors still bribe their way through the process.

In 2006, authorities in Dongguan, a major shoe, clothing and electronics production hub in Guangdong province, imposed heavy fines on Fountain Set, a leading knitted fabric manufacturer that produced for Gap, Calvin Klein, Nike and Victoria's Secret, on the grounds that the factory had been dumping polluted wastewater directly into a local river.

The following year, Dongguan's mayor warned polluting Hong

Kong factories in the city that they had a year to clean up their operations. Polluting factories in industries like electroplating, dyeing and printing would be denied new licenses to operate.[19]

Andy Rothman, China macro strategist for brokerage CLSA, wrote in a note to investors that the Communist Party's growing attention to water pollution would have a growing impact on the investment environment. The party's drive to clean up its water supply "represents a significant risk for firms in the sectors that produce the most industrial wastewater: chemicals, power, steel and nonferrous metals, textiles, processed food and paper."[20]

The Guangdong government has started publishing a black list of companies that violate the labor law. In September 2005, the province's department of labor and social security released a list of 20 employers that had failed to pay wages or broken the rules in other ways. The following summer, it published a list of 30 companies, including foreign-invested firms, that owed back wages of more than $2.6 million to thousands of workers.[21] Shenzhen authorities have also started naming, shaming and fining companies that violate the labor law. And the central government's State Environmental Protection Administration has started drawing up lists of companies that violate environmental laws.

These are still token gestures—killing the chicken to scare the monkey, as the Chinese saying goes. Even as these black lists were being published, it was business as usual for countless other factories violating the law in Guangdong province and across the country. Law enforcement cannot be a token gesture. Otherwise it has no credibility, no teeth.

"The state is the only organization with anything approaching the capacity . . . to ensure compliance with law," says one Hong Kong–based consultant who works with factories and brands to improve compliance. "And the only way this works is as it works in the U.S. Most companies in the U.S. will never be audited by an industrial hygienist from the state of whatever state they're in. But what keeps them on their toes is that they might be. Some guy might come waltzing into your factory one day and say, 'Okay, here's my badge, and I'm here to check. And if you've got a violation of this sort, you're shut down. And if you don't shut down, we've got the police around this afternoon arresting you.'"[22]

Of course, no country, including the United States, enforces its labor and environmental laws perfectly. But a more even enforcement of the laws on the books would serve the Chinese government's interests in several ways. It would help discourage investment in the resource-intensive, energy-intensive polluting industries that the government is, in theory at least, trying to keep in check.

Better law enforcement would compel factory managers to find ways to work more efficiently. It would reduce medical bills for occupational illness by reducing the hazards on the job. It would help defuse trade disputes by raising the price of Chinese-made goods. And it would get foreign critics off China's back by showing that the government is serious about raising its labor and environmental standards.

Violations of labor rights are already provoking widespread unrest, which threatens the social stability that is the foundation of the Communist Party's legitimacy, economic growth and the country's attractiveness as a destination for foreign investment. And by failing to enforce its laws, China limits its own potential in manufacturing. More sophisticated industries require a more sophisticated regulatory structure.

Of course, more even enforcement of the law would doubtless threaten the cozy relationships between local officials and the industries they are supposed to be supervising. A lot of golf outings, Rolex purchases, and red envelope stuffing would have to be canceled. Government officials would have to divest their shares in local businesses. Officials from labor inspection bureaus might have to leave their air conditioned offices more often.

This might be more than these local governments could tolerate. And the dislocation of jobs that might occur were officials to start cracking down on more than a handful of investors cannot be dismissed. It would be significant.

But the alternative is clear. Without better law enforcement, China will have to continue to contend with the political and economic consequences of rising labor activism, worsening pollution, a mounting health care bill and a widening income gap. These problems are not going away on their own.

Chapter 9

THE FUTURE OF THE
CHINA PRICE

SAM SLIDES BEHIND THE WHEEL of his new black Honda and noses the car into Friday morning traffic. It's a hot, sunny June morning in Changsha, capital of central Hunan province, and everything seems to be falling into place.

Beside him sits his wife Jasmine, eight months pregnant and radiant in a yellow dress. High school sweethearts, they married at 21. Now, at 23, they're about to start a family in a brand-new gated community. Sam, whose name, like those of other members of his family, has been changed, is looking forward to making use of the development's two swimming pools and basketball court. In a few years, they plan to build a house in the mountains where they can entertain family and friends on the weekends.

The Honda heads out of town into the verdant countryside toward Jasmine's father's towel factory. Towels, a key Hunan export, have been the family's mainstay for nearly two decades. Sam married into the job of overseeing the plant's $5 million in annual sales.

The road narrows and Sam slows to accommodate farmers swaying on bicycles. On either side are rice paddies and family farm plots. That's where the first sign of changes ahead appears. Trees.

Several years ago, farmers on the outskirts of Changsha realized they could make good money growing trees. They planted family plots in Hunan's fertile soil and hung signs on trees near the road advertising their cell phone numbers. Soon enough, the farmers who worked at Sam's factory were demanding higher wages because they could make better money from trees.

The factory, which relies mostly on local labor, had no choice but to capitulate. "Salaries are going up and up," Sam sighs from behind the wheel. The labor market has tightened, too, as other factories have opened in the area. The government is hiking the minimum wage in Changsha. Sam figures he has three, maybe five more years before his factory loses its competitive edge.

This is where the next boom in Chinese manufacturing is supposed to take place. Conventional wisdom holds that rising costs of everything from labor to land on the coasts are driving factories in labor-intensive consumer industries deep into the country's heartland, to provinces like Hunan, in pursuit of lower prices. But in China's fast-forward economy, investors are finding things aren't as cheap or plentiful as they used to be. And the workers aren't pushovers, either.

Thanks in part to Chinese government policies, the country's labor-intensive export factories have for most of the past decade operated almost in defiance of the rules of economics, enjoying stagnant wages, ample coastal land near the ports and a seemingly endless supply of pliant labor. Government incentives, including subsidized electricity and generous tax breaks, have helped keep the ordinary forces of a market economy at bay. The low prices that this combination of factors produced earned China the enviable position of the world's dominant producer in a huge variety of products. But this fortuitous situation couldn't last. "This is an advantage that expires," says Arthur Kroeber, managing director of Dragonomics, a research and advisory group that specializes in the Chinese economy.[1]

Jonathan Anderson, former head of Asian economics at invest-ment bank UBS, calls it "the end of China's supposed absolute man-ufacturing domination."[2] He argues that China will revert to a more normal trading pattern, where it gains market share in some areas and loses it in others. For any other country, this would be a natural assumption, devoid of drama. For the world's emerging superpower and a world hooked on its cheap products, it is anything but.

SAM'S FACTORY is a series of gloomy, medieval rooms arranged in a U shape, a century behind the modern plants on the coasts. In one dark, humid room, a man uses a long metal pole to stuff tan towel fabric into a hole in the side of a machine. The machine spits out the towels bleached white. Another room houses enormous towel-printing machines and buckets of viscous paint. In yet another room sit rows of sewing machines and stacks of finished towels.

The room where the factory greets customers is equally spar-tan. Lined with black overstuffed sofas and matching chairs, it buzzes with horseflies. The windowsills are still wrapped in plastic from the manufacturer. Off this room is the boss's office and a tiny, windowless showroom hung with dozens of beach towels. If you have ever bought a towel from a small store near the beach, it prob-ably came from a factory like this.

This is the oldest towel factory in town. In 1987, Sam's father-in-law, Fang, was the village chief. He decided to go into business making towels and exporting them. Fang borrowed the equivalent of just under $40,000 at today's exchange rates, hired 20 of his neighbors, and started making towels that he sold to foreign cus-tomers through a trade association. Over time, the factory ex-panded to employ 400 people, producing 20,000 towels a day. Fang wouldn't even consider an order smaller than 2,000 towels. Business was good in the early days of China's export manufacturing boom: As recently as 1996, Fang was earning margins of 20 percent.

But, inevitably, competition arrived. Towel manufacturing took off, not only in Hunan but around the country. Cotton prices soared. So did wages, especially as the tree business matured. By the summer of 2006, when we spoke, Fang claimed he was paying his workers $105 a month, a wage comparable to what they might have earned in coastal areas. In Chinese factories, it's hard to know for sure how much managers actually pay their employees. But it's clear that the legal minimum wage in Changsha is rising.

Labor, which once accounted for 5 percent of his costs, had risen to 15 percent, Fang said. But the surge in towel factories—Fang counts 20 main competitors—was driving prices down every year. "Wages are going up, prices are coming down," Fang says matter-of-factly, sitting in the factory's fly-infested conference room. "Our profits are smaller."

It is the refrain of every Chinese factory. Like many other industries in which competition in China has beat prices down to next to nothing, Chinese towel makers are now facing international sanction because of their low prices. The United States has imposed quotas on Chinese towel imports. Taiwanese towel makers, outraged by the dominance of Chinese towels in their domestic market, took Beijing to the World Trade Organization in 2006.

Fang is unmoved by the changing market situation, perhaps because at 50 years old, he hopes to hand over the business to his son-in-law, perhaps because he can still make a living here in Hunan. Moving the factory elsewhere would be difficult because he'd have to train another group of workers. He has employees who have been working for him for five years, an eternity in coastal China. "We're considering the situation," he says.

Fang is tall, with a flat face and a thick Hunan accent, delivered through teeth etched with dark brown stains. At meals, Fang rolls up his pants to his knees, exposing two skinny, hairless calves. He likes a strong drink, especially with friends, and is partial to the clear local liquor that burns going down. He works a seven-day week, starting each day at 7:30 A.M., and smokes three packs of cigarettes a day.

Sam, however, is looking past this daily grind. He is watching the trends in global manufacturing carefully. "Within fifteen years, because costs in China are too high, many factories will open in India and Pakistan, and also in Vietnam. In these places, costs are very cheap—the cost of workers, of yarn," he says.

Later that day, Fang and Sam meet two of Fang's friends and business associates at an empty local restaurant. The friends arrive with women in tow. The women, not the men's wives, have long, permed hair and high heels and embroidered jeans—eye candy in this farming town. Women are an important part of deal making in China, where prostitutes are often part of the entertainment of customers and other contacts. That night, Sam will arrange for a striking young lady to accompany a visiting customer for an evening of dinner, drinking and karaoke. ("In business, we have to be a little spoiled," the customer told me. "Otherwise, it doesn't work.")

The women drink milk while the men polish off two bottles of the clear liquor. Lunch is gourd with peppers, egg yolks cooked on a bed of green peppers, winter melon soup, broiled fish and bowls of white rice. The decibel level rises as the liquor takes effect.

This is not Sam's idea of a good time. As he watches his father-in-law tuck into a bottle of liquor, he says quietly, "If I ran a factory, I think I would drink every day." Sam has seen the writing on the wall for Hunan towels and staked his future away from his father-in-law's factory. He is cultivating relationships with bank managers, whom he entertains on a regular basis over karaoke and dinner. He has also started a trading business, sourcing T-shirts and slippers from other Chinese factories for customers in Europe and the United States. It's a decision based on economic as well as quality-of-life considerations. "If I worked in the factory, I'd be busy every day. I don't like that," he says. "If I ran a trading company, I'd work five and a half days a week and I could go out and drink beer at night."

Ten years from now, he'd like to move into fashion, or real estate. Then he'll buy a BMW, Sam says. He has already test-driven a 5-series, just to see how it felt.

CHINA HAS BECOME a victim of its own success as the world's leading manufacturer of labor-intensive consumer goods. The rush of investment in factories has driven down profit margins and driven up prices of everything from raw materials to labor to power.

As is inevitable as any economy develops, some of China's competitive advantages as a labor-intensive manufacturing powerhouse over the past three decades are eroding. The forces that will shape China's manufacturing sector in coming decades are already clear: rising wages and material costs, greater demand for unionization, a higher risk of litigation, a dwindling supply of cheap workers, calls for better product quality and safety and substantial downward pressure on margins.

Some factories will try to mitigate these factors by moving up the value chain into design, research and development, and by creating their own brands. Others will look to acquire rivals and increase economies of scale. Some will go out of business.

Wages are rising fast in both coastal and inland cities. In Wuhan, in Hubei province, the urban minimum wage has nearly tripled since 1995, rising to $76 a month in February 2007. The city of Wuxi in Jiangsu province also nearly tripled its wage over the same period. The government in Changsha, near Sam's factory, raised the legal minimum wage in its central district from $63 a month in 2005–2006 to $79 the following year. Wages in districts already attracting heavy manufacturing investment, such as Ningbo, are rising even faster.

The gap between China's wages and the rest of the world's means that manufacturing pay in China is likely to remain lower than in the United States or Europe for years. But the gap is shrinking fast. David Dollar, the World Bank's country director for China, has estimated that wages in China are growing two to three times faster than in other low-wage Asian economies.[3]

Even if most factories do not pay the minimum wage, as we've seen to be the case so far, as the economy develops, managers will face increasing market pressure from higher wages in other industries and regions. In Luzhou, a city in Sichuan province that has historically exported its labor to other provinces, the service sector has expanded rapidly to include McDonald's, shopping centers and hotels. In 2003, restaurants in the city's Jiangyang district paid staff $33 a month, in addition to free accommodation and meals. By the following year, wages had risen to between $53 and $59, similar to the minimum wage in Dongguan in Guangdong province at the time.

The hopes that China's hinterland would offer rock-bottom costs were misplaced. "Labor costs in China must rise very quickly. Not slowly, very fast. The phase of low-cost labor is over," says Su Zhi, deputy director of the Bureau of Health Supervision, which is affiliated with the Ministry of Health. Labor is not the only input that is becoming more dear. Costs of raw material and land are rising as well. Crucially, the renminbi is being slowly revalued.

The China price has been rising since 2004. As Jonathan Anderson of UBS pointed out in an April 2007 report, Chinese manufacturing export prices fell in U.S. dollar terms an average of 2 percent every year between 1996 and 2003. But since 2004, the trend has reversed: Export prices in U.S. dollar terms have been rising an average 2 percent every year.[4] Export prices are rising for everything from clothing to electronics. Anderson also notes that prices from other low-end export countries such as the Philippines, Taiwan, Thailand and Malaysia have been rising in tandem with those from China.

Li & Fung, the Hong Kong-based sourcing company, said that it saw a 2 percent to 3 percent increase in the prices its clients were paying for goods in 2006, the first such rise in more than six years.[5]

This shift has global implications. If in the late 1990s China was accused of "exporting deflation," could it now be "exporting inflation"? As the rising export prices became clear, economists began to debate this possibility. So far, there is no clear evidence that this is the case. Kroeber, the Dragonomics consultant, disagrees with the idea that China ever exported deflation, since it lowered the prices of manufactured goods but also raised the price of commodities at the same time. "China is not exporting inflation," he told me. "China is losing the lowest end of its exports."

Indeed, it's hard to imagine the brands and retailers whose customers have come to expect constant price declines paying substantially more for the goods they buy from overseas. Retailers and brands will have to find other ways to improve efficiency and cut costs out of their supply chains. They will also have to look for countries that can provide lower prices—along with the industry clusters, quality and reliability that China offers—or persuade their shareholders to tolerate slimmer profit margins, which seems unlikely. Most buyers in China cannot conceive of lowering their margins, even as they continue to squeeze their suppliers' margins.

Higher export prices from China are already driving some buyers elsewhere. A veteran Hong Kong–based buyer who supplies Wal-Mart says he will start considering buying from other countries. An executive from a Spanish retail chain says she plans to lower the portion of goods she orders in China from 50 percent of her total purchasing to 30 percent. She is looking seriously at India, Vietnam, Bangladesh and Sri Lanka. One buyer from a major U.S.

restaurant chain that buys hundreds of millions of dollars' worth of goods per year says that he is planning to buy more from China but is also looking at "Vietnam, a bit at India and, eventually, at Africa." Stephen Frost, director of CSR Asia, the Hong Kong consultancy, says electronics companies he works with are considering shifting manufacturing to countries like Malaysia, Indonesia and Thailand because of higher costs.

Some manufacturing capacity in southern China has already migrated to Vietnam. Some 46 percent of the labor-intensive industries that moved from China to Vietnam in the second half of 2005 had been located in Guangdong, according to one academic.[6] Others, including the automotive industry, are looking to India, lured by investment incentives and the large pool of cheap assembly-line labor and engineers. Foreign direct investment in Vietnam and India is rising, though it is still a fraction of the amount of money that continues to pour into China.[7]

Increasingly, there is talk in Japanese business circles of a "China-plus-one" strategy: having operations in China as well as another country in the region to hedge against political and other risks in the world's fastest-growing economy.[8] To protect itself from the impact of potential trade disputes, Uniqlo, the Japanese apparel store, decided in 2006 to lower the share of clothing it sources from China from 90 percent to 60 percent.[9]

To be sure, no one is talking about leaving China entirely. There are strong forces that will keep manufacturing within its borders. China has the infrastructure in place—airports, ports, roads, workers—to remain a powerful force in manufacturing for decades to come. One of China's key competitive advantages is its use of industrial clusters. For some labor-intensive goods, the entire supply chain has moved to China, so that all the components, machinery repair shops and raw materials are clustered together within a two-hour drive of the factory. The faster lead times industries like clothing demand are harder to achieve without these clusters. It will take time to replicate the cluster effect in other countries with lower costs than China.

Not to mention the allure of the Chinese domestic market. Part of the attraction of shifting manufacturing to China has always been better access to its 1.3 billion consumers. "What is the real motivation for manufacturing abroad?" asks Kasra Ferdows, the Heisley Family chair of Global Manufacturing at Georgetown's McDonough School of Business. "The main motivation for putting production abroad is to be closer to their customers. It is not to make something cheap and bring it back."[10]

Of course, by this argument, companies that shift some manufacturing to other countries will gain access to those markets as well. Still, with the exception of India, no other market compares with China in terms of size. And, as destinations for contract manufacturing, other emerging markets in Asia lack some of China's charms. Vietnam's strong labor unions make it a more challenging place to operate. Ultimately, Vietnam's manufacturing workforce is tiny compared with China's: The entire population of Vietnam is only 85 million people, less than the population of Guangdong province.

India's infrastructure, including roads and ports, also lags far behind China's. According to one estimate, the total shipping time from India to the United States is between eight and 10 weeks, much longer than the two to three weeks for vessels heading from China to the United States.[11] It is harder to run the mammoth factories common in China in India. The country's labor activism also scares off some international investors.[12]

"The next ten years, I will guarantee you that China will be the force in production in every category of the world. I can almost guarantee that. In fact, I would put my money and bet on that today," says Bruce Rockowitz, president of the trading arm of Li & Fung, the large Hong Kong–based sourcing and logistics group.[13] Rockowitz predicts that as manufacturing of different products has been dispersed around the world over the past few decades, so in the future will it be distributed around China.

It's possible that the current search for cheaper manufacturers in Vietnam, Malaysia and elsewhere is evidence of a transition. After 1978, with significant investment from Hong Kong and Taiwan, light industry developed on the coasts, creating the clusters that make China so competitive. Now, as costs on the coasts rise, factories are looking for new locations where the cost savings outweigh the expense of moving. Low-end manufacturing may not end up in Hunan, but it could well flourish in other provinces, like Jiangxi. It won't stay for long, however, if costs continue to rise.

China is continuing to ascend the value chain in manufacturing, moving into the export of cars and motorcycles, industrial machinery and ships. In 2005, China exported more car parts than it bought from overseas for the first time. Exports of machinery and transportation equipment hit $352 billion in 2005, a sharp increase from five years earlier. The country is expected to replace Germany as the world's third-largest car manufacturer.[14] Already, Honda Motor produces cars for export in China. China's auto exports doubled in 2006.[15] It is expected to overtake South Korea as the largest shipbuilding country in the world.[16] Ford is expanding its purchases of parts in China. "We're barely scratching the surface in China," Bill Ford, the carmaker's chairman, told the *Wall Street Journal*.[17]

Indeed, the spring 2007 Canton Fair featured an entire hall full of industrial machinery. There were vacuum-packing machines, ice cream machines, golf carts, motorcycles and cars—all made in China. "The China price still exists," says Kroeber. "It's just migrating to a different category of goods, which is not necessarily good for people outside China."

And yet it is far from certain that China will be able to replicate its dominance in low-end manufacturing at the high end.

Lax law enforcement, an abundant supply of unskilled labor

and short-termist management served China well during this first phase of rowdy, rapid industrial development. But these factors will work against the country as it tries to move into industries where success is determined by technical skill, innovation and the soft skills of marketing and modern financial management.

The trend toward "modularization" of manufacturing, in which the process is broken up into steps that can be done by separate factories, has given Chinese plants an important role in the global supply chain—as low-margin commodity producers, not as innovators. Daniel Rosen, a consultant and visiting fellow at the Peter G. Peterson Institute for International Economics, argues that China's abundant supply of labor has made its factories much less reliant on machinery and technology than those in Japan and the West. This tendency "stacks the deck against Chinese producers" in less labor-intensive industries, he wrote in the *China Economic Quarterly*.[18]

Rosen argues that other features of the Chinese economy and business world—its inefficient financial markets, its relatively small patent base, its undeveloped legal system, its firms' reluctance to use information technology to bring greater transparency into their operations—will handicap its companies in the years to come, particularly as Chinese companies try to expand overseas. To be fair, these are all areas Beijing is trying to improve.

Chinese companies need not only better laws and regulations, but also a history of judicial interpretation in order to have greater predictability and clarity about activities in the marketplace. A reliable, predictable legal system is essential as China moves into higher-value-added goods.

Rosen cites the example of encouraging Chinese farmers to switch from producing grain to cultivating shiitake mushrooms, the more expensive variety prized in Japan. Exporting shiitake mushrooms is potentially much more lucrative (perhaps $10 a pound, compared to 10 cents a pound for grain) and well suited to China's large labor force. "The only problem," Rosen told me, "is that you can't get people to pay $10 a pound for anything if there's no assurance that there's no toxic residue all over the product."

Kroeber, whose company publishes the *China Economic Quarterly*, agrees. "The higher you move up the value chain, the more the regulatory framework, if it's well designed, actually becomes an advantage," he says. "The people who make the most money are actually the people with the best regulatory regimes."[19]

Other issues will handicap China's advantage as well. The dynamic now playing out on the streets of Shenzhen, where there are many unskilled middle school graduates like Luyuan, Meng and her colleagues but relatively few high school or college graduates with the skills that the city's electronics factories require, is being replicated around the country. The high cost of education relative to rural incomes has left a serious skills gap.

China has a severe shortage of skilled labor. That shortage doesn't mean it won't succeed in the higher levels of manufacturing, but it does mean it will have to invest to move up the ladder. Workers can be trained, and machines can be bought. In this respect, China's overarching labor supply problem, the result of its family planning policies, could work to its advantage by forcing faster mechanization.

For now, however, China needs to find jobs for millions of people every year. Some 300 million people are expected to migrate to Chinese cities over the next two decades.[20] Chinese leaders Hu Jintao and Wen Jiabao's focus on a "harmonious society" will doubtless put employment near the top of the agenda. Keeping migrant workers happy is increasingly a central policy challenge. If life in the cities doesn't work out for migrants, Ching Kwan Lee, associate professor of sociology at the University of Michigan, contends, China could be faced with a difficult problem. "It's kind of a time bomb," she says. "If the city doesn't provide enough, these people have nowhere else to go."

The upward momentum will also cause dislocation in China. Just as the China price shuttered factories in the United States, Mexico and elsewhere, leaving millions of former factory employees out of work, it is already forcing factories in southern China to shrink or shut and move farther inland. The dilemma facing the governor of Guangdong province is not so different from the dilemma facing the governor of South Carolina or Illinois.

Zhang Dejiang, the province's Communist party head, warned in May 2007 that the province was facing "unprecedented challenges to its development," including increased competition from overseas, rising costs and trade protectionism. "Strengthening innovation is the core of our economic upgrading," Zhang said. "We have to transform a resource-driven economy to an innovation-driven economy."[21]

China does have a large pool of engineering graduates and young professionals. But it's not clear how many of them are the people China needs to move industry to the next level. Multinationals in China say less than 10 percent of local job applicants meet their requirements, according to a study by the McKinsey Global Institute.[22]

MGI points to universities' emphasis on theory rather than practical problems, to candidates' poor English and, interestingly, to graduates' lack of mobility. Unlike less educated Chinese, who formed the mass migration to toil in factories, only one-third of Chinese graduates move to other provinces for work, according to the institute's analysis.[23]

In one of the quirks of the Chinese economy, unemployment among recent university graduates has become a national issue serious enough to merit a meeting of China's State Council (its cabinet) in 2006. Chinese academics warn that the country's universities are failing to prepare students for the business world. There has even been a report, possibly bogus, that 286 graduates and postgraduates applied for 11 jobs as street cleaners in Guangzhou.[24]

THESE FACTS HAVE not been lost on the Chinese government. Facing growing social unrest, trade tensions, excess capacity across many sectors and environmental degradation, Beijing has pledged to reposition its economy away from heavy reliance on exports. The new policy reflects a recognition that China's rapid growth will be more sustainable if it is rooted more in domestic consumption.

In December 2004, Chinese leaders at the Central Economic Work Conference, an annual event, agreed to shift the economy away from reliance on investment and exports toward domestic consumption[25]—what one Chinese report called a move away from the two "strong horses" of investment and international trade and toward the "weak donkey" of consumption.[26] The government has been slashing incentives for exporters in energy- and resource-intensive industries and heavily polluting sectors, lowering or removing tax rebates on thousands of categories of exports, expressly to take the wind out of trade conflicts in sensitive areas like textiles.[27] Simultaneously, it has been raising rebates for exporters of high-technology products.

As part of its attempt to raise the growth of domestic consumption relative to the growth of exports and investment, Beijing is increasing its spending on rural health care, for example, and introducing pilot programs to insure urban residents.

Still, some economists reckon that despite efforts by the government to increase its spending, stimulate consumption and reform the currency, so far they haven't had much impact. The Chinese economy is still hooked on exports. And so is the rest of the world.

The human legacy of this mutual dependency will remain long after low-end manufacturing has moved on to other countries. Chinese workers' slice of the profits from global supply chains has and will continue to lift countless families out of poverty. The lure of a better life in the cities will continue to stretch the horizons of young men and women. But the country will also face a mounting health care bill in caring for the hundreds of thousands, if not millions, of people who have fallen ill as a result of exposure to environmental pollution or occupational hazards. Caring for these casualties of the country's rapid economic expansion will put extra burdens on the country's ailing health care system.

Updating the supply chains in industries with lagging safety and health standards will cost money, too. A.T. Kearney, the management consultancy, has estimated that upgrading China's food safety process to improve standards, training, transportation and warehousing will cost $100 billion.[28] For sure, that will add to the cost of food from China.

Some of the enduring costs of the China price are harder to measure in figures. If China continues to produce low-quality exports that violate safety standards, it could risk losing some of its manufacturing business.

At the same time, the willingness of individuals to stand up for their rights in public could act as a brake on economic growth by derailing projects that might have helped nudge China's GDP even higher. It could also make China less attractive to foreign investors seeking political stability and predictability. As China becomes more tightly knit into the fabric of global commerce, its choices about how it responds to popular protests carry consequences for its international reputation.

Ultimately, however, this kind of individual rights awareness has an effect that is at once prosaic and momentous: It makes China more like other countries. It forces government officials in China to consider the public's views, at least occasionally. That isn't democracy, but it's a step toward a more balanced political system.

The government's efforts to introduce a new labor law and encourage the establishment of ACFTU branches are evidence of Beijing's recognition that the downsides of the China price threaten its interests. But there are more fundamental challenges ahead, the most substantial of which is improving the rule of law and the legal system. China needs to end official collusion with industry at the expense of workers' and ordinary citizens' health, safety and liveli-hood. It needs to make the legal system a reliable, predictable chan-nel for people to resolve disputes. It needs to substantially expand inspections of factories and mines for labor and environmental law violations and make its punishments stick. It needs to create an organization that truly represents workers, particularly migrants, in their negotiations with government agencies, the judicial system and employers. It's not unthinkable that this organization could be the ACFTU, but the state-backed union would need to undergo substantial reform in order to serve workers more effectively. It needs to loosen the reins on the media so it can serve as a watchdog on polluting industries, law-breaking factories and corrupt officials.

China needs to dramatically improve its capability to prevent and treat occupational disease. The health care system, particularly in rural areas, is ill equipped to handle the volume of sick workers the country is producing. Likewise, it must increase its research on the environment's impact on health.

Reforms of this magnitude will take decades, if they happen at all. Ironically, one of the factors that first lured foreign investors to China—the bottomless pool of labor—could make it harder for China to improve its labor and environmental record. The need to keep such a large number of people employed could work against the need to strengthen enforcement of labor laws and regulations, as well as the need to move up the value chain to less labor-intensive industries.

That said, when the Chinese government puts its mind to a certain task, it gets the job done. If China applied the same elbow grease to policing its factories that it does to policing political de-bate on the Internet, it would improve the standard of its manufac-turing base, reduce the caseload of lawsuits and protests by disgruntled workers and ease tensions with its trading partners. Indeed, any country that has to go to the lengths that China is having to go to to control its economic growth could afford to sacrifice some of its competitiveness through more consistent enforcement of the law.

In the end, as much as the responsibility seems to lie with Beijing, it also lies with the global consumer. Our appetite for the $30 DVD player and the $3 T-shirt helps keep jewelry factories filled with dust, illegal mines open and 16-year-olds working past midnight. We all pay the China price.

AFTERWORD

"H OW MUCH ARE THE bananas?" the woman in the blue jacket wanted to know.

"Two and a half renminbi for the ones from Thailand, two for the ones from Guangdong," Li Luyuan answered.

The woman scurried away into the cold.

For three months, Luyuan had been repeating this conversation with a procession of stingy, anonymous passersby. For three months, she had been watching her savings drain into this ice-cold fruit stand in a blue collar district of Shanghai, hundreds of miles and a lifetime away from the Shenzhen real estate agency where she used to work. Almost as quickly as it had expanded, Shenzhen's real estate market had collapsed, forcing thousands of agents, Luyuan among them, out of their jobs.

As property prices began to slide, Luyuan had heard from Liu Jun, a former colleague from the real estate agency who had moved to Shanghai to open a fruit store. Jun, whose name has been changed, was in his mid-thirties and had always had a thing for Luyuan. Though Luyuan considered him a friend and nothing more, Jun promised her a steady wage, a roof over her head, and most tempting, an education in business. He had a solid retail strategy, he told her: his fruit stand would be much nicer than those in Shanghai, with freshly painted wooden shelves, imported exotic fruits nestled in Styrofoam netting, and brightly colored posters on the walls.

Luyuan quit the agency, said goodbye to her friends, and splurged on a flight to Shanghai. It was the first time anyone in her family had flown on an airplane.

But Luyuan was so exhausted, she slept through the entire flight. When the stewardess shook her awake, the plane was empty, sitting motionless on the tarmac in the country's financial capital. Luyuan asked for a few moments to appreciate her surroundings. She was sad to have missed the sensation of being suspended in air, high above the earth.

Luyuan's first days in Shanghai were disappointing. Jun took her out to see the sights—the Bund along the Huangpu River, where American and European banks and trading houses established their outposts more than a century ago, the Shanghai Museum of Chinese art.

Luyuan found Shanghai too old for her taste. She preferred the clean streets and strictly modern architecture of Shenzhen, a city only slightly older than she was. The apartment she shared with Jun was in a gray concrete 1950s-era building peopled mostly by retired employees of state-owned enterprises. Some threw their waste directly out of their windows. "Trash city," Luyuan called her neighborhood.

Even more disheartening was the fruit stand. Every morning, Jun would leave the apartment just after dawn to buy fruit at the wholesale market. With the prices of fruit and other kinds of food rising, he paid about 600 renminbi, or $87, for a day's supply. The problem was they usually only sold about 600 renminbi worth of fruit a day. Luyuan prepared two meals a day for the couple in a makeshift kitchen balanced on fruit crates in the back of the store. The icy water she used to wash their food, and the long winter days and nights in the unheated store and apartment, had left her hands swollen and bruised, like eggplants.

Between the cost of supplies, rent for the store and apartment, and food, Luyuan and Jun hadn't made a penny. They were going broke fast.

LIFE MOVES QUICKLY in China, more quickly, perhaps, than anywhere else in the world today. In the months since *The China Price* was published, the pressures it describes have accelerated. The combination of rising raw material costs, a strengthening renminbi, higher wages, declining demand from America, and the repeal of the export tax rebate for many products created a perfect storm for Chinese manufacturers. Nearly 60,000 factories have gone out of business in Guangdong alone, and this is only the beginning.

The closures have extended beyond the traditional exporting provinces. Sam, the Hunan towel factory manager who predicted in the summer of 2006 that his factory would lose its competitive advantage in three to five years, shut down the plant about 18 months after we spoke. Yarn prices and workers' wages rose too high too quickly. Sam still lives in Changsha, except now he is purely an exporter, selling sleeping bags and towels made by other factories. "Business is really very tough," he told me, then asked whether I had any ideas of products he might sell.

Factories that remain in business have put their prices up. Starting in late 2007, Chinese factory managers began to ask their customers for price increases of as much as 50 percent. Most retailers balked at hikes of that magnitude, but many had to pay slightly more for their Chinese-made products for the first time. Some brands, in shoes and clothing for example, passed some of the increase on to the consumer. Others went back to their suppliers and tried to cut out more costs in their product's design, using three screws where before there were four, substituting cheaper metals, buying cheaper cashmere and passing it off as the same quality.

And others traveled to Vietnam in search of lower prices. Not everyone was happy with what they found. Rising fuel and food costs drove consumer prices up sharply, and contributed to a wave of hundreds of strikes at Vietnamese factories.

Nor was the quality of the output in Vietnam on par with that in China. A sourcing executive at a big American discount chain said that he was dismayed with what he saw on a trip to Vietnam: while many of his Chinese suppliers now helped him design products, coming up with new ways to add features or lower production costs, the Vietnamese factories he visited did little more than snap parts together. Nor were the costs of doing business that much lower. The cheapest room at the Sheraton Saigon Hotel & Towers now goes for $270.

Higher oil prices only added to the rising costs of Chinese exports. The cost of shipping a 40-foot container from Shanghai to America has increased from $3,000 in the early 2000s to $8,000 today.[1] Throughput growth at the ports in Shenzhen slowed dramatically in the first half of 2008, a reflection of both higher prices of goods in China and American consumers' reduced appetite for shopping.

And yet for the Chinese government, things could have been worse. The factories going out of business were those that lacked the management skills to survive. These were the low value-added plants that cities like Shenzhen had been trying to expel for years.

Indeed, Beijing was the architect of most of the changes that shook China's manufacturing sector between 2007 and 2008. Many factory managers blamed the new labor contract law that came into effect on January 1, 2008, for raising the costs of doing business. In fact, what really hurt their profit margins was the rapid appreciation in the value of the renminbi and the sharp increase in the cost of raw materials. For extremely low-margin producers, the repeal of the export tax rebate was the last straw.

The new labor dispute law that came into effect in May 2008 triggered a surge in the number of labor-related cases filed with the government. In the first month after its introduction, the number of cases filed in Shanghai's Pudong district more than tripled compared to the year before.[2] Labor disputes in Guangdong province tripled in 2008.

Chinese people's desire for justice has only increased. After a massive earthquake shook Sichuan province on May 12, burying thousands of children under collapsed schools, volunteers distributed pamphlets published by the government reminding victims that they could sue government officials for certifying the shoddy buildings. (Li Gang, the self-trained legal adviser who lost his arm in an industrial accident, Tang Manzhen, the widow of the jewelry worker Deng Wenping, and Chen Wei, the worker who dreamed of becoming a trader, who all come from the area hit by the quake, were not affected.)

To address the problems migrant workers still face in getting paid and receiving social welfare benefits, Beijing created a Department of Migrant Workers' Affairs within the newly formed Ministry of Human Resources and Social Security. State media reported that the government was upgrading local labor supervision and inspection departments to bureau status and allocating them more funding. And in the summer of 2008, Shenzhen proposed a draft labor regulation that would require companies to establish a mechanism for negotiating with their employees over issues including overtime, and would create a stronger role for the All-China Federation of Trade Unions relative to management. Most important, the extensive media coverage of the new labor laws showed millions of workers that they had rights.

As China raised its standards for factories, America toughened its stance toward them as well. American lawmakers passed the most profound overhaul of product safety legislation in more than a decade, increasing funding for the Consumer Product Safety Commission, requiring third-party testing for certain children's toys, and providing protection to whistleblowers within retailers, distributors, and manufacturers.

IF ENFORCED, these laws will help protect generations of Chinese factory workers. But none of them had much meaning for Luyuan and the other girls of room 817, most of whom had already left the factories. Yuan Meng, the maternal girl who dreamed of becoming a beautician, moved back to the countryside outside Chongqing with her parents and little sister. Zhang Juan was already a mother of one, living in southwestern Sichuan province with her husband. Only Jie Yuying remained in the trenches of China's modern industrial revolution, except now she had been promoted to management.

Luyuan had been begging Jun to let her leave Shanghai and return to Shenzhen. She was cold and miserable. Luyuan and Jun had run out of things to talk about in their first week on the job. Now, they spent their days in silence, Jun smoking packs of Honghe cigarettes and Luyuan listening to the radio on her cell phone and waiting for someone to ask her the price of bananas. In the evening, they would throw out the fruit that had rotted during the day. "It's not ideal," Jun said when I asked him how business was going one chilly afternoon in March 2008. "It's confusing. There are a lot of fruit shops like this one in Shenzhen, shops with this kind of decoration, and they're making a lot of money."

In the two years since she had left Shenzhen Rishen Cashmere Textile, Luyuan had been knocked up and then down by the waves of China's economic growth. Shenzhen's real estate boom had earned her more money than anyone in her family had ever imag-

ined, but now the country's mushrooming food inflation was sending her quickly back toward poverty.

In the spring, Luyuan persuaded Jun to let her go. Her boyfriend, another colleague from the real estate agency, sent her money
for a train ticket to Shenzhen. When I saw her there weeks later, the
swelling in her hands had gone down and she was grinning.

Over bowls of sweet bean soup at a teahouse across the street
from the agency, her boyfriend Little Zhang at her side, Luyuan
told me of her plans to return to selling real estate during the day.
At night, she would make up for the years she had lost sewing
sweaters and making parts for DVD players. Luyuan, at 24, was
going back to school, starting where she left off: junior high.

Acknowledgments

MUCH OF THE ACTION in Guangdong occurs behind a veil of secrecy. Despite the huge scale of economic activity there, only a handful of foreign journalists are based in the province. The Chinese government keeps close tabs on international reporters across the border in Hong Kong.

Foreign journalists in the former British colony, which returned to China in 1997 but is now run as a special administrative region, must apply for a special visa to visit the mainland. As part of that application, journalists must submit letters of invitation from the people they plan to interview. These procedures ensure that not many people in China get to talk to a foreign reporter from Hong Kong.

My application as a journalist to cover a labor conference in Guangdong was refused and the conference canceled. An admitted former spy from the People's Liberation Army would offer to drive me around while I was in southern China. At other times, a different government official sat in on my interviews.

Because of these experiences, in early 2006, I retired from journalism for a while. I took a leave of absence from the *Financial Times* and became a visiting fellow at the University of Hong Kong's Hong Kong Institute of Economics and Business Strategy (HIEBS).

I am eternally grateful to the wonderful people at HIEBS, particularly Michael Enright, Alan K.F. Siu and Angelina Hung, for very generously allowing me the means to research and write this book. Editors at the *Financial Times*, particularly John Ridding, Dan Bogler and Victor Mallet, graciously granted me leave and extended it when I needed more time.

Scores of other people helped bring this book to life. Dan Mandel, my ever-supportive agent, believed in my ideas and cheerfully answered my endless questions around the clock. Scott Moyers and Vanessa Mobley, my editors at The Penguin Press, were everything I could have dreamed of: brilliant, inspiring and savvy. Not to mention patient. Everyone at Penguin, including Lindsay Whalen and Laura Stickney, was equally fantastic to work with.

Audrey Zhou tirelessly pursued minute details, transcribed countless hours of interviews, and combed Web sites for information on my behalf. Tracy Tu and Cara He provided hospitality and valuable research assistance earlier in the project.

Robin Munro, Stephen Frost and Melissa Brown were all extremely generous with their time, insights and assistance. Liam Casey went beyond the call of duty to provide me with use of his driver and his office, and the company of his talented colleague Christina Zhang.

My mother Andy and brother Brendan, Jason Kindopp, Mary Gallagher, John Ruwitch, Shawn Donnan and Elizabeth Balkan, who all had their hands full with family and work, graciously read part or all of this book and provided extremely helpful suggestions. Pietra Rivoli was kind enough to read some and share her thoughts as well.

Johnny Che, Liyi Chang and James Wang were generous, wise guides to their country, helping me understand not only what people were saying but also how China works. Jill Tucker gave me great insights into the world of social compliance. Sharmila Whelan spoiled me with hospitality and encouragement.

Martin Ma, Liu Kaiming, Hu Kanping, Yang Li, Ben Davide Erro, Ross O'Brien, Bill Anderson, Lynne O'Donnell, Judith Banister, Dorothy Solinger, Gary Bass, Kate Kelly and Kyle Pope, Susan Murcko, Davide Meale, Nancy Leou, Bao Pu, Monina Wong, Parry Leung, Andrew Batson and Amy Wong all went out of their way to be helpful. My parents and grandfather offered sustenance and encouragement from afar.

Some of the people who were instrumental in this book have asked to remain anonymous, and I deeply regret not being able to thank them by name. Luyuan and the girls of room 817 welcomed me into their lives, taught me Chinese and cooked me some of the best meals I have ever eaten. Tang Manzhen and the man known here as Li Gang spent hours walking me through the sometimes-painful details of their life experiences. Zhang Yisheng patiently explained his thinking and kept me very well fed. By accepting me into their worlds, these people changed the way I saw mine.

Colin Beere, to whom this book is dedicated, was superhuman during this entire process. I will always be grateful for his superb editing, his willingness to discuss the China price at any hour of the day or night, his unfailing belief in me and his understanding and support. Every author should have a Colin.

All of these people helped me during the research and writing of this book, but any errors are entirely mine.

Notes

INTRODUCTION: THE BETTER MOUSETRAP

1. Ted Fishman, "The Chinese Century," *New York Times*, July 4, 2004.
2. Pete Engardio, Dexter Roberts, and Brian Bremner, "The China Price," *BusinessWeek*, December 6, 2004, 102.
3. Bill Powell, "It's All Made in China Now," *Fortune*, March 4, 2002, 121.
4. David Luhnow, "Up the Food Chain: As Jobs Move East, Plants in Mexico Retool to Compete," *Wall Street Journal*, March 5, 2004.
5. Engardio et al., "China Price."
6. Peter Marsh, "US to Lose Role as World's Top Manufacturer by 2020," *Financial Times*, May 24, 2007.
7. Ibid.
8. Dominic Ziegler, "The Export Juggernaut," *Economist*, A Special Report on China and its Region, March 31, 2007, 8.
9. Liu Baijia, "Samsung Aims to Buy More in China," *China Daily*, April 22, 2006. Available at http://www.chinadaily.com.cn/bizchina/2006-04/22/content__574083.htm.
10. "Export Juggernaut." *The Economist*, March 31, 2007, 10.
11. Robert E. Scott, "China Trade Costs Jobs in Every State," Economic Policy Institute Briefing Paper No. 219, July 30, 2008, available at http://www.epi.org/content.cfm/bp219. Not everyone agrees with these figures about American job losses. See Guy de Jonquieres, "China Manufacturing Myths," *Financial Times*, April 3, 2006.
12. Senators Schumer and Graham introduced a bill in 2005 that would have imposed a temporary 27.5 percent tariff on all goods imported from China. Their press release is available at http://www.senate.gov/~schumer/SchumerWebsite/pressroom/press__releases/2005/PR4111.China020305.html.
13. Richard L. Wilkey, testimony on behalf of the National Association of Manufacturers before the House Committee on Ways and Means, April 14, 2005. Available at http://www.nam.org/s__nam/sec.asp?CID=170&DID=168.
14. Katya Adler, "Spanish Fury over Chinese Shoes," BBC News, September 24, 2004. Available at http://news.bbc.co.uk/2/hi/europe/3687602.stm.

15. C. Fred Bergsten et al., *China: The Balance Sheet* (New York: Public Affairs, 2006), 74. See also David Luhnow, "Up The Food Chain," *Wall Street Journal*, March 5, 2004, and Geri Smith, "Wasting Away: Despite SARS, Mexico Is Still Losing Export Ground to China," *BusinessWeek*, June 2, 2003, 42.

16. Malgorzata Halaba, "Polish Firms Fend Off Rivals in China," *Wall Street Journal*, October 12, 2005.

17. Craig Timberg, "The China Effect Hits Nigeria," Washington Post Foreign Service, published in the *Miami Herald*, January 8, 2007.

18. Erin Lett and Judith Banister, "Labor Costs of Manufacturing Employees in China: An Update to 2003–04," *Monthly Labor Review*, November 2006, 40–41. There is good reason to believe that this actually understates the total manufacturing employment in China, because of the exclusion of undocumented migrant workers from some statistics. See Judith Banister, "Manufacturing Employment and Compensation in China," U.S. Department of Labor, Bureau of Labor Statistics, November 2005, 34–35. Available at http://www.bls.gov/fls/home.htm.

19. Robert M. Campbell, Jimmy Hexter, and Karen Yin, "Getting Sourcing Right in China," in *The McKinsey Quarterly 2004 Special Edition: China Today* (New York: McKinsey & Company, 2004), 36.

20. Banister, "Manufacturing Employment," 26.

21. Ibid.

22. James Kynge, *China Shakes the World: The Rise of a Hungry Nation* (London: Weidenfeld & Nicolson, 2006), 30–31.

23. Bergsten et al., *China: The Balance Sheet*, 89. Because China uses the total value of finished goods, rather than the value added locally, in its trade data, some observers believe that its export figures overstate the value it is adding.

24. Bergsten et al., *China: The Balance Sheet*, 106.

25. Wu Lifang, Yue Xiaohang, and Thaddeus Sim, "Supply Clusters: A Key to China's Cost Advantage," *Supply Chain Management Review*, Vol. 10, no. 2, (March 1, 2006), 46.

26. Ibid.

27. Cited in Michael J. Enright, Edith E. Scott and Chang Ka-mun, *Regional Powerhouse: The Greater Pearl River Delta and the Rise of China* (Singapore: John Wiley & Sons, 2005), 62, as quoted in "Clean up Your Computer: Working Conditions in the Electronics Sector," (report, Catholic Agency for Overseas Development, London, January 26, 2004).

28. Ibid., 57.

29. Keith Bradsher, "China's Industrial Boom Is Seriously Inflating Commodity Prices," *New York Times*, October 16, 2004.

30. Walt Bogdanich and Jake Hooker, "From China to Panama, a Trail of Poisoned Medicine," *New York Times*, May 6, 2007.

31. Robert Lee Hotz, "Asian Air Pollution Affects Our Weather," *Los Angeles Times*, March 6, 2007, A-1.

32. Liang Qiwen, "Guangdong Faces Population Pressure," *China Daily*, February 16, 2005. The 2000 census, however, reported a population of only 85 million people.

33. Sun Yunlong, ed., "South China's Guangdong Sees Slow Income Growth," *China Daily*, March 13, 2007. Available at http://news.xinhuanet.com/english/2007-03/13/content_5838063.htm.

34. All renminbi to dollar conversions in the book have been made at a rate of $1 to Rmb7.59, the rate on July 5, 2007.

CHAPTER 1: HOOKED

1. From unpublished pages of Harry S. Truman's memoirs, as quoted in Alfred E. Eckes, Jr., *Opening America's Market: US Foreign Trade Policy Since 1776* (Chapel Hill: University of North Carolina Press, 1995), 158. As Eckes points out, the ideological framework for this embrace of freer trade as a means to meet foreign policy goals had been put in place in the 1930s by Cordell Hull, who served as secretary of state under Franklin D. Roosevelt.

2. Conversation with Pietra Rivoli, associate professor at Georgetown University's Mc-Donough School of Business, August 9, 2007.

3. Ellen Israel Rosen, *Making Sweatshops: The Globalization of the US Apparel Industry* (Berkeley: University of California Press, 2002), 37.

4. Ibid., 106.

5. Pietra Rivoli, *The Travels of a T-Shirt in the Global Economy: An Economist Examines the Markets, Power and Politics of World Trade* (Hoboken, NJ: John Wiley & Sons, 2005), 84.

6. Bonacich, Edna, et al., eds., *Global Production: The Apparel Industry in the Pacific Rim* (Philadelphia: Temple University Press, 1994), 22.

7. Jane L. Collins, *Threads: Gender, Labor, and Power in the Global Apparel Industry* (Chicago: University of Chicago Press, 2003), 108.

8. Bonacich et al., *Global Production*, 23.

9. American Apparel and Footwear Association, *Trends: An Annual Compilation of Statistical Information on the US Apparel & Footwear Industries* (Washington, D.C.: AAFA, June 2007), 3.

10. Bonacich et al., *Global Production*, 87.

11. Patricia A. Wilson, *Exports and Local Development: Mexico's New Maquiladoras* (Austin: University of Texas Press, 1992), 37, 139.

12. Hong Wang, *China's Exports Since 1979* (New York: St. Martin's Press, 1993), 27.

13. Jonathan Spence, *Mao Zedong* (New York: Viking, 1999), 132–33.

14. Jonathan Spence, *The Search for Modern China* (New York: W. W. Norton, 1990), 583.

15. Nicholas R. Lardy, *China in the World Economy* (Washington, D.C.: Institute for International Economics, 1994), 33.

16. Spence, *Mao Zedong*, 150.

17. Jonathan R. Woetzel, *China's Economic Opening to the Outside World: The Politics of Empowerment* (New York: Praeger, 1989), 34.

18. Ibid., 88, and Hong Wang, *China's Exports*, 36.

19. Joe Studwell, *The China Dream: The Elusive Quest for the Greatest Untapped Market on Earth* (London: Profile Books, 2002), 43.

20. Ezra F. Vogel, *One Step Ahead in China: Guangdong Under Reform* (Cambridge, MA: Harvard University Press, 1989), 342, 338–339.

21. Hong Wang, *China's Exports*, 40.

22. Laurence J. C. Ma, *Commercial Development and Urban Change in Sung China (960–1279)* (Ann Arbor: Department of Geography, University of Michigan, 1971), 35.

23. Valery M. Garrett, *Heaven is High, the Emperor Far Away: Merchants and Mandarins in Old Canton* (Oxford: Oxford University Press, 2002), 45.

24. Vogel, *One Step Ahead in China*, 83.

25. Ibid., 85–86.

26. Ibid., 348–350.

27. Ibid., 144, and Mary Elizabeth Gallagher, *Contagious Capitalism: Globalization and the Politics of Labor in China* (Princeton, NJ: Princeton University Press, 2005), 39.

28. Dori Jones Yang and Maria Shao, "China's Push for Exports Is Turning into a Long March," *BusinessWeek*, September 15, 1986, 66.
29. Vogel, *One Step Ahead in China*, 69.
30. Studwell, *China Dream*, 45–46.
31. "Coleco's Cabbage Patch Kids 'Born' in China, Hong Kong," *Wall Street Journal*, December 8, 1983.
32. "Sony Color Televisions Will Be Made in China," *Wall Street Journal*, February 6, 1984.
33. Dori Jones Yang and Thane Peterson with Neil Gross, "The Year of the Cheap Chinese TV," *BusinessWeek*, October 17, 1988, 102E.
34. Ibid.
35. Lardy, *China in the World Economy*, 31.
36. Ibid., 32.
37. Jason Dean, "The Forbidden City of Terry Gou," *Wall Street Journal*, August 11, 2007.
38. Lardy, *China in the World Economy*, 34.
39. Orville Schell, *Mandate of Heaven: The Legacy of Tiananmen Square and the Next Generation of China's Leaders* (New York: Touchstone, 1994), 334.
40. Wang Gan, "Conspicuous Consumption, Business Networks, and State Power in a Chinese City" (PhD diss., Yale University, 1999), 83.

CHAPTER 2: THE FIVE-STAR FACTORY

1. Victor Fung, "Beijing Opens a Window of Opportunity," *Asian Wall Street Journal*, July 7, 2005.
2. Jason Dean and Pui-Wing Tam, "The Laptop Trail," *Wall Street Journal*, June 9, 2005.
3. Edward S. Steinfeld, "Chinese Enterprise Development and the Challenge of Global Integration" (background paper for World Bank's *Innovative East Asia: The Future of Growth*, revised November 2002), 4–6.
4. Kasra Ferdows, "New World Manufacturing Order," *Industrial Engineer* 35, no. 2 (February 2003): 28.
5. Steinfeld, *Chinese Enterprise*, 18.
6. Stephenson Harwood & Lo, *China Legal*, March 2006, 3.
7. Andy Rothman with Carole Liu and Julia Zhu, "China's Capitalists: Special Report," CLSA Asia-Pacific Markets, September 2005, 23.
8. Peter Wonacott, "China's Factories Compete—with Each Other," *Wall Street Journal Europe*, November 14, 2003.
9. See http://www.dol.gov/compliance/topics/wages-overtime-pay.htm.
10. Interview with Auret van Heerden, February 15, 2006.
11. Interview with Philip Lam (pseudonym), May 20, 2007.
12. Some labor groups send researchers into factories undercover to document labor abuses, often with cameras. These researchers are anathema to Chinese factory managers. Typically, the factory suffers more than its customer when the exposés that result from this kind of research are published, since the customer launches an investigation and then may pull its orders.
13. Judith Banister, "Manufacturing Employment and Compensation in China," U.S. Department of Labor, Bureau of Labor Statistics, November 2005, 36.
14. Ibid., 37.
15. Rosey Hurst, Hilary Murdoch and Daniella Gould, "Changing Over Time" (report, Impactt), January 2006, 4, 6. Available at http://www.impacttlimited.com/site/publications

.asp. In an article entitled "The Problem with Supplier Audits" in the August/September 2005 edition of *Corporate Responsibility Management*, Daniella Gould, then Impactt's director of North America and East Asia, noted that it was "common for workers to be at their stations for 270–390 hours per month and some workers have been seen to work 450 hours."

16. U.S. Department of Labor, Employment Situation Summary, "The Employment Situation: May 2007." Available at http://www.dol.gov/dol/highlights/infocusarchive-2006.htm.

17. Verité, "Excessive Overtime in Chinese Supplier Factories: Causes, Impacts and Recommendations for Action" (research paper, September 2004), 12.

18. Fifty-three percent of workers surveyed said their main motivation for working overtime was to earn extra income. Seventy-three percent of workers considered overtime income "important," "very important" or "essential." Verité, "Excessive Overtime," 15.

19. Interview with an anonymous Western factory owner, February 18, 2006.

20. Interview with Auret van Heerden, February 15, 2006.

21. Anita Chan, *China's Workers Under Assault: The Exploitation of Labor in a Globalizing Economy* (Armonk, NY: M. E. Sharpe, 2001), 11.

22. China Labour Bulletin, "Falling Through the Floor: Migrant Women Workers' Quest for Decent Work in Dongguan, China," CLB Research Series No. 2 (September 2006): 11.

23. Ibid., 12, 15.

24. Verité, "Excessive Overtime," 24.

CHAPTER 3: THE PHYSICAL COST

1. "Investigating the Top Occupational Illness," *China Daily*, December 21, 2006.

2. "The State of Equity in China: Social Security and Public Expenditure," *China Human Development Report* (United Nations Development Program, 2005), 27. Available at www.undp.org.cn/downloads/nhdr2005/08chapter4.pdf.

3. "China's Workers at Greater Risk of Illness, Injury on Job," *Xinhua*, July 17, 2006.

4. Jasper Becker, "Cases of Mining Disease Silicosis Top Million in China," *South China Morning Post*, Business Post supplement. April 2, 2002.

5. Josephine Ma, "Migrant Work Still Fraught with Risks; Despite a Decline in Job-Related Deaths, Many Laborers Face Grave Dangers," *South China Morning Post*, June 19, 2004.

6. Mao Nongxi, "Pneumonconiosis Is the Most Serious Occupational Illness in China," *Workers' Daily*, December 20, 2006.

7. Ma, "Migrant Work."

8. David Rosner and Gerald Markowitz, *Deadly Dust: Silicosis and the On-Going Struggle to Protect Workers' Health* (Ann Arbor: University of Michigan Press, 2006), 78–81.

9. Ibid., 96–97.

10. Centers for Disease Control, National Institute for Occupational Health and Safety, "Fatal and Nonfatal Injuries, and Selected Illnesses and Conditions." *Worker Health Chartbook 2004*.

11. Igor Fedotov, "The ILO/WHO Global Programme for the Elimination of Silicosis (GPES)." (presentation, IOHA 2005 6th International Scientific Conference, September 19–23, 2005). Available at http://www.Saioh.org/ioha2005/proceedings/PPT/Keynotes/Keynote9PPTweb.pdf.

12. Changqi Zou, Yun Gao, and Qingyan Ma, "Pneumoconiosis in China: Current Situation and Countermeasures," *Mineral Dusts and Prevention of Silicosis*, vol 4, no. 2 (September 1997). Available at http//www.oit.org/public/english/region/asro/bangkok/asiaosh/newsletr/silicosi/zou.htm.

13. Ibid.
14. Fedotov, "ILO/WHO Global Program," 2. The World Health Organization Fact Sheet No. 238: Silicosis (May 2000) reports that between 1991 and 1995, China reported more than 500,000 cases of silicosis and more than 24,000 deaths every year.
15. "China's Workers at Greater Risk of Illness, Injury on Job," *Xinhua*, July 17, 2006.
16. China Labor Bulletin, "Deadly Dust: The Silicosis Epidemic among Guangdong Jewellery Workers and the Defects of China's Occupational Illness Prevention and Compensation System," CLB Research Series No. 1, (December 2005): 2.
17. D. Wen, quoted in Max Tuñón, "Internal Labor Migration in China: Features and Responses," ILO Office, Beijing, April 2006.
18. China Labor Bulletin, "Deadly Dust," 12.
19. Interview with Auret van Heerden, February 15, 2006.
20. Interview with a former government inspector, June 30, 2006.
21. Cited in Tuñón, "Internal Labor Migration," 14.
22. Ibid., 14.
23. "State of Equity in China," 27.
24. Ibid., 1.
25. Fei-ling Wang, *Organizing Through Division and Exclusion: China's Hukou System* (Stanford, CA: Stanford University Press, 2003), 63–67.
26. Hualing Fu and D. Y. Choy, "From Mediation to Adjudication: Settling Labor Disputes in China," *China Rights Forum*, No. 3, (2004): 20.
27. Interview with Fu Hualing, January 31, 2007.
28. Zhou Litai, interview with the author, January 6, 2007; Fu and Choy, "From Mediation to Adjudication," 21.
29. Interview with Robin Munro, January 15, 2007.
30. Fu and Choy, "From Mediation to Adjudication," 21.
31. Interview with Alex Pei Keung (lawyer at China Labor Bulletin), February 15, 2007.
32. Mary E. Gallagher, "Mobilizing the Law in China: 'Informed Disenchantment' and the Development of Legal Consciousness," *Law & Society Review*, Vol. 40, no. 4 (2006): 804.
33. Ibid., 799.
34. "Network to Provide Free Legal Aid for Migrant Workers," *Xinhua*, February 27, 2007.
35. Interview with a labor lawyer, February 15, 2007.
36. Interview with Mary Gallagher, February 1, 2007.
37. "Help or Hindrance to Workers: China's Institutions of Public Redress," China Labor Bulletin Research Reports, April 23, 2008, available at http://www.china-labour.org.hk/en/node/10244.
38. "China Must Do More to Prevent Occupational Diseases," *Xinhua*, April 5, 2007.
39. "China's Workers at Greater Risk of Illness, Injury on Job," *Xinhua*, July 17, 2006.
40. "China Must Do More."
41. sina.com.cn, September 11, 2002.
42. Wang Xiao-Rong and David C. Christiani, "Occupational Lung Disease in China," *International Journal of Occupational and Environmental Health* vol. 9, no. 4: (2003): 322.
43. Liu Yuanli, "Development of the Rural Health Insurance System in China," *Health Policy and Planning*, vol. 19, no. 3 (May 2004), 160.
44. Amnesty International, "Internal Migrants: Discrimination and Abuse. The Human Cost of an Economic 'Miracle'," March 1, 2007. Available at http://www.amnestyusa.org/document.php?id=ENGASA170082007; Office of the World Health Organization Representative in China and Social Development Department of China State Council

Development Research Center. *China: Health, Poverty and Economic Development* (Beijing, June 2006), 24.

45. Amnesty International, "Internal Migrants."
46. Liu, "Development of the Rural Health Insurance System," 160.
47. World Health Organization, *China*, 17.
48. Kristine Kwok, "2020 Set as Goal for National Insurance Plan," *South China Morning Post*, October 13, 2006.
49. Amnesty International, "Internal Migrants."
50. World Health Organization, *China*, 18; Liu, Development of the Rural Health Insurance System,"; "State of Equity in China."
51. "China Vows to Give More Migrant Workers Industrial Injury Insurance," *Xinhua*, November 22, 2006.
52. Luan Shanglin, ed., "Migrant Workers to Get Basic Job Health Care," *Xinhua*, April 24, 2006.
53. Paul French, "Welcome to Bubble Town," *Asian Wall Street Journal*, May 27, 2004, cited in Judith Banister, "Manufacturing Employment and Compensation in China" (U.S. Department of Labor, Bureau of Labor Statistics, November 2005), 46.
54. "Work Injury Insurance Covers 13.4 Percent of Migrant Workers in China," *Xinhua*, April 25, 2007.
55. "Ministry of Labor—Enterprises Will Be Forced to Enroll in Insurance System for Migrant Workers," *China Youth Daily*, September 9, 2006.

CHAPTER 4: THE GOLD RUSH

1. Elizabeth C. Economy, *The River Runs Black: The Environmental Challenge to China's Future* (Ithaca, NY: Cornell University Press, 2004), 72.
2. Ibid., 72. In fact, because of widespread power shortages in industrial areas in southern China, many factories end up installing their own generators. These generators run on diesel (or some other kind of fuel), which is highly polluting and helps explain the deterioration in air quality in the area, including Hong Kong.
3. Rujun Shen, "As China's Small Mines Stay Shut, Crisis Grows," Reuters, July 13, 2008; "Coal Mines' Safety Record Improves in 1H2008," *China Daily*, July 9, 2008, available at http://www.china.org.cn/government/central_government/2008-07/09/content _15977406.htm.
4. "Rehabilitating China's Killer Coal Mines," *People's Daily*, November 5, 2004. Translated by Guo Xiaohong and Li Jingrong. Available at http://www.china.org.cn/english/ 2004/ Nov/111285.htm.
5. Elspeth Thomson, *The Chinese Coal Industry: An Economic History* (London: Routledge, 2003), 143.
6. Ibid., 191.
7. See China Labor Bulletin's coal report, *"You xiao de Gongren zuzhi: baozhang kuanggong shengming de biyou zhilu"* ("Bloody Coal: An Appraisal of China's Coal Mine Safety Management System"), March 2006, at http://iso.china-labour-org.hk/public/contents/ article?revision%5fid=39557&item%5fid=17033 for ample documentation.
8. Interview with Trevor Houser (director of the energy practice at China Strategic Advisory), August 14, 2007.
9. Keith Bradsher and David Barboza, "Pollution from Chinese Coal Casts a Global Shadow," *New York Times*, June 11, 2006.

10. China Labor Bulletin, *"You xiao de Gongren zuzhi: baozhang kuanggong shengming de biyou zhilu"* ("Bloody Coal: An Appraisal of China's Coal Mine Safety Management System"), March 2006, 10.

11. "If Shanxi Can Do It (Clean Up), Anybody Can," report from U.S. Embassy, Beijing, June 2001. Available at http://www.usembassy-china.org.cn/sandt/Shanxi.htm.

12. Tai Hang, "From Gray to Blue: Taiyuan Polishes Its Dirty Image," *Beijing Review*, April 2004, http://www.bjreview.cn/EN/200444/Cover-200444(B).htm.

13. Chen Zhonghua, *"Taiyuan youjian baiyun piao—Taiyuan zhili huanjing wuran ji,"* ("Taiyuan Sees Clouds Again—A Record of Taiyuan's Environmental Pollution Controls"), *Taiyuan Evening News*, June 6, 2000.

14. Zhang Yunxing, "Working for Blue Skies in Taiyuan," China.org.cn, February 20, 2006. Available at http://www.china.org.cn/english/MATERIAL/158627.htm.

15. Chen, "Taiyuan Sees Clouds."

16. Zhu Guoliang, He Zhanjun and Teng Junnei, *"Wuran chao zai 'heibeizi' xia de san da chengshi"* ("Three Overpolluted Cities Under a 'Black Quilt' "), *Xinhua*, January 25, 2007.

17. World Health Organization, United Nations Development Program, "Environment and People's Health in China," 2001, 25. Available at http://www.wpro.who.int/NR/rdonlyres/FD5E0957-DC76-41F2-B207-21113406AE55/0/CHNEnvironmental Health.pdf.

18. Zhang Yu, *"Chi mu zhong de Taiyuan "Chengshiguancha"* ("Taiyuan in the Twilight of Life"), *Market News*, May 10, 2002.

19. "Air Pollution, Children's Illnesses Increase Dramatically," *Xinhua*, December 26, 2006.

20. Andreas Lorenz, "'The Chinese Miracle Will End Soon,'" *Spiegel Online International*, March 7, 2005. Translated by Patrick Kessler. Available at http://www.spiegel.de/international/spiegel/0,1518,345694,00.html.

21. Shi Jiangtao, "500b-Yuan Loss from Sulfur Cloud," *South China Morning Post*, August 4, 2006.

22. Economy, *River Runs Black*, 69.

23. Ibid., 88.

24. Ibid., 82.

25. "China's Environment Reaches Critical Point: Industrialization Moving Too Rapidly Increases Pollution," Agence France-Presse, published in *Vancouver Sun*, November 14, 2006.

26. Shai Oster and Mei Fong, "Village Battle Against Pollution Shows China's Enduring Struggle," *Wall Street Journal Asia*, July 19, 2006, 16.

27. Sarah Schafer, "Taking China to Court: Environmentalists Have Found an All-American Way to Challenge the Worst Polluters—Class-Action Lawsuits," *Newsweek International*, November 20, 2006.

28. Economy, *River Runs Black*, 85.

29. World Health Organization, "Environment and People's Health"; Economy, *River Runs Black*, 85.

30. World Health Organization, "Environment and People's Health," 46. In fact, this figure may be even higher. In July 2007, the *Financial Times* reported that Beijing had lobbied to exclude from a World Bank report its finding that the number of people dying prematurely in China from pollution every year was much higher, at 750,000. See Richard McGregor, "750,000 a Year Killed by Chinese Pollution," *Financial Times*, July 2, 2007.

31. Bill Saradove, "The High Cost of an Economic Miracle," *South China Morning Post*, August 4, 2006.

32. See " 'Green GDP' Index System Is Approaching: Interview," *People's Daily Online*, September 15, 2004, http://english.people.com.cn/200409/15/eng20040915_157149.html.
33. There have been cases of environmental protest in Taiyuan, and there is evidence that the public is increasingly willing to complain about it. As Anna Brettell describes in "Environmental Disputes and Public Service Law: Past and Present," (Wilson Center, China Environment Series, Issue 4, 66–68), farmers in Taiyuan have complained about the contamination of their crops by piles of coal dust generated by the No. 2 Thermal Power Plant that were dumped by a river. In response to the farmers' complaints to the government, the river was cleaned up, but the farmers were never compensated for their losses. The dispute resurfaced later, and the provincial Environmental Protection Bureau intervened, but the power plant still refused to compensate the farmers. Ms. Brettell quotes an EPB official as saying that nothing can be done because the power plant in question is a provincial government priority. See http://www.wilsoncenter.org/topics/pubs/ACF3DE.pdf.
34. Su Yuan, "*Shanxi Mei Lao Ban Zhen Xiang*" ("The Reality of Coal Mine Bosses"), *Southern People Weekly*, October 27, 2005.
35. "China's Efforts to Build a Clean Government Paying Off," *Xinhua*, published by *People's Daily Online*, January 8, 2007.
36. Jiang Zhuqing, "Officials Found Reluctant to Retract Stakes in Coal Mines," *China Daily*, September 23, 2005.
37. "The Chaotic Phenomenon of Fake Reporters in Datong, Shanxi," *Beijing News*, February 1, 2007. Translated by EastSouthWestNorth at http://www.zonaeuropa.com/20070204__1.htm.
38. Sun Chunlong, "*Shanxi Guan Mei Gou Jie Hei Mu Chong Chong, Di Fang Guan Cheng Bu Gan Zai Cha*" ("The Collusion between Government and Coal Mine Is Serious, Complicated and Kept Underground, Local Officals Say They Dare Not Carry Out Further Inspections"), *Oriental Outlook*, November 14, 2005.
39. Shai Oster, "Illegal Power Plants, Coal Mines in China Pose Challenge for Beijing," *Wall Street Journal*, December 27, 2006.
40. The Chaotic Phenomenon of Fake Reporters in Datong, Shanxi," *Beijing News*, February 1, 2007.
41. China Labor Bulletin, "Bloody Coal," 17.
42. "Coal-Rich Province Improves Mine Safety," *Xinhua*, February 22, 2007.
43. Li Fangchao, "Penalties Prescribed for Safety Violations: Corruption Seen as Major Reason for Rising Number of Workplace Accidents," *China Daily*, November 23, 2006.
44. "The Chaotic Phenomenon of Fake Reporters in Datong, Shanxi," *Beijing News*, February 1, 2007.
45. Irene Wang, "Safety Watchdog Lashes State-Owned Mine Chiefs," *South China Morning Post*, November 11, 2006.
46. Tom Miller, "China Could Become Top Air Polluter Next Year," *South China Morning Post*, March 1, 2007.
47. Tim Appenzeller, "The Coal Paradox," *National Geographic*, March 2006, 101.

CHAPTER 5: THE STIRRING MASSES

1. Interview with Stephen Frost, June 22, 2007.
2. Dorothy Solinger, *Contesting Citizenship in Urban China: Peasant Migrants, the State, and the Logic of the Market* (Berkeley: University of California Press, 1999), 49.
3. Ibid., 50–51.

4. Ibid., 164.

5. Ibid., 159–160.

6. Quoted in ibid. at 71–72.

7. Huang Ping and Zhan Shaohua, "Internal Migration in China: Linking It to Development" (paper prepared for the Regional Conference on Migration and Development in Asia, Lanzhou, China, March 14–16, 2005), 6.

8. Huang and Zhan, "Internal Migration," 6.

9. Rachel Murphy, *How Migrant Labor Is Changing Rural China* (Cambridge: Cambridge University Press, 2002), 91.

10. Solinger, *Contesting Citizenship*, 180.

11. Ibid., 182.

12. Ibid., 174.

13. Cai Fang, "Invisible Hand and Visible Feet: Internal Migration in China," Chinese Academy of Social Sciences, Institute of Population and Labor Economics, *Working Paper Series* No. 5, 7. Available at http://iple.cass.cn/e/e.htm.

14. Solinger, *Contesting Citizenship*, 206–207.

15. Wang Fei-ling, *Organizing Through Division and Exclusion: China's Hukou System* (Stanford: Stanford University Press, 2003), 65–66.

16. Solinger, *Contesting Citizenship*, 90.

17. Wang, *Organizing Through Division*, 79.

18. Interview with Liu Kaiming (director, Institute of Contemporary Observation), August 9, 2006.

19. Wang, *Organizing Through Division*, 78.

20. Li Zhang, *Strangers in the City: Reconfigurations of Space, Power, and Social Networks Within China's Floating Population* (Stanford, CA: Stanford University Press, 2001), 35.

21. Wang, *Organizing Through Division*, 77–78.

22. Nicolas Becquelin, "Enforcing the Rural-Urban Divide: Use of Custody and Repatriation Detention Triples in 10 Years," *Human Rights in China*, February 23, 2003. Available at http://www.hrichina.org/public/contents/article?revision%5fid=4150&item%5fid=4149.

23. Solinger, *Contesting Citizenship*, 72.

24. Wang, *Organizing Through Division*, 91.

25. Ibid., 120.

26. Qiao Jian, dean of labor relations and head of the labor union department at the China Institute of Industrial Relations, says China's welfare and labor relations systems make the country's migrant workers outcasts "whose status is no better than the 'untouchables' in the Indian caste system." Vivien Cui and Kevin Huang, "China's Neglected 'Untouchables,' " *South China Morning Post*, May 1, 2006.

27. Wang, *Organizing Through Division*, 127.

28. Amnesty International, "Internal Migrants: Discrimination and Abuse. The Human Cost of an Economic 'Miracle,' " March 1, 2007. Available at http://www.amnestyusa.org/document.php?id=ENGASA170082007.

29. Wang, *Organizing Through Division*, 197.

30. Alice Yan, "Changes Urged to Registration System," *South China Morning Post*, February 27, 2007; Kristine Kwok, "More Cities to Allow in Rural Residents," *South China Morning Post*, October 16, 2006.

31. Wang, *Organizing Through Division*, 198.

32. Tom Miller, "One Step Forward . . . ," *China Economic Quarterly*, Q3 2005, 37.

33. Li Lianjiang, "Driven to Protest: China's Rural Unrest," *Current History*, September 2006, 250–254.

34. Interview with Zeng Feiyang, March 12, 2007.

35. Interview with Han Dongfang, April 6, 2007.

36. Interview with Ching Kwan Lee, March 13, 2007.

37. Jonathan Anderson, "The New China—Back to the Real World," UBS Investment Research, Asian Economics Perspectives, March 1, 2007, 14.

38. Thomas Lum, "US-Funded Assistance Programs in China," Congressional Research Service Report for Congress, May 18, 2007, 4. The State Department's Web site seems to suggest that Congressional funding for the Human Rights and Democracy Fund was even more generous, at about $71 million. See http://www.state.gov/g/drl/p/.

39. Lum, "US-Funded Assistance," 6.

40 Mary Elizabeth Gallagher, *Contagious Capitalism: Globalization and the Politics of Labor in China* (Princeton, NJ: Princeton University Press, 2005), 83.

41. Gordon White, Jude Howell, and Shang Xiaoyuan, *In Search of Civil Society: Market Reform and Social Change in Contemporary China* (Oxford: Clarendon Press, 1996), 41–42.

42. Ibid., 46.

43. Gallagher, *Contagious Capitalism*, 90.

44. Firmina Chen, "Labor Unions and FIEs," *China Law & Practice*, April 2005, 1.

45. Chen Feng, "Between the State and Labour: The Conflict of Chinese Trade Unions' Double Identity in Market Reform," *China Quarterly* 176 (2003): 1016.

46. Ibid., 1019.

47. U.S. Department of State, Bureau of Democracy, Human Rights and Labor, "Country Reports on Human Rights Practices, China" (2005). Available at http://www.state.gov/g/drl/rls/hrrpt/2005/61605.htm.

48. U.S. Department of State, Bureau of Democracy, Human Rights and Labor, "Country Reports on Human Rights Practices, China" (2006). Available at http://www.state.gov/g/drl/rls/hrrpt/2006/78771.htm.

49. Mei Fong and Ann Zimmerman, "Showdown Looms for Wal-Mart in China," *Asian Wall Street Journal*, May 15, 2006.

50. Guo Wencai, "Union Accepts Migrant Workers," *China Daily*, September 3, 2003.

51. Cao Desheng, "Trade Unions Help Migrants Receive Their Backpay," *China Daily*, January 6, 2005.

52. Cui and Huang, "China's Neglected 'Untouchables'."

53. Carl Goldstein, "Wal-Mart in China," *The Nation*, December 8, 2003, 7.

54. John Ruwitch, "With Wal-Mart Unionized in China, Now What?" Reuters News Service, March 25, 2007.

55. Interview with Robin Munro, April 30, 2007.

56. Ibid.

57. Workers' dissatisfaction with factory food sparks a surprising number of labor protests in China. Often, anger about food is a reflection of anger at management for more substantial abuses. See Chow Chung-yan, "Workers at Toy Factory Arrested After 3-Day Riot," *South China Morning Post*, July 26, 2006, for one example.

58. "*Sheng laodong he shehui baozhang ting fu ting zhang jie shao shang tiao si da yuanyin*" ("Provincial Ministry of Labor and Social Security's Vice Director Introduces Four Reasons for the Wage Hike"), www.chhuber.com. March 1, 2007.

59. Richard Welford and Dennis Cheung, "Chinese Investment Heads Inland," *CSR Asia Weekly*, vol. 2, week 24, (July 14, 2006).

60. Barboza, "Sharp Labor Shortage."
61. See http://eng.newwelfare.org.
62. Peng Xiujian and Dietrich Fausten, "Population Aging and Labor Supply Prospects in China from 2005 to 2050," *Asia-Pacific Population Journal*, December 2006, 48.
63. Cary Huang, "Aging Population Set to Slow Growth," *South China Morning Post*, November 11, 2006.

CHAPTER 6: THE GIRLS OF ROOM 817

1. Chen Hong, "Feeling the Pinch of a Growing Population," *China Daily*, July 23, 2005.
2. See http://english.sz.gov.cn/economy/200509/t20050929_484.htm.
3. Craig Simons, "Thriving Shenzhen Tests China's Future," *Atlanta Journal-Constitution*, February 11, 2007.
4. Austin Ramzy, "The China Connection," *Time*, June 18, 2007, 39.
5. "Shenzhen Steps Up Efforts to Control Population," *China Daily*, May 16, 2007. Available at http://www.china.org.cn/english/China/210936.htm.
6. Zhao Lei, "*2006 Shenzhen xinfang shang zhang yue 3 cheng 2007 fanggjia hai jiang shang yang?*" ("House Prices Increased by Around 30% in 2006, What About 2007?"), *Southern Metropolis News*, January 4, 2007.
7. Hu Zheye, "SZ Unveils Innovation Law," *Shenzhen Daily*, March 16, 2006.

CHAPTER 7: ACCOUNTS AND ACCOUNTABILITY

1. Bob Ortega, *In Sam We Trust: The Untold Story of Sam Walton and How Wal-Mart Is Devouring America* (New York: Times Books, 1998), 245.
2. E-mail communication with E. J. Bernacki (Levi's corporate communications), June 27, 2007.
3. Telephone conversation with Gare Smith, June 19, 2007.
4. Dara O'Rourke, "Smoke from a Hired Gun: A Critique of Nike's Labor and Environmental Auditing in Vietnam as Performed by Ernst & Young," Transnational Resource and Action Center, (1997) 6. Available at http://nature.berkeley.edu/orourke/PDF/smoke.pdf.
5. Vernon Loeb, "Sports Shoe Companies Run for Indonesia's Cheap Labor," Knight-Ridder News Service, published in *Austin American-Statesman*, February 16, 1992.
6. Nena Baker, "The Hidden Hand of Nike Series: Nike's World Power and Profit (1st. of 3 parts)," *Portland Oregonian*, August 9, 1992.
7. Ortega, *In Sam We Trust*, 238; Frank Swoboda, "Sears Agrees to Police Its Suppliers; Retailer Addresses Issue of Forced Labor," *Washington Post*, March 31, 1992.
8. Ortega, *In Sam We Trust*, 224, 242–43.
9. Ibid., 225.
10. Ibid., 242.
11. Ibid., 244-46.
12. Ibid., 246.
13. Ibid., 246.
14. Telephone conversation with Gare Smith, June 19, 2007.
15. Ortega, *In Sam We Trust*, 250.
16. Ibid.
17. Ibid.
18. Ibid, 318–319.
19. Robert J. S. Ross, *Slaves to Fashion: Poverty and Abuse in the New Sweatshops* (Ann Arbor: University of Michigan Press, 2004), 230.

20. Kimberly Ann Elliott and Richard B. Freeman, *Can Labor Standards Improve Under Globalization?* (Washington, D.C.: Institute for International Economics, 2003), 57.
21. Ibid., 58.
22. Ibid.
23. Ibid., 148–50.
24. Dara O'Rourke, "Monitoring the Monitors: A Critique of PricewaterhouseCoopers (PwC) Labor Monitoring," September 28, 2000, 2. Available at http://nature.berkeley.edu/orourke/PDF/pwc.pdf.
25. Wal-Mart Stores, Inc., "2006 Report on Ethical Sourcing," 3.
26. Ibid.
27. Daniella Gould, "The Problem with Supplier Audits," *Corporate Responsibility Management*, August–September 2005, 24–30.
28. Telephone conversation with Doug Cahn, November 30, 2006.
29. Reebok International Ltd., "2005 Human Rights Report," 29. Available at http://www.reebok.com/static/global/initiatives/rights/reports/rhrreport2005.html.
30. Edwin Markham, *Cosmopolitan*, series starting August 1906, as quoted in Arthur and Lila Weinberg, eds., *The Muckrakers* (Urbana: University of Illinois Press, 2001), 368.
31. Lei Jianqiao, *"Mao Shu You Xi Yan Xiu Ban"* ("Training Course for the Game of Cat and Mouse"), *Southern Weekend*, December 15, 2005.
32. The company's Web site can be found at http://www.super-net.cn/eng__index.asp.
33. This advertisement was located by the excellent sleuths at CSR Asia, the Hong Kong–based consultancy. See http://www.csr-asia.com/index.php?p=9717.
34. Translation from online advertisement found at http://www.chinadada.com/noshine company/dativ7415.html.
35. Obtained from a Hong Kong NGO.
36. Dexter Roberts and Pete Engardio with Aaron Bernstein and Stanley Holmes, "Secrets, Lies and Sweatshops," *BusinessWeek*, November 27, 2006, 50.
37. Association for Sustainable & Responsible Investment in Asia, "Toxic Chemicals—Asian Investors Are At-Risk," January 2007, 7. Available at http://www.asria.org/publications.
38. Interview with the head of compliance, September 5, 2006.
39. Telephone conversation with Sam Porteous, Mary 26, 2005.
40. Wal-Mart, "2006 Report," 3.
41. Interview with Ron Martin, November 30, 2006.
42. Gap Inc., "Facing Challenges, Finding Opportunities: 2004 Social Responsibility Report," 9. Available at www.gapinc.com/public/SocialResponsibility/socialres.shtml.
43. American Apparel and Footwear Association, "ShoeStats 2007," 3. Available at http://www.apparelandfootwear.org/statistics.asp.
44. Gary McWilliams, "Discounts Pinch Retailers," *Wall Street Journal*, December 21, 2006, 5.
45. Telephone conversation with Stephen Frost, May 16, 2007.
46. E-mailed response to written questions sent by June Ip on July 3, 2007.
47. Interview with a former auditor, May 10, 2007.
48. Telephone conversation with Sam Porteous, May 26, 2005.
49. Gould, "The Problem with Supplier Audits," 24.
50. Interview with Auret van Heerden, February 15, 2006.
51. Telephone conversation with Dara O'Rourke, December 20, 2006.
52. Gould, "Problem with Supplier Audits."

316   NOTES

53. Telephone interview with Rajan Kamalanathan and Beth Keck, March 19, 2007.
54. Email correspondence with Alannah Goss, (public relations executive based in Hong Kong).
55. Disney's labor standards are available at http://corporate.disney.go.com/corporate/intl__labor__standards.html.
56. Target Corporation, "Target Corporate Responsibility Report: Social Responsibility," 16–18. Available at http://sites.target.com/site/en/corporate/page.jsp?contentId=PRD03-004325.
57. Kohl's Corporation, "Report to Shareholders on Social Responsibility," March 2007, 9. Available at www.kohlscorporation.com/InvestorRelations/-Investor12.htm.
58. Ibid., 5.
59. Corporate responsibility report available at http://corporate.homedepot.com/wps/.
60. Telephone conversation with Doug Cahn, November 30, 2006.
61. I am grateful to Melissa Brown for calling this article to my attention.
62. Michael E. Porter and Mark R. Kramer, "Strategy and Society: The Link Between Competitive Advantage and Corporate Social Responsibility," *Harvard Business Review*, December 2006, 78.
63. Ibid., 82.
64. Ibid.
65. Hau L. Lee, "The Triple-A Supply Chain," *Harvard Business Review*, October 2004, 107.
66. Ibid., 112.
67. See "The Consumer and Sweatshops November 1999," survey commissioned by Mammount University's Center for Ethical Concerns. Available at http://www.marymount.edu/news/garmentstudy/overview.html.
68. Monica Prasad et al., "Consumers of the World Unite: A Market-Based Response to Sweatshops," *Labor Studies Journal* 29, no. 3 (Fall 2004), 63.
69. Ibid., 65–7.
70. Ibid., 69.
71. Jonathan Brown, "Ethical Shopping: The Red Revolution," *Independent*, January 27, 2006.

CHAPTER 8: THE NEW MODEL FACTORY
1. Matthew R. Miller and Clare Cheung, "Fraud Trial Shows China's Banking Flaws; Manager Links Bank of China Executives to $482 Million Case," Bloomberg News, published in *International Herald Tribune*, November 21, 2006.
2. Drew Thompson, "Healthcare Reform in China: Design by Committee," *China Brief* volume 7, no. 14 (July 11, 2007). Available at http://www.jamestown.org/china__brief/article.php?articleid=2373539.
3. Telephone conversation with Jason Kindopp, August 10, 2007.
4. Ibid.
5. Global Labor Strategies, "Behind the Great Wall of China," 2. Available at http://laborstrategies.blogs.com/global__labor__strategies/about__us/index.html.
6. US-China Business Council, "Comments on the Draft Labor Contract Law of the People's Republic of China (Draft of March 20, 2006)," April 19, 2006, 1. Available at http://www.uschina.org/public/documents/2007/04/proposed-labor-contract-law-position.html.
7. Global Labor Strategies, "Behind the Great Wall," 2.
8. Aaron Halegua, "The Debate over Raising Chinese Labor Standards Goes International,"

Harvard Law & Policy Review Online. http://www.hlpronline.com/2007/04/halegua__ 01.html.

9. US-China Business Council, "The US-China Business Council's Position on China's Proposed Labor Contract Law," April 5, 2007. Available at http://www.uschina.org/public/ documents/2007/04/proposed-labor-contract-law-position.html.

10. Geoff Dyer, "China's Labor Law Raises US Concerns," *Financial Times,* May 2, 2007.

11. From an unofficial translation by law firm Baker & McKenzie.

12. Associated Press, "China's Legislature Approves New Labor Law," June 29, 2007.

13. Edward Alden, Richard McGregor and Raphael Minder, "US Textile Sector Not Impressed by China Export Levy," *Financial Times,* December 14, 2004.

14. Brian Ho, "Shenzhen Stock Exchange Instruction on CSR," *CSR Asia Weekly* 2, Week 24 (June 14), 2006, 4–5.

15. Tom Miller, "Labor Pains," *South China Morning Post,* March 31, 2006.

16. He Huifeng, "Bad Publicity over Sweatshop Label Stirs Delta Factory Chiefs to Better Workers' Lot," *South China Morning Post,* April 9, 2007.

17. See http://www.apple.com/hotnews/ipodreport/.

18. Telephone conversation with Stephen Frost, May 16, 2007.

19. Ivan Zhai, "Dongguan Mayor Gives HK Factories a Year to Clean Up," *South China Morning Post,* February 7, 2007.

20. Email from Andy Rothman, sent July 18, 2006, entitled "Thirsty China Update: The Fountain Set Example."

21. Liang Qiwen, "30 Firms Blacklisted for Defaulting Wages," *China Daily,* June 26, 2006, 3.

22. Interview with a consultant, July 11, 2006.

CHAPTER 9: THE FUTURE OF THE CHINA PRICE

1. Interview with Arthur Kroeber, May 28, 2007.

2. Jonathan Anderson, "The New China—Back to the Real World," UBS Investment Research, Asian Economic Perspectives, March 1, 2007, 30.

3. Dominic Ziegler, "The Export Juggernaut," *Economist.* A Special Report on China and Its Region, March 31, 2007, 9.

4. Jonathan Anderson, "No, Really, How Competitive Are China's Exports?" UBS Investment Research, Asian Focus, April 17, 2007, 3.

5. Tom Mitchell, "The Rising Cost of Commerce in the South," *Financial Times,* April 12, 2006.

6. "Academic Sees End to Guangdong Labor Shortage," *China Daily,* October 8, 2006. The academic was Li Youhuan, an economics professor at the Guangdong Academy of Social Sciences.

7. "Vietnam Attracts Almost 4 Billion USD of FDI," Ministry of Foreign Affairs of Vietnam, September 1, 2006, http://www.mofa.gov.vn/en/nr050807104143/nr040807105039/ ns060825093300. FDI flows into India were expected to exceed $11 billion in 2006–2007, against $5.5 billion the year before, as reported by Amy Yee, "FDI in India Expected to Double," FT.com, December 28, 2006.

8. Mariko Sanchanta, "China-Japan Trade: Canny Japanese Companies Prefer China Plus One," *Financial Times,* Japan Special Report, October 11, 2005. Available at http:// www.ft.com/cms/s/7f7a64c6-39ac-11da-806e-00000e2511c8,dwp__uuid=dc5b2c94-47bb-11da-a949-00000e2511c8.html.

9. "The Problem with Made in China," *Economist,* January 13, 2007, 69.

10. Telephone conversation with Kasra Ferdows, November 14, 2006.

11. Joe Leahy, "Case Study: Hong Kong Clothes Company Considers Its Options," *Financial Times*, October 9, 2006.

12. Anand Giridharadas, "In India, 'Next Great' Industrial Story," *International Herald Tribune*, May 31, 2006.

13. Interview with Bruce Rockowitz, June 5, 2006.

14. Andrew Batson, "China's Rise as Auto-Parts Power Reflects New Manufacturing Edge," *Wall Street Journal*, August 1, 2006.

15. "China's Auto Exports Doubled in '06—Numbers Indicate Rising Challenge to the Competition," *Wall Street Journal*, January 2, 2007.

16. Choe Sang-Hun, "South Korean Business Feels Pinch between China and Japan," *International Herald Tribune*, March 29, 2007.

17. Gordon Fairclough, "Ford's Foray into China Shows Asian Ambitions," *Wall Street Journal Asia*, October 27–29, 2006.

18. Daniel H. Rosen, "Comparative Disadvantage: What China Can't Do," *China Economic Quarterly*, Q3 2006, 45–51.

19. Interview with Arthur Kroeber, May 28, 2007.

20. Elaine Wu, "300m Expected to Move to Cities over Next Two Decades," *South China Morning Post*, August 3, 2006.

21. Leu Siew Ying, "Guangdong Faces Unique Problems, Says Party Chief," *South China Morning Post*, May 22, 2007.

22. Diana Farrell and Andrew J. Grant, "China's Looming Talent Shortage," *McKinsey Quarterly* 4, (2005), 56.

23. Ibid., 57.

24. Cary Huang, "Bleak Future for Millions of Graduates," *South China Morning Post*, November 23, 2006, 8.

25. Nicholas R. Lardy, "China: Rebalancing Economic Growth" (paper presented at The China Balance Sheet in 2007 and Beyond, conference held by Center for Strategic and International Studies and the Peterson Institute for International Economics, May 2007).

26. "China to Adjust Export Tax Rebate Mechanism," Newsgd.com, July 24, 2006. http://www.newsgd.com/business/laws/200607240033.htm.

27. On April 13, 2007, *Xinhua* reported that the government was preparing to cut the export tax rebate on textile products. "Analysts say low-value-added textile products and garments are major exports and often spark trade disputes," *Xinhua* reported. "The textile industry would be a likely target in the government's campaign to suppress the trade surplus." The report went on to say that such a move would lower the growth rate in garment exports from 25 percent to 10 per cent. See http://news.xinhuanet.com/english/2007-04/13/content__5971993.htm.

28. A. T. Kearney, Inc., "Fixing China's Food Safety Issues Will Require a $100 Billion Investment, According to New A. T. Kearney Research," June 26, 2007, http://www.atkearney.com/main.taf?p=1,5,1,190.

AFTERWORD

1. Larry Rohter, "Shipping Costs Start to Crimp Globalization," *New York Times*, August 3, 2008.

2. TransAsia Lawyers, PRC Employment Law Newsletter, vol. 9, no. 6, June 27, 2008.

Bibliography

American Apparel & Footwear Association. *Trends: An Annual Compilation of Statistical Information on the U.S. Apparel and Footwear Industries.* Washington, D.C.: AAFA, June 2004.

Amnesty International. "Internal Migrants: Discrimination and Abuse. The Human Cost of an Economic 'Miracle'." March 1, 2007. http://www.amnestyusa.org/document.php?id=ENGASA170082007.

Anderson, Jonathan. "The New China—Back to the Real World." UBS Investment Research, Asian Economic Perspectives, March 1, 2007.

———. "No, Really, How Competitive Are China's Exports?" UBS Investment Research, Asian Focus, April 17, 2007.

Andors, Stephen. *China's Industrial Revolution: Politics, Planning, and Management, 1949 to the Present.* New York: Pantheon Books, 1977.

Appenzeller, Tim. "The Coal Paradox." *National Geographic,* March 2006.

Association for Sustainable & Responsible Investment in Asia. "Toxic Chemicals—Asian Investors Are At-Risk." January 2007. http://www.asria.org/publications.

A. T. Kearney, Inc. "Fixing China's Food Safety Issues Will Require a $100 Billion Investment, According to New A.T. Kearney Research." June 26, 2007. http://www.atkearney.com/main.taf?p=1,5,1,190.

Banister, Judith. "Manufacturing Employment and Compensation in China." U.S. Department of Labor, Bureau of Labor Statistics, November 2005.

Becker, Jasper. *Hungry Ghosts: Mao's Secret Famine.* New York: Henry Holt and Company, 1996.

Becquelin, Nicolas. "Enforcing the Rural-Urban Divide: Use of Custody and Repatriation Detention Triples in 10 Years." *Human Rights in China,* February 23, 2003. http://www.hrichina.org/public/contents/article?revision%5fid=4150&item%5fid=4149.

Bergsten, C. Fred, Gill Bates, Nicholas R. Lardy, and Derek Mitchell. *China: The Balance Sheet.* New York: Public Affairs, 2006.

Bettleheim, Charles. *Cultural Revolution and Industrial Organization in China: Changes in Management and the Division of Labor.* Translated by Alfred Ehrenfeld. New York: Monthly Review Press, 1974.

Bonacich, Edna, Lucie Cheng, Norma Chinchilla, Nora Hamilton, and Paul Ong, eds. *Global Production: The Apparel Industry in the Pacific Rim.* Philadelphia: Temple University Press, 1994.

Cai Fang. "Invisible Hand and Visible Feet: Internal Migration in China." Chinese Academy of Social Sciences, Working Paper Series No. 5. http://www.cfr.org/publication/12943/.

Campbell, Robert M., Jimmy Hexter, and Karen Yin. "Getting Sourcing Right in China." *The McKinsey Quarterly 2004 Special Edition: China Today.* New York: McKinsey & Company, 2004.

Centers for Disease Control, National Institute for Occupational Health and Safety. "Fatal and Nonfatal Injuries, and Selected Illnesses and Conditions." Chapter Two in *Worker Health Chartbook 2004.*

Chan, Anita. *China's Workers Under Assault: The Exploitation of Labor in a Globalizing Economy.* Armonk, NY: M.E. Sharpe, 2001.

Chen, Feng. "Between the State and Labour: The Conflict of Chinese Trade Unions' Double Identity in Market Reform." *China Quarterly* 176 (2003): 1006–28.

Chen, Firmina. "Labor Unions and FiEs." *China Law & Practice,* April 2005.

China Labor Bulletin. *Deadly Dust: The Silicosis Epidemic among Guangdong Jewellery Workers and the Defects of China's Occupational Illnesses Prevention and Compensation System.* CLB Research Series No. 1. December 2005.

———. *Falling Through the Floor: Migrant Women Workers' Quest for Decent Work in Dongguan, China.* CLB Research Series No. 2, September 2006.

———. *You xiao de gongren zuzhi: baozhang kuanggong shengming de biyou zhilu (Bloody Coal: An Appraisal of China's Coal Mine Safety Management System).* CLB Research Series, March 2006.

Collins, Jane L. *Threads: Gender, Labor, and Power in the Global Apparel Industry.* Chicago: University of Chicago Press, 2003.

Eckes, Alfred E., Jr., *Opening America's Market: U.S. Foreign Trade Policy since 1776.* Chapel Hill: University of North Carolina Press, 1995.

Eckstein, Alexander. *Communist China's Economic Growth and Foreign Trade: Implications for U.S. Policy.* New York: Council on Foreign Relations, 1966.

Economist Intelligence Unit. "China: Tense Trade." *Business China* 306, December 8, 2003.

Economy, Elizabeth C. *The River Runs Black: The Environmental Challenge to China's Future.* Ithaca, NY: Cornell University Press, 2004.

Elliott, Kimberly Ann, and Richard B. Freeman. *Can Labor Standards Improve Under Globalization?* Washington, D.C.: Institute for International Economics, 2003.

Engardio, Pete, Dexter Roberts, and Brian Bremner. "The China Price." *BusinessWeek,* December 6, 2004.

Enright, Michael J., Edith E. Scott, and Chang Ka-mun. *Regional Powerhouse: The Greater Pearl River Delta and the Rise of China.* Singapore: John Wiley & Sons, 2005.

"Export Juggernaut, The." *Economist, A Special Report on China and Its Region,* March 31, 2007.

Farrell, Diana and Andrew J. Grant. "China's Looming Talent Shortage." *McKinsey Quarterly,* No. 4, 2005.

Fedotov, Igor. "The ILO/WHO Global Programme for the Elimination of Silicosis (GPES)." Presentation at the IOHA 6th International Scientific Conference, September 19–23, 2005.

———. "The ILO/WHO Global Programme for the Elimination of Silicosis (GPES)." Presentation at the 13th Session of the Joint ILO/WHO Committee on Occupational Health, December 9–12, 2003.

Ferdows, Kasra. "New World Manufacturing Order." *Industrial Engineer* 35, no. 2, (February 2003): 28–34.

Fishman, Charles. *The Wal-Mart Effect: How the World's Most Powerful Company Really Works—and How It's Transforming the American Economy.* New York: Penguin Press, 2006.

Frazier, Mark. "Pensions, Public Opinion, and the Greying of China." *Asia Policy* 1 (January 2006): 43–68.

———. *The Making of the Chinese Industrial Workplace: State, Revolution, and Labor Management.* Cambridge: Cambridge University Press, 2002.

Freese, Barbara. *Coal: A Human History.* New York: Penguin Books, 2003.

Fu, Hualing, and D. Y. Choy, "From Mediation to Adjudication: Settling Labor Disputes in China." *China Rights Forum* 3 (2004): 17–22.

Gallagher, Mary E. "Mobilizing the Law in China: 'Informed Disenchantment' and the Development of Legal Consciousness," *Law & Society Review* 40, no. 4 (2006): 783–816.

———. *Contagious Capitalism: Globalization and the Politics of Labor in China.* Princeton, NJ: Princeton University Press, 2005.

Gap Inc. "Facing Challenges, Finding Opportunities: 2004 Social Responsibility Report." www.gapinc.com/public/SocialResponsibility/socialres.shtml.

Garrett, Valery M. *Heaven is High, the Emperor Far Away: Merchants and Mandarins in Old Canton.* Oxford: Oxford University Press, 2002.

Global Labor Strategies. "Behind the Great Wall of China." http://laborstrategies.blogs.com/global_labor_strategies/about_us/index.html.

Goldstein, Carl. "Wal-Mart in China." *The Nation,* December 8, 2003.

Gould, Daniella. "The Problem with Supplier Audits." *Corporate Responsibility Management* 2 no. 1, (August/September 2005).

Halegua, Aaron. "The Debate over Raising Chinese Labor Standards Goes International." *Harvard Law & Policy Review Online.* http://www.hlpronline.com/2007/04/halegua 01 .html.

Ho, Brian. "Shenzhen Stock Exchange Instruction on CSR." *CSR Asia Weekly* 2, Week 24, June 14, 2006.

Hong Kong Christian Industrial Committee. "Report on the Working Conditions of Soccer and Football Workers in Mainland China, Revised Version." May 2002.

Huang, Ping, and Zhan Shaohua. "Internal Migration in China: Linking It to Development." Paper prepared for the Regional Conference on Migration and Development in Asia, Lanzhou, China, March 14–16, 2005.

Hurst, Rosey, Hilary Murdoch, and Daniella Gould. "Changing over Time." Impactt. http://www.impacttlimited.com/site/publications.asp.

Kennedy, Gareth L. "Silica—The Next Asbestos?" *Future Fellows* (2005). http://www.casact.org/admissions/futfell/dec05/issues.htm.

Kohl's Corporation. "Report to Shareholders on Social Responsibility." March 2007. http://www.kohlscorporation.com/InvestorRelations/pdfs/reportsbareholders2006.pdf.

Kynge, James. *China Shakes the World: The Rise of a Hungry Nation.* London: Weidenfeld & Nicolson, 2006.

Lardy, Nicholas R. *China in the World Economy.* Washington, D.C.: Institute for International Economics, 1994.

———. "China: Rebalancing Economic Growth." Paper presented at *The China Balance Sheet in 2007 and Beyond* conference held by Center for Strategic and International Studies and the Peterson Institute for International Economics, May 2007.

Lee, Hau L. "The Triple-A Supply Chain." *Harvard Business Review,* October 2004.

Lett, Erin, and Judith Banister. "Labor Costs of Manufacturing Employees in China: An Update to 2003–04." *Monthly Labor Review,* November 2006.

Li, Lianjiang. "Driven to Protest: China's Rural Unrest." *Current History,* September 2006.

Liker, Jeffrey K., and Thomas Y. Choi. "Building Deep Supplier Relationships." *Harvard Business Review,* December 2004.

Liu, Yuanli. "Development of the Rural Health Insurance System in China." *Health Policy and Planning* 19, no. 3 (May 2004): 159–165.

Lum, Thomas. "US-Funded Assistance Programs in China." Congressional Research Service Report for Congress, May 18, 2007.

Ma, Laurence J. C. *Commercial Development and Urban Change in Sung China (960–1279).* Ann Arbor, MI: Department of Geography, University of Michigan, 1971.

Miller, Tom. "One step forward . . ." *China Economic Quarterly,* Q3 2005, 34–37.

Murphy, Rachel. *How Migrant Labor is Changing Rural China.* Cambridge: Cambridge University Press, 2002.

Office of the United States Trade Representative. "Statement from USTR Spokesman Regarding China Labor Petition." July 21, 2006. http://www.ustr.gov/Document_ Library/Press   Releases/2006/July/Statement_from_USTR_Spokesman_Regarding_ China_Labor Petition html.

Office of the World Health Organization Representative in China and Social Development Department of China State Council Development Research Center. *China: Health, Poverty and Economic Development.* Beijing: June 2006.

O'Rourke, Dara. "Monitoring the Monitors: A Critique of PricewaterhouseCoopers (PwC) Labor Monitoring." September 28, 2000. http://nature.berkeley.edu/orourke/ PDF/pwc.pdf.

———. "Oursourcing Regulation: Analyzing Nongovernmental Systems of Labor Standards and Monitoring." *Policy Studies Journal* 31, no 1 (2003).

———. "Smoke from a Hired Gun: A Critique of Nike's Labor and Environmental Auditing in Vietnam as Performed by Ernst & Young." Transnational Resource and Action Center, 1997. http://nature.berkeley.edu/orourke/PDF/smoke.pdf.

Ortega, Bob. *In Sam We Trust: The Untold Story of Sam Walton and How Wal-Mart Is Devouring America.* New York: Times Books, 1998.

Peng, Xiujian, and Dietrich Fausten. "Population Aging and Labor Supply Prospects in China from 2005 to 2050." *Asia-Pacific Population Journal,* December 2006.

Porter, Michael E., and Mark R. Kramer. "Strategy and Society: The Link Between Competitive Advantage and Corporate Social Responsibility." *Harvard Business Review,* December 2006.

Powell, Bill. "It's All Made in China Now." *Fortune,* March 4, 2002.

Prasad, Monica, Howard Kimeldorf, Rachel Meyer, and Ian Robinson. "Consumers of the World Unite: A Market-Based Response to Sweatshops." *Labor Studies Journal* 29, no. 3, (Fall 2004).

"Problem with Made in China, The." *Economist,* January 13, 2007.

Ramzy, Austin. "The China Connection." *Time,* June 18, 2007.

Reebok International Ltd. "2005 Report on Ethical Sourcing."

Rivoli, Pietra. *The Travels of a T-Shirt in the Global Economy: An Economist Examines the Markets, Power, and Politics of World Trade.* Hoboken, NJ: John Wiley & Sons, 2005.

Roberts, Dexter. "How Rising Wages Are Changing the Game in China." *BusinessWeek,* March 27, 2006.

———, and Pete Engardio with Aaron Bernstein and Stanley Holmes. "Secrets, Lies and Sweatshops." *BusinessWeek,* November 27, 2006.

Rosen, Daniel H. "Comparative Disadvantage: What China Can't Do." *China Economic Quarterly,* Q3 2006.

Rosen, Ellen Israel. *Making Sweatshops: The Globalization of the U.S. Apparel Industry.* Berkeley: University of California Press, 2002.

Rosner, David, and Gerald Markowitz. *Deadly Dust: Silicosis and the On-Going Struggle to Protect Workers' Health.* Ann Arbor: University of Michigan Press, 2006.

Ross, Robert J. S. *Slaves to Fashion: Poverty and Abuse in the New Sweatshops.* Ann Arbor: University of Michigan Press, 2004.

Rothman, Andy, with Carole Liu and Julia Zhu. "China's Capitalists: Special Report." *CLSA Asia-Pacific Markets,* September 2005.

Schafer, Sarah. "Taking China to Court: Environmentalists Have Found an All-American Way to Challenge the Worst Polluters—Class-Action Lawsuits." *Newsweek International,* November 20, 2006.

Schell, Orville. *Mandate of Heaven: The Legacy of Tiananmen Square and the Next Generation of China's Leaders.* New York: Touchstone, 1994.

Scott, Robert E. "Costly Trade With China." Economic Policy Institute Briefing Paper No. 188, May 2, 2007. http://www.epi.org/content.cfm/bp188.

Solinger, Dorothy. *Contesting Citizenship in Urban China: Peasant Migrants, the State, and the Logic of the Market.* Berkeley: University of California Press, 1999.

Spence, Jonathan. *Mao Zedong,* New York: Viking, 1999.

———. *The Search for Modern China.* New York: W. W. Norton, 1990.

Steinfeld, Edward S. "Chinese Enterprise Development and the Challenge of Global Integration." Background paper for the World Bank's *Innovative East Asia: The Future of Growth.* Revised November 2002.

Stephenson Harwood & Lo. *China Legal.* March 2006.

Studwell, Joe. *The China Dream: The Elusive Quest for the Greatest Untapped Market on Earth.* London: Profile Books, 2002.

Tai, Hang. "From Gray to Blue: Taiyuan Polishes Its Dirty Image." *Beijing Review,* 2004.

Target Corporation. "Target Corporate Responsibility Report: Social Responsibility." http://sites.target/com/site/en/corporate/page.jsp?contentId=PRD03-004325.

Thomson, Elspeth. *The Chinese Coal Industry: An Economic History.* London: Routledge, 2003.

Tuñón, Max. "Internal Labor Migration in China: Features and Responses." ILO Office, Beijing, April 2006. http://www.ilo.org/public/english/region/asro/beijing/downbad/training/lab_migra.pdf.

United Nations Development Program. "The State of Equity in China: Social Security and Public Expenditure." *China Human Development Report,* 2005. http://www.cfr.org/publication/12943.

US-China Business Council. "The US-China Business Council's Position on China's Pro-

posed Labor Contract Law." April 5, 2007. http://www.uschina.org/public/documents/
2007/04/proposed-labor-contract-law-position.html.

———. "Comments on the Draft Labor Contract Law of the People's Republic of China
(Draft of March 2006)." April 19, 2006. http://www.uschina.org/public/documents/
2007/04/proposed-labor-contract-law-position.html.

United States Department of Labor. "The Employment Situation: May 2007." Employment
Situation Summary. http://www.dol.gov/dol/highlights/infocusarchive-2006.htm.

United States Department of State, Bureau of Democracy, Human Rights and Labor. "Country Reports on Human Rights Practices, China." (2005) http://www.state.gov/g/drl/rls/
hrrpt/2005/61605.htm.

———. "Country Reports on Human Rights Practices, China." (2006) http://www.state.gov/
g/drl/rls/hrrpt/2006/78771.htm.

United States Embassy, Beijing. "If Shanxi Can Do It (Clean Up), Anybody Can." June
2001. http://www.usembassy-china.org.cn/sandt/Shanxi.htm.

Verité. "Excessive Overtime in Chinese Supplier Factories: Causes, Impacts and Recommendations for Action." Research Paper, September 2004.

Vogel, Ezra F. *One Step Ahead in China: Guangdong Under Reform.* Cambridge, MA: Harvard
University Press, 1989.

Wal-Mart Stores, Inc. "2005 Report on Ethical Sourcing." 2006.

———. "2006 Report on Ethical Sourcing." 2007.

Wang, Fei-ling. *Organizing Through Division and Exclusion: China's Hukou System.* Stanford,
CA: Stanford University Press, 2003.

Wang, Gan. *Conspicuous Consumption, Business Networks, and State Power in a Chinese City.*
PhD diss., Yale University, 1999.

Wang, Hong. *China's Exports Since 1979.* New York: St. Martin's Press, 1993.

Wang, Xiao-Rong, and David C. Christiani. "Occupational Lung Disease in China." *International Journal of Occupational and Environmental Health* vol. 9, no. 4 (2003): 320–25.

Webb, Alysha. "As Labor Costs Rise, the 'China Price' Isn't Quite as Nice." *Automotive News,*
November 21, 2005.

Weinberg, Arthur, and Lila Weinberg eds. *The Muckrakers.* Urbana: University of Illinois
Press, 2001.

Welford, Richard, and Dennis Cheung. "Chinese Investment Heads Inland." *CSR Asia Weekly*
2, week 24, July 14, 2006.

White, Gordon, Jude Howell, and Shang Xiaoyuan. *In Search of Civil Society: Market Reform
and Social Change in Contemporary China.* Oxford: Clarendon Press, 1996.

Wilson, Patricia A. *Exports and Local Development: Mexico's New Maquiladoras.* Austin: University of Texas Press, 1992.

Woetzel, Jonathan R. *China's Economic Opening to the Outside World: The Politics of Empowerment.* New York: Praeger, 1989.

World Health Organization, United Nations Development Program. "Environment and People's Health in China." 2001. http://www.wpro.who.int/NR/rdonlyres/FD5E0957-
DC76-41F2-B207-21113406AE55/0/CHNEnvironmentalHealth.pdf.

Wu, Lifang, Xiaohang Yue, and Thaddeus Sim. "Supply Clusters: A Key to China's Cost Advantage." *Supply Chain Management Review* 10, no. 2 (March 1, 2006).

Yang, Dali L. "China's Looming Labor Shortage." *Far Eastern Economic Review,* January/Feb-
ruary 2005, 19–24.

Ziegler, Dominic. "The Export Juggernaut." *Economist: A Special Report on China and Its Region.* March 31, 2007.

Zhang, Li. *Strangers in the City: Reconfigurations of Space, Power, and Social Networks within China's Floating Population.* Stanford, CA: Stanford University Press, 2001.

Zou, Changqi, Gao Yun, and Ma Qingyan. "Pneumonconiosis in China: Current Situation and Countermeasures." *Mineral Dusts and Prevention of Silicosis,* vol. 4, no. 2 (September 1997). http://www.oit.org/public/english/region/asro/bangkok/asiaosh/newsletr/silicosi/zou.htm.

subcontracting
  advantages of, 47
  as common practice, 46
  in jewelry industry, 81–82
  monitoring as impossible, 47
  Wal-Mart as aware of, 51–52
sulfur dioxide, 89, 90, 92, 93, 95
Sun Zhigang, 114–15
Su Zhi, 57–58, 83, 84, 85–86, 278
sweatshops
  consumer concern about, 231–34
  consumer ignorance about, 186
  Foxconn accused of, 266–67
  Levi Strauss wants to avoid
    association with, 185
  malfunctioning auditing system
    allows, 184
  See also antisweatshop movement
Sykes, Eslie, 3

Taiwan
  as Asian Tiger, 20
  investment in China, 29, 282
  rising export prices in, 279
  and special economic zones, 28
  "Taiwan price," 19
Taiyuan
  air pollution in, 91–92
  coal mining near, 89
  journalist beaten to death outside, 100
  Ningxia St. Edenweiss in, 150
  pollution-related health problems in,
    92–93
Taiyuan Steel Group, 92
Tak Shun Technology Group, 144
Tang, Barry, 224
Tang Manzhen, 56–64, 72–75, 76–78,
  86–87
Target, 225–26
tariffs (duties), 6, 18, 19
televisions, 17, 30–31, 209
Tepper Marlin, Alice, 191–92
textile industry
  corporate social responsibility
    initiative in, 262–65
  manufacturing moves to Asia, 19–22
  speeding production process for,
    36–37
  towels, 272, 274–75
  See also clothing (apparel)

Thailand, 21, 54, 144, 250, 279, 280
Thompson, Drew, 67, 257
Three Gorges Dam, 104
Tian Chengping, 84–85
Timberland
  agrees to higher prices, 182–83
  auditing factories by, 194, 238–39, 240
  and Fair Factories Clearinghouse
    database, 222
  open approach adopted by, 226
  works with Social Accountability
    International, 240–41
time cards, falsified, 44, 45, 197, 202–3
Tommy Hilfiger, 267
toothpaste, 2, 14
Top Form International, 30, 144
towels, 272, 274–75
town and village enterprises, 48
toys
  Cabbage Patch dolls, 30
  for climbing manufacturing ladder, 20
  in development of Chinese
    manufacturing, 31
  International Council of Toy
    Industries, 192
  recall of Chinese-made, 2, 14–15
Truman, Harry S., 18, 19
Tucker, Jill, 219–20, 228
Turner, Jennifer, 95
turnover, employee, 52–53, 142, 241,
  244, 253, 265
TÜV Rheinland, 194, 265

unemployment among university
  graduates, 285
unfair trading practices
  China accused of, 3
  dumping, 3, 6, 264
Uniqlo, 251, 280
United States
  average manufacturing workweek in,
    48
  China's manufacturing output
    compared with, 4
  Chinese air pollution affects, 2, 14,
    89–90
  Chinese exports to, 5, 31
  Chinese government harasses
    companies that support labor rights,
    135–36